S. 7.

Times Wide World

CHARLES G. DAWES, ambassador to England, goes duck hunting in Nebraska. ∽ "Hell and Maria" helps make him Vice President (p. 198)

CHARLES E. MITCHELL, chairman of the National City Bank of New York, who started work as a clerk in Chicago. ∽ The window of a skyscraper helps him sell bonds (p. 203)

THOMAS A. EDISON at work in his laboratory at Llewellyn Park, N. J. ∽ He compares electricity to a dachshund (p. 207)

International

U. & U.

THEODORE N. VAIL, late head of the American Telephone and Telegraph Company. ∽ He made a new kind of map p. 190)

ADMIRAL WILLIAM S. SIMS, commander of the American battle fleet in the World War, on the courts of Newport. ∽ As an "upstart" lieutenant he defied the whole Navy Department (p. 191)

International

A STAR BOOK

STRATEGY IN HANDLING PEOPLE

By

EWING T. WEBB

and

JOHN B. MORGAN, Ph.D.

Associate Professor of Psychology
Northwestern University

ILLUSTRATED

GARDEN CITY PUBLISHING COMPANY, INC.

GARDEN CITY, NEW YORK

TO

ELIZABETH JACKSON WEBB

Whose devoted work over a period of several years in gathering and sifting biographical data has alone made this book possible, and whose enthusiasm has kept alive in us all the true spirit of adventure, this book is gratefully dedicated.

THANKS ARE DUE TO
THESE SCIENTISTS

In the effort to make some of the useful principles of psychology more interesting to young business men and more immediately helpful, the authors have adopted an unusual plan of presenting this material. They wish now to acknowledge a debt of gratitude to the following members of the American Psychological Association who gave timely encouragement in the early stages of this work by expressing their approval of the method used:

PROFESSOR GORDON W. ALLPORT
  Dartmouth College
PROFESSOR W. C. BAGLEY
  Columbia University
PROFESSOR C. HOMER BEAN
  Louisiana University
PROFESSOR CHARLES SCOTT BERRY
  University of Michigan
DEAN FREDERICK E. BOLTON
  University of Washington
PROFESSOR FREDERICK G. BONSER
  Columbia University
PROFESSOR WARNER BROWN
  University of California
PROFESSOR WILLIAM M. BROWN
  Washington and Lee University
DR. B. R. BUCKINGHAM
  Harvard University
PROFESSOR WILLIAM H. BURNHAM
  Clark University
PROFESSOR C. MACFIE CAMPBELL
  Harvard Medical School
PROFESSOR LEONARD CARMICHAEL
  Brown University
PROFESSOR HARVEY A. CARR
  University of Chicago
DEAN WILL GRANT CHAMBERS
  Pennsylvania State College
PROFESSOR HARRY WOLVEN CRANE
  University of North Carolina
PROFESSOR ELMER CULLER
  University of Illinois

PROFESSOR JOHN FREDERICK DASHIELL
  University of North Carolina
PROFESSOR JUNE E. DOWNEY
  University of Wyoming
PROFESSOR RICHARD M. ELLIOTT
  University of Minnesota
PROFESSOR HORACE B. ENGLISH
  Antioch College
PROFESSOR J. E. EVANS
  Iowa State College
PROFESSOR PAUL R. FARNSWORTH
  Stanford University
PROFESSOR SHEPHERD IVORY FRANZ
  University of California
PROFESSOR FRANK N. FREEMAN
  University of Chicago
PROFESSOR CORA LOUISA FRIEDLINE
  Randolph-Macon Woman's College
PROFESSOR SVEN FROEBERG
  Gustavus Adolphus College
DR. PAUL HANLY FURFEY
  Catholic University of America
PROFESSOR HENRY E. GARRETT
  Columbia University
PROFESSOR THOMAS RUSSELL GARTH
  University of Denver
PROFESSOR ARTHUR I. GATES
  Columbia University
DEAN ESTHER ALLEN GAW
  Ohio Wesleyan University
PROFESSOR ARNOLD GESELL
  Yale University

STRATEGY IN HANDLING PEOPLE

PROFESSOR A. R. GILLILAND
  Northwestern University
PROFESSOR SHELDON GLUECK
  Harvard Law School
PROFESSOR HENRY HERBERT GODDARD
  Ohio State University
PROFESSOR H. M. HALVERSON
  Yale University
PROFESSOR SAMUEL P. HAYES
  Mt. Holyoke College
PROFESSOR ARTHUR W. KORNHAUSER
  University of Chicago
PROFESSOR HOWARD SCOTT LIDDELL
  Cornell University
DR. D. I. MACHT
  Johns Hopkins University
PROFESSOR MARK A. MAY
  Yale University
PROFESSOR W. A. McCALL
  Columbia University
PROFESSOR MAX FREDERICK MEYER
  University of Missouri
PROFESSOR WALTER R. MILES
  Stanford University
PROFESSOR GEORGE HAINES MOUNT
  University of Southern California
PROFESSOR SIDNEY M. NEWHALL
  Yale University
PROFESSOR H. K. NIXON
  Columbia University
DEAN FRANKLIN CRESSEY PASCHAL
  Vanderbilt University
PROFESSOR G. T. PATRICK
  University of Iowa
DEAN LOUIS A. PECHSTEIN
  University of Cincinnati
PROFESSOR F. A. C. PERRIN
  University of Texas
PROFESSOR WALTER B. PILLSBURY
  University of Michigan
PROFESSOR A. T. POFFENBERGER
  Columbia University
DR. LOUISE E. POULL
  Columbia University

PROFESSOR SAMUEL RENSHAW
  Ohio State University
DR. A. A. ROBACK
  University Extension Lecturer
  Commonwealth of Massachusetts
PROFESSOR CHRISTIAN A. RUCKMICK
  University of Iowa
PROFESSOR HENRY ALFORD RUGER
  Columbia University
DEAN C. E. SEASHORE
  University of Iowa
PRESIDENT WALTER DILL SCOTT
  Northwestern University
PROFESSOR M. ALLEN STARR
  Columbia University
PROFESSOR EDWARD K. STRONG
  Stanford University
PROFESSOR JOHN W. TODD
  University of Southern California
PROFESSOR CHARLES H. TOLL
  Amherst College
PROFESSOR EDWARD CHACE TOLMAN
  University of California
PROFESSOR M. R. TRABUE
  University of North Carolina
DEAN KARL T. WAUGH
  University of Southern California
PROFESSOR LOUIE WINFIELD WEBB
  Northwestern University
PROFESSOR ALBERT P. WEISS
  Ohio State University
PROFESSOR MARY T. WHITLEY
  Columbia University
PROFESSOR R. S. WOODWORTH
  Columbia University
PROFESSOR HELEN THOMPSON WOOLLEY
  Columbia University
PROFESSOR CLARENCE S. YOAKUM
  University of Michigan
PROFESSOR KIMBALL YOUNG
  University of Wisconsin
PROFESSOR PAUL THOMAS YOUNG
  University of Illinois

Note: The men and women listed above are among the 159 scientists who approved of the basic plan of this book: to illustrate psychological principles with incidents from the careers of successful men. Their approval was given to the authors in response to a letter asking their estimate of various methods of presentation. There was, in some cases, a difference of opinion as to what additional methods should be used, but all agreed on the essential point.

CONTENTS

CHAPTER   PAGE

I   ARE GREAT MEN DIFFERENT FROM ME? . . .   3

II   THE SECRET OF MAKING PEOPLE LIKE YOU .   7

III   AN EASY WAY TO MAKE NEW FRIENDS . . .   13

IV   HOW TO INTEREST AND CONVINCE PEOPLE . .   23

V   LETTING THE OTHER FELLOW DO THE TALKING   35

VI   THE KNACK OF GETTING CO-OPERATION . . .   43

VII   STRATEGY THAT FEW CAN RESIST   50

VIII   TRADING PENNIES FOR DOLLARS   60

IX   HOW TO MAKE PEOPLE SAY YES   66

X   MORE DETECTIVE WORK   79

XI   THREE SUCCESSFUL SALESMEN AND THEIR ONE SECRET   92

XII   WINNING YOUR WAY AGAINST OPPOSITION . .   97

XIII   HOW TO AVOID MAKING ENEMIES   110

XIV   A SURE WAY TO WIN PEOPLE'S GOOD WILL .   118

XV   SIZING UP THE OTHER FELLOW   128

XVI   THINGS TO LOOK FOR IN JUDGING PEOPLE . .   141

CONTENTS

CHAPTER   PAGE

XVII   A SIMPLE WAY TO DEVELOP PERSONALITY . .   156

XVIII   MAKING MEN GLAD TO WORK   160

XIX   TUNING IN ON PEOPLE   167

XX   RIGHT AND WRONG METHODS OF PRAISING PEOPLE   172

XXI   HOW TO GET CREDIT FOR WHAT YOU DO . .   181

XXII   CREATING YOUR REPUTATION   189

XXIII   PUTTING YOUR IDEAS ACROSS   203

XXIV   HAVE YOU A POKER FACE?   215

XXV   PLAYING YOUR CARDS TO WIN   225

XXVI   MISTAKES TO AVOID IN USING HUMOR   238

XXVII   WHEN AND HOW TO PUT UP A FIGHT   244

APPENDIX   253

INDEX   258

"Many of us think of salesmen as people travelling around with sample kits. Instead, we are all salesmen, every day of our lives. We are selling our ideas, our plans, our energies, our enthusiasm to those with whom we come in contact."

CHARLES M. SCHWAB

Strategy
in Handling
People

CHAPTER I

ARE GREAT MEN DIFFERENT FROM ME?

Why Hoover Talked
The Knack of Influencing People

To SHOW HOW ABLE MEN have handled our own familiar problems in dealing with people, to make plain why their methods so often bring surprising results, is the purpose of this book. . . .

For a quarter of an hour Herbert Hoover has said "Yes" or "No" and little else.

Chubby-cheeked, amiable, he sits in the big easy chair — waiting.

Paul Leach, star correspondent of the *Chicago Daily News*, is worried. Here he is on Hoover's special train, in Hoover's private car, with the undivided attention of Hoover himself. What a chance for an interview! And yet — he is drawing a blank.

Hoover will not or cannot talk.

One after another Leach has touched on Hoover's pet subjects, has tried to draw him out.

But no real flicker of interest has stirred in those shrewd, blue-gray eyes.

Leach is up against a problem which all of us have faced. He wants to impress a man who is older and more important than himself. But the important person is indifferent.

How can Leach put himself across with Hoover?

By sheer accident he blunders into a familiar trick of interviewing.

"Just as I despaired the most," says Leach, "luck came to my aid and I *made a misstatement of fact about something he knew very well.*

"The train was crossing Nevada.

"'This,' I said, looking at the dreary waste, with the hazy purple mountains in the distance, 'is still the country of the pick-and-shovel prospector.'"

Hoover took him up immediately: "'Modern methods,' he said, 'have displaced the old aimless prospecting' . . . For nearly an hour he talked about mining . . . the talk switched to petroleum, to airplane mail, to half a dozen other things." [1]

At that moment Hoover was one of the most important men in the world. As Republican candidate for the presidency, he was on his way to the notification ceremonies at Palo Alto. In his private car, many important guests were waiting impatiently to get his attention. And yet for nearly two hours he devoted himself to a young man whom he barely knew.

Leach made a deep impression on Hoover. And he did it *not* by showing how clever he was — but by exactly the opposite method. He won out by revealing his own ignorance and giving Hoover a chance to correct him.

Why did this strategy produce such a remarkable effect upon Hoover?

This question is not difficult to answer. But it will take us far.

The device used accidentally by Paul Leach is only one of many simple yet unusual methods which able men employ in dealing with people.

It is these methods which we are about to examine.

We will observe, for example, how Dwight Morrow attracts and charms important people by merely asking questions; how Benjamin Franklin made a lifelong friend of an enemy by requesting a favor; how Herbert Hoover laid the cornerstone of his career by pretending he could use the typewriter; how Theodore Roosevelt quickly turned strangers into ardent supporters through one small precaution that most of us neglect.

In hundreds of little dramas of this sort, we will see how the very problems which we all face every day have been solved by the world's most successful men.

In each incident we will find a clear-cut, simple method of influencing others. We will learn why it works and how we can use it ourselves. Also we will discover one answer to a question that has been asked many times: "Are great men different from me?"

One and all, great leaders are far more careful than most men in dealing with people. They take many precautions which lesser men neglect. They know that only through other people is it possible to succeed.

When we stop to consider our own difficulties today, and our successes or setbacks in the past, do we not find other people at the root of most of them: a superior or subordinate, an associate or customer, a friend or a relative?

We all know men, particularly young men, who always seem to be blocked by people whom they cannot control. Often they have those vital qualities, industry and honesty. But they have not bothered to learn how to deal with people.

It is no accident that Charles Schwab has been recognized for thirty years as "America's greatest salesman." [2] No accident that Theodore Roosevelt had a "genius in personal contacts." [3] No accident that Owen D. Young is noted for his insight into other people's problems and Henry Ford, for his understanding of their needs and wishes.

One of the chief objectives of such men is to establish their influence over others.

The Knack of Influencing People

These men have acquired what William Storey, president of the Santa Fe Railroad, calls the "knack" of handling people.

Their strategy, as we shall see, is very simple. Yet for years it has been surrounded by a sort of mystery.

When, for instance, Matthew Brush, head of the American International Corporation, was asked what he considered the best way of "winning success," he made this reply:

"Learn its principles from a successful man, the way you would study music under a master musician." [4]

Undoubtedly, nearly all leaders possess knowledge about influencing people which they cannot easily put into words.

Because they watch other people more closely than most of us, they have learned more about human nature. Actually they control others very largely by making use of a few principles of psychology. But often they have come to count on these laws without fully understanding them. As a rule, they cannot clearly explain the very methods which they themselves employ.

Here perhaps we find one reason that so many secretaries and clerks of big men have themselves gone far in the world: These assistants have had the opportunity of watching their employers in action day in and day out.

Samuel Insull worked in this way with Thomas Edison; John Raskob with Pierre du Pont; Andrew Carnegie with Thomas Scott; George Cortelyou with Theodore Roosevelt; J. H. Barringer with John Patterson; James Simpson with Marshall Field.

Hundreds of prominent executives have started their careers as confidential assistants to some outstanding leader. From behind the scenes they have been able to observe his actual methods of controlling people.

It is this personal strategy of successful men which we are going to explore. We will find that it is very practical. It will help us solve many problems in handling the people whom we encounter every day at our work and at home.

JOHN D. ROCKEFELL-
ER, one-time Cleve-
land clerk. The
creator of Standard
Oil ready for golf at
Ormond Beach, Flo-
rida. ∞ He praises a
man who failed (p.
177)

CALVIN COOLIDGE takes in the hay on
his father's farm in Vermont. ∞ He
is modest, but no shrinking violet
(p. 181)

CHARLES M. SCHWAB, the ex-stake driver who built Bethlehem Steel. ∞ He gives away his watch (p. 179)

GENERAL GEORGE W. GOE-THALS, soldier, engineer and leader of men; builder of the Panama Canal. ∞ He dodged all ceremonies (p. 183)

CHAPTER II

THE SECRET OF MAKING PEOPLE
LIKE YOU

Why Carnegie and Franklin Asked Favors
One Thing the Other Fellow Always Wants
A Plan Used by Many Able Men

IN THEIR EARLY STRUGGLES, both Andrew Carnegie and Benjamin Franklin make use of the same interesting bit of strategy.

Both are facing a familiar obstacle: Their plans are opposed by another man. Carnegie is blocked by a balky associate; Franklin by a man who dislikes him.

And both Carnegie and Franklin get their own way easily and quickly by precisely the same method. Just how they managed it has been described by Carnegie and Franklin themselves with much good-hearted glee.

Almost overnight Franklin turned an enemy into a lifelong friend.

Franklin was still young, owner of a small printing business in Philadelphia. He had just been re-elected clerk of the Pennsylvania Assembly.

But trouble loomed ahead. Before the election a new member had made a long speech against him. Now this man deliberately ignored Franklin on the floor of the House.

Franklin was much worried about this unexpected enemy. What could he do? He himself has told us:

"I therefore did not like the opposition of this new member who was a gentleman of fortune and education with talents

7

that were likely to give him great influence in the House which, indeed, afterward happened. I did not, however, aim at gaining his favor by paying any servile respect to him but, after some time, took this other method.

"Having heard that he had in his library a certain very scarce and curious book, I wrote a note to him, expressing my desire of perusing that book and requesting that he would do me the favor of lending it to me for a few days.

"He sent it immediately," Franklin continues, "and I returned it in about a week with another note expressing strongly my sense of the favor.

"When next we met in the House, he spoke to me (which he had never done before) and with great civility; and he ever afterward manifested a readiness to serve me on all occasions, so that we became great friends and our friendship continued to his death." [1]

By asking a favor, the right kind of a personal favor, Benjamin Franklin swiftly won the warm liking of a man who started by slighting him and opposing him.

Perhaps even Franklin himself was surprised at the power of his strategy.

Andrew Carnegie, a wide reader, may well have picked up this idea from Franklin's own autobiography. He uses the same device to deal with a rebellious partner.

His own lieutenant, quaint, lovable Colonel Piper, is about to desert him in an emergency.

Both men are in St. Louis trying to collect money on a bridge which Carnegie's company has just built. But the good Colonel, growing homesick, has decided to take the night train back to Pittsburgh.

Carnegie finds his entire plan of action endangered by this childish notion of the Colonel's.

It is by asking his partner for help along entirely different lines that Carnegie induces him to stay in St. Louis and carry on with his part of the job.

Colonel Piper, as Carnegie is aware, is very fond of fine horses. So Carnegie tells him that he has heard that St. Louis is a noted place for them, that he wants to buy a span as a gift for his sister, and he asks Piper to stay over to select the horses.

The Colonel is delighted.

"The bait took . . . " writes Carnegie. "We held the bridge. 'Pipe' made a splendid Horatius." [2]

To keep his lieutenant in town, to secure obedience without friction, Carnegie, like Franklin, asked a favor of a special sort.

One Thing the Other Fellow Always Wants

Who has not noticed that people enjoy granting small favors, particularly favors that touch on some hobby or interest of their own?

On the surface the plan seems clever enough. But few of us would count on it heavily.

Yet what impressive results Carnegie and Franklin secure with it!

The force of this strategy rests on one of the underlying laws of human nature. Let us see how this law worked in the case of Franklin and the influential member of the Assembly.

Why did this man's hatred of Franklin disappear almost overnight? What awakened in him that swift glow of friendliness? The answer is not difficult.

In his little comedy, Franklin made the other man the star. He himself took the minor part. The older man was cast for the benefactor. Franklin was seeking help.

He made the other fellow feel superior and important.

Psychologists would say that Franklin had raised his *ego*.

Ego, of course, is simply the Latin word for "I." Psychologists use it to describe the *opinion* which we have *of ourselves*. It is the picture we form of our own importance, our estimate at any moment of our own worth.

One of the strongest desires that moves all people is to uphold their *ego*.

When we give a man a better opinion of himself, we earn his good will because we satisfy one of his basic needs. Here is the true secret of making people like us: to help them sustain their *ego*. There are many easy ways to do this. Among them is the method that Franklin and Carnegie used: to arrange for the other fellow to assist us in some way which he will enjoy and which is little trouble to him.

A Plan Used by Many Able Men

Do we not ourselves recall with pleasure such assistance that we have given others — small favors which were gratefully received?

And are there not, on the other hand, people whom we at times rather avoid because we are too heavily in their debt?

When we ourselves help other people our *ego* is raised. But when they help us our *ego* is likely to suffer.

This does not apply, of course, to those little courtesies which people so often show us, those friendly acts of consideration which impose no obligation. These are altogether delightful: evidence that we are important to the other fellow. It is wise and pleasant to offer many such attentions to others.

But it is unwise to place people under obligations which they cannot return. If we do *too much* for them they will in time often dislike us either secretly or openly.

Hugh Fullerton, a famous newspaper writer with hundreds of friends, says that his worst enemies are men for whom he has done a great deal.

One precaution all leaders observe: When they help the other fellow, *they make it easy for him to cancel the obligation.* Thus they safeguard his pride and also give him a strong incentive to help them in return.

They solve many different problems by letting people grant them favors.

Henry Stanton, a well known Chicago advertising man, found that one of his good friends was growing cool, drifting away from him. So he asked this man, who was an engineer, to look over the plans for the water-supply system on his new estate and to give him advice.

The engineer took the blue prints, worked over them far more carefully than Stanton expected, and presently returned them with practical suggestions. From that day on, the old cordiality was restored.

In the early career of Donald Smith, one of the builders of the Canadian Pacific Railway, later known as Lord Strathcona, we find a similar incident. Forced by his work as fur buyer to make friends with a hostile trapper, Smith asked shelter for the night as the first move in winning him over.

And that arch diplomat, King Edward VII, exerting all his skill to charm the new American ambassador, Joseph Choate, took especial pains to request a small favor at their first meeting. He asked Choate to send him photographs of McKinley and Roosevelt.

People are all different. Yet because this strategy rests on a universal human need, it succeeds with almost any normal person: with superiors and subordinates, with strangers and relatives, with people who like us and those who dislike us. The only points of difference in these people that we must be careful to take into account are their personal interests, their habits and hobbies: It is a small favor touching one of their own special interests which they most enjoy doing for us.

We win people's good will, gain their attention in a pleasant way, when we ask them to do us a favor which they enjoy granting.

This is one of many friendly methods by which leaders influence others. Like all the devices of this type which we find them using, its success rests on something within themselves — something which we too can cultivate: They are *deeply and genuinely interested in other people.*

If used coldly, this plan of asking a favor is a mere bit of trickery. But when we wish the other man well and really want his friendship, it becomes a way to make this feeling known to him.

Back of the strategy which able men employ lies their understanding of other people's needs and their sincere desire to please them. Theodore Roosevelt is a striking example of this fact.

"Roosevelt's great personal popularity was due largely to his interest in other people and their affairs," [3] writes a keen student of men. His outstanding characteristic was a deep natural liking for his fellow human beings and a warm sympathy with them.

This same trait we find in all those leaders whom we most admire — such men as Charles Schwab, Owen D. Young, Henry Ford, Benjamin Franklin, Andrew Carnegie, Abraham Lincoln and hundreds of others.

Charm, poise, "personality" — all arise from this feeling of genuine interest in people. It is this alone which can give power to our strategy. Fortunately this inner warmth can be developed by very simple methods. To show what the methods are and how any one can use them, is one of the objects of this book.

CHAPTER III

AN EASY WAY TO MAKE NEW FRIENDS

How Theodore Roosevelt Fascinated Strangers
Mark Hanna Turns an Enemy into a Supporter
William Howard Taft Dances the "Rigadon"

ACROSS THE BANQUET TABLE, Theodore Roosevelt sees a cluster of strange faces. They belong to Republicans whose names begin with "T."

These men know Roosevelt, of course — but coldly, from a distance. Of every one, before the banquet ends, he wishes to make a devoted follower.

Just back from Africa, Roosevelt is in Omaha on his first campaign trip with the 1912 election ahead.

And for these strangers at banquets, he is prepared. He has a plan that hinges on asking a single question.

"After cross-cover introductions," writes Dr. Victor Rosewater, who sat beside him, "Colonel Roosevelt bent closer and said to me quietly, 'Tell me, Rosewater, something about these fellows in front of me.' Complying, I gave him a brief characterization of each."

Now Theodore is ready to fascinate these men whom he has never seen before. It is easy. He has learned what each one is proud of, what he has done, what he likes.

Here, from behind the scenes, we see Roosevelt's "genius in personal contacts" at work.

"Possessed of this information," continues Dr. Rosewater, "Colonel Roosevelt immediately had topics of conversation to fit every one of his table companions." [1]

In order to win these strangers, Roosevelt has taken the trouble to post himself ahead of time about their affairs. So he is able to start them talking about themselves — able to make known his *interest* in *them*. Each of these men will leave the table delighted and impressed.

With Roosevelt this strategy was a fixed habit. At the White House, says Isaac Marcosson, the noted journalist, he "found out everything about a man before that man came to see him . . . Most people are vain, and nothing flatters their vanity more than to realize that facts about them are known and not forgotten." [2]

By one of the simplest of all methods, Roosevelt raised the *ego* of people whom he wished to charm.

He showed *sincere* respect for the things that were close to them, respect for their special interests.

Great leaders keep this all-important fact always before them: *People are all different and must be treated differently.*

They know that the points of difference in people, easiest to pick up and to use, lie in their personal interests. To a surprising extent these are common knowledge: the people and the things that have formed a part of their lives; the things that belong to them; the things they themselves have said and thought and done, their habits, their hobbies and their opinions.

"The other fellow's playground" is what one able salesman has called this little private world in which every one of us lives and moves.

Much of the power of the great man comes to him merely because he meets people on their own "playground."

On first becoming head of the United States Steel Corporation, Elbert H. Gary found himself completely blocked.

His associates disliked him. He received little co-operation. He could make no progress. Gary himself has described his difficulties.

"He told me at one time," says a man who knew him well, "that most of the men who had been his associates in the early days of the Steel Corporation, . . . did not like him at first, and he had to study the reason for this and cultivate their friendships before he could make any progress in obtaining their co-operation." "A favorite topic of Judge Gary was the making of friends." [3]

How did he solve his problem, this eminent captain of industry?

One of his answers, a method which he employed regularly, has been described to the authors by Walter Dill Scott, the psychologist who is president of Northwestern University.

"In his business letters," says President Scott, "Gary always put a personal note. He would include just a line or two about the other man's hobbies, or achievements, his family or friends; a word, perhaps, about their last conversation."

This method of showing people that they are important to us is very simple indeed. And the results are often astonishing.

Mark Hanna Turns an Enemy into a Supporter

A young New York business man dislikes Mark Hanna. For two days he has refused even to meet him.

Mark Hanna, magnate of Cleveland, is about to become a world famous figure, political overlord of the United States. Here, at the Republican Convention of 1896, he is making McKinley president, putting the country on a gold standard.

But to the young New Yorker, Hanna is "foulness compact," the "Red Boss" of Cleveland. Newspaper mud slinging has misled William Beer. This high-minded amateur of politics has come to St. Louis to watch the convention, to work for his beliefs. But he has avoided Hanna like a plague spot.

Now Beer has yielded to friends who tell him that it is vital for him to meet the Republican boss.

In a crowded, noisy room at the Southern Hotel, he is led up to a calm, gray-clad figure, "deep in a chair beside a bottle of mineral water."

Beer is presented, Hanna speaks.

And Beer, to his amazement, finds that Hanna is talking about *him*, about *his* father, a Democratic judge; about *his* uncle; about *his* views on the platform:

"'You from Ohio? . . . Son of Judge Beer?' The young man was startled. 'H'm, your dad cost some friends of mine in the oil business a lot of money once. . . . Some Democratic judges,' said Mr. Hanna impersonally, 'are a damn sight more honest than lots of Republican judges. . . . Let's see, . . . Got an uncle down at Ashland, haven't you? . . . And now . . . what's it you want to tell me about the platform?'

"The amateur spoke . . . His throat was raw when he stopped talking.

"'Very interesting,' said Mr. Hanna." [4]

A new chapter has opened in the life of William Beer.

In a few days Hanna will have one more enthusiastic follower. During this convention and for eight years to come, Beer's chief interest will be to serve this man whom he had hated with all his heart.

To Charles Schwab, the one-time stake-driver who has built the Bethlehem Steel Corporation, the personal interests of other men are a recognized instrument of leadership.

As head of the Emergency Fleet Corporation during the War, we find him using this tool to delight and inspire one of his most important subordinates.

To the admiral in charge of the Hog Island shipyards Schwab offers "the best Jersey cow in America" if he will turn out fifty ships that year instead of the thirty-one called for by the program. The Admiral is delighted. He sets out enthusiastically to make the high record: Somehow Schwab has learned that Jersey cows are his special hobby.

It was as a very young man that Cyrus Curtis, millionaire publisher of the *Saturday Evening Post* and the *Ladies' Home Journal*, learned the power of this strategy.

Barely graduated from selling dry goods behind a counter in Portland, Maine, he was struggling to establish the *Ladies' Home Journal*.

But none of the well known authors would write for his obscure magazine. In the front rank of these scornful folk was Louisa M. Alcott, one of the most popular writers of her day. Yet it was she who soon turned the tide for him.

Curtis discovered that Miss Alcott "had a charity in which she was vitally interested."

"So to Miss Alcott the energetic author-chaser returned,"

writes Edward Bok, "with the proposition that he would pay one hundred dollars for a column article for her charity. This proved too strong a temptation for the woman with a pet charity. She sent Mr. Curtis an article and he sent her a check for a hundred dollars." [5]

By merely altering his offer to include Louisa Alcott's hobby, Curtis changed her scorn to liking, rounded a dangerous corner in his career as a publisher.

By a similar plan, Lord Frederick Hamilton, a distinguished British diplomat, once managed a difficult old gentleman when he himself was just beginning his career.

One of Hamilton's first jobs in the diplomatic service was to establish a friendly personal contact with this particular man, the Papal Nuncio in Lisbon.

Hamilton found out ahead of time one fact about this Italian archbishop which others had overlooked. The great prelate had a pet hobby: good food and skilful cooking. Hastily, Hamilton collected enough information about Italian cooking to show an intelligent and sincere interest in this topic.

"After that," he says, "I was the Nuncio's most welcome visitor." They discussed this subject "until the excellent prelate's eyes gleamed and his mouth began to water."

"I felt rewarded for my trouble," Hamilton concludes, "when my chief, the British Minister, informed me that the Nuncio considered me the most intelligent young man he knew. He added further that he enjoyed my visits, as my conversation was so interesting." [6]

Many men set up special methods of collecting and using this sort of information.

Fred Kelly, a well known newspaper man, says that one of the most successful salesmen whom he knows keeps a little card index of the hobbies and personal interests of his customers.

Walter Dill Scott describes a manager who maintains a tickler record of all his employees' birthdays in order to give each his raise in salary on that particular day.

This strategy is especially effective when we can give the other fellow a pleasant surprise. Often all we have to do is to make use of what we already know about him.

Hugh Fullerton tells how Roosevelt charmed and pleased him merely by speaking, time after time when they met, of a point which they had in common, a point dating back many years: "How is baseball?" Teddy always asked, "Is Captain Anson still playing?" [7]

It is a method that will work equally well with the humblest and with the most important people.

"The most eminent of men," writes Isaac Marcosson, famous for his interviews with notables of the world, "is flattered when you can recall to him what he said in a passing conversation the last time you met him." [8]

Not long ago an advertising man was discussing the youthful bank president, Lawrence Whiting, he of the swift, brilliant career in Chicago finance:

"He knows how to ask questions. He is always asking you about yourself, a few words in passing. Shows that he remembers what you are doing, what you are interested in, little things you would think he had forgotten. I'm not important to him, he barely knows me. But when I see him there's always a smile and a question. 'Are you still breaking ninety?' 'Been down to Nashville again?' 'That boy of yours winning any more races?'" [9]

It is easy to make a practice of doing this — and so easy also to forget about it altogether. How often we are thinking not of the other fellow but of ourselves!

Leaders take the trouble to keep their mind on the other man. They solve many problems by showing their respect for the things which are close to him.

William Howard Taft Dances the "Rigadon"

Night after night William Howard Taft nimbly guides his famous bulk — dances the Spanish "Rigadon." Twenty times in forty days he weaves intricate steps with light-footed Filipino women.

He is chairman of the Philippine Commission after the Spanish War and the insurrection. He is traveling from province to province, selling new plans of government to the hostile natives. To win their good will he has studied the "Rigadon" and now dances it night after night with dusky beauties.

"The personal influence of this man was irresistible," says Oscar Davis. "He found the Filipinos sullen, suspicious . . . He made them all friends." [10]

Taft displayed his sincere respect for the other fellow's customs by himself adopting one of them.

So also Calvin Coolidge made his bow to the farm vote by posing for photographers in his overalls, pitchfork in hand; complimented our Indians by donning a feathered headdress.

When General Goethals took charge of building the Panama Canal, he astonished every one by laying aside his uniform and appearing in civilian clothes. Statesmen and soldiers were shocked. But the vast civilian force of laborers and engineers was pleased and reassured.

Benjamin Franklin, arch diplomat of America, suave master of men, learned this strategy only by first scorching his fingers. Working far from home in a London printing house, he tried to buck traditions. In the composing room he refused to pay the tax levied by the workmen on all newcomers. For several weeks he endured all manner of annoyances — then gave in, "convinced of the folly of being on ill terms with those one is to live with constantly." [11] Soon he gained great influence over his fellow workers.

He who hopes to lead must first show respect for the habits of the group, whether it is a club, a nation, a trade or a school. On the stranger who disregards our customs, whose ways are different, we cannot help looking with coolness and suspicion. He is exhibiting a sort of contempt for the things which we revere. Franklin, it appears, made the mistake only once.

As American representative in France, years later, he literally rebuilt himself into a Frenchman, gained a popularity in that country unequaled by any American until the days of the Great War and Myron T. Herrick.

Able men often draw the other fellow to them by merely showing respect for his name — the one thing which is close to every one's *ego*.

It was as a boy, the son of a poor weaver in Scotland, that Andrew Carnegie, the great "Iron Master," first used this strategy.   At that time he was engaged in raising rabbits.

"My first business venture," he says, "was securing my companions' services for a season as an employer, the compensation being that the young rabbits, when such came, should be named after them. . . . Many . . . were content to gather dandelions and clover for a whole season with me, conditioned upon this unique reward — the poorest return ever made to labor.   Alas! what else had I to offer them! . . .

"I treasure the remembrance of this plan as the earliest evidence of organizing power upon the development of which my material success in life has hung." [12]

Later on Carnegie employed this same plan to sell steel rails. One of his biggest customers was the Pennsylvania Railroad. When his great new rail mill was built in Pittsburgh he linked this customer to him for good and all: He set up a lasting mark of respect for John Edgar Thomson, president of the Pennsylvania, by naming the new mill the "Edgar Thomson Steel Works" in his honor.

With people in all walks of life, Andrew Carnegie followed this same policy: He exhibited esteem for their names.

It was one of his delights, we are told by Samuel Gompers, the noted labor leader, to describe how he called his men by name, "Bill," or "John."   And it was one of his boasts that no strike had ever occurred in his mills when he was personally in charge.

Many are the industrial leaders who make it a point to know the names of their subordinates by the hundreds and by the thousands, and to speak to them always by name.

The force of this precaution is strikingly illustrated by the way in which Hugh Chalmers was lured away from the National Cash Register Company.   Roy Chapin and Howard Coffin, having formed the Thomas-Detroit automobile company, decided they needed Chalmers.   But he was already earning seventy thousand a year where he was.   And he refused all offers until one provision was added: that they would rename the company in his honor.   This Chalmers could not resist.

So the Chalmers-Detroit Motor Car Company came into being.

In many different ways able men take pains to exhibit their respect for the things which other people revere.

We see Leonard Wood, Protestant, walking down a sun-scorched street of Santiago, Cuba, solemnly swinging a Catholic censer. A Catholic canopy shades his Protestant head, a mitered bishop is by his side. The crowds cheer. Governor of Cuba after the Spanish War, General Wood is winning over resentful, suspicious Cubans, turning a fever-ridden, disorderly island into a self-governing republic. Now he is showing his genuine respect for the church which the Cubans revere.

It was in this spirit that Arthur Balfour, the British statesman, visiting this country during the Great War, publicly praised Herbert Hoover, James Gerard, and our American weather; talked frequently of "democracy"; showed himself "democratic" by cracking jokes and riding a bicycle; remarked that, like Woodrow Wilson, he enjoyed detective stories; started his address to Congress by "reminding his audience that he was himself a member of a free assembly like their own." [13]

William Wrigley, Jr., the salesman who has made himself a millionaire captain of industry, literally built his career around this type of strategy. "Wherever I went to sell goods," he recently told the authors, "I got the atmosphere of the town and the people and talked to dealers in their own terms."

When selling soap, for example, to French-Canadians, he announced himself in each store by tapping his chest and exclaiming, *"Savon minéral!"* This phrase for mineral soap was all the French he knew and, after using it once, he lapsed immediately into English. But these two words did the work. The merchants were delighted just to be greeted in their native tongue. Few other salesmen had taken the trouble to show them this small courtesy.

To win the other fellow's liking and co-operation, remember that his personal interests are different from your own. Keep in mind his habits and hobbies; the things he has done, the things he owns; his knowledge, his opinions, and his name; the people and the things he reveres; his wants and his needs.

Take the trouble to exhibit your respect for these interests of his.

Show him that you know what they are and that you esteem them. Make full use of the small points which you remember about him.

With people who are especially important to you, it often pays to post yourself ahead of time on their interests and perhaps to work out some plan for keeping yourself posted.

When dealing with groups, you can often display sincere respect for their customs and habits by yourself adopting some of them.

CHAPTER IV

HOW TO INTEREST AND CONVINCE PEOPLE

A Telegraph Boy Makes Presidents His Friends
Gerard Swope Loses a Big Contract
Alexander Graham Bell Offers to Make a Piano Sing
Amos Cummings Lands a Job in New York

WHEN EDWARD BOK, editor and builder of the *Ladies'
Home Journal*, was only thirteen, he won the personal
attention of the greatest men of his day by merely
writing a special sort of letter to each of them.

At that time Bok was an obscure immigrant boy working as
a Western Union messenger in Brooklyn. Yet with very little
trouble, he quickly established friendships with General and
Mrs. Grant, Rutherford Hayes, General Sherman, Mrs. Abraham Lincoln, Jefferson Davis, and many others.

And later, it was one of these new friends, Rutherford Hayes,
as president of the United States, who smashed precedents in
Bok's behalf by writing for his *Brooklyn Magazine* an article
which started it toward success.

Hundreds, thousands, as we know, clamor for the bare attention of such noted men.

Yet little Edward Bok easily outstripped these thousands.

It was a special sort of letter, as already pointed out, that
he wrote to each of his celebrities.

Bok had read short biographies of these noted men. Here
was his well of magic.

"He decided to test the correctness of the biographies," says
Beard, "and with the simple directness of a Dutch boy he wrote

to General James A. Garfield asking if the story of his once
being a boy on the tow-path was true, and telling him why he
asked.   General Garfield answered him fully and cordially.
Then the idea came to the boy to procure other letters from
noted men, not only for their autographs, but also for the sake
of learning something useful. . . .

"So he started, asking why one man did this or that, or the
date of an occurrence in his life. . . .   Several authors asked
Edward to come and see them, so the boy watched to see when
distinguished men arrived in Brooklyn and then he would go
and call on those to whom he had sent letters and thank them
personally." [1]

Many of us must win and hold the notice of important
strangers, must capture fortresses.   What of our ammunition?
Do we, like Bok, look into the *other fellow's* experience to find it?

The first problem in influencing people, of course, is *to gain
and hold their attention.*

This was Bok's real achievement.   He did it by a method
that all able men employ: He approached each celebrity
through *that man's special interests.*

Sheer good luck enabled Andrew Carnegie to use this strategy
at a critical moment.   Carnegie found that he had lost the contract for "the most important railroad bridge that had been
built up to that time."

Now he was trying to persuade the directors of the bridge
company to change their decision.   But they were totally ignorant about the big point involved: that wrought iron was superior to cast iron.   Carnegie was making little headway.

Then, says Carnegie, came "something akin to the hand of
Providence."

One of the directors, it developed, had recently smashed a
cast iron lamp-post by running his buggy into it in the dark.

Gleefully, Carnegie pounced upon this trifle.   "Ah, gentlemen, there is the point." [2]   And now at last they were really
listening to him!   Now he could show them why wrought iron
was superior to cast iron.

With this incident to work upon, Carnegie saved the day,
snatched the big contract from the rival company whose bid

the directors had already decided to accept. After everything else failed, Carnegie held the attention of these directors by the same method which little Edward Bok employed: through an appeal to their own personal experience.

When we see a man's eyes wandering as we talk to him, feel his attention slipping away from us, it usually is because we have neglected this strategy: We have forgotten to consider *his* experience. We have not come close enough to his special interests. A serious blunder in the career of Gerard Swope strikingly illustrates this point.

Gerard Swope Loses a Big Contract

At a critical period in his business life Gerard Swope lost a large contract.

President, now, of the General Electric Company, Swope was at that time a youthful salesman for Western Electric. He was hoping to become head of a branch office.

And then came this misfortune. A carefully prepared report, submitted to the governors of a penitentiary, fell flat.

He "had to learn another lesson. . . . " writes Keene Sumner. "It was Swope the engineer, not Swope the salesman, that made out that report, for it was filled with such a mass of bewildering details that the governors hadn't the remotest idea what it meant. The result was that a rival company won the contract." [3] Swope, with his elaborate report, made no impression whatever.

What a contrast there is between this report of Swope's and the method employed by Andrew Carnegie!

With his yarn about a broken lamp-post, Carnegie was able to snatch a contract from under the very nose of a competing firm.

But Swope failed even to hold the attention of the men whom he hoped to convince.

Swope used unfamiliar language, ignored the other fellow's personal interests.

Carnegie gripped the attention of the directors by approaching them through their own experience.

The closer we come to the other man's special interests, the more closely we rivet his attention.

Every newspaper we read is built upon this strategy. Says Kent Cooper, general manager of the Associated Press:

"The first big fact which the editor keeps in mind is that you are most interested in yourself. The second fact is a corollary of the first. You are interested in the people whom you know and the things which you have seen." "There were some very important despatches from Europe on the front and second pages of the paper this morning, but you gave them hardly a glance. . . . For the present you are more interested in what your income tax is going to be, whether there will be a new subway, so that you won't be so crowded on your way home at night; whether real estate values on your street are going up or down; whether someone whom you know has died, and whether the report of the dinner which took place last night contains your name as 'among those present.'" [4]

"The most interesting person in the world to anyone is himself," says Karl A. Bickel, the president of the United Press. "If you can't read something about yourself, you want to read about someone you know either personally or by reputation." [5]

This is why Babe Ruth holds our attention more readily than, for example, Gaston Doumergue, president of France. Doumergue is a more important person. But most of us know Babe better. He is closer to *us* and *our* personal interests.

This is why our own name leaps out at us from a printed page, no matter how small the type in which it appears. It is a part of ourselves.

For this same reason we follow with bated breath the adventures of the hero on the screen or through the pages of a novel. In reality it is ourselves that we are watching. When he shoots, we pull the trigger; when he flees, we spur his horse. And those newspaper headlines about nameless people — "Masked bandit holds up man and wife" — why do they stop us? Because for the moment, we ourselves are that man who faced the bandit's revolver. "People like to read about . . . the things that might conceivably have happened to themselves," says Kent Cooper, "about the dramas, and the tragedies in

which they might have been the heroes or the victims." [6]
"Human interest stuff" it is called by newspaper men: stories
in which we ourselves can step into the leading rôle. It is in
ourselves that we are really interested.

Watch a friend the next time you hand him some snapshots.
Almost always he will linger longest over those in which he
himself is included. He cannot help doing this. None of us
can.

In the Edison laboratories at West Orange, New Jersey,
Thomas Edison has worked out an ingenious method of discovering what part of the work really interests his young
employees most deeply. He gives little heed to what they themselves say. He gets the actual facts in a quite different way:
through a system that shows him the things to which they *give
their attention* most frequently.

"At all times," his son, Charles Edison, recently told the
authors, "we have four young men whose sole duty it is to
wander around through shops on tours of inspection. Each
day they make reports with suggestions, criticisms and comments. Many valuable ideas come to us from these reports.
But, even more important, we learn what it is that genuinely
interests these men — what field they are best suited for.

"A man, for instance, is a chemical engineer and tells us
that chemistry is his chosen line. Nevertheless, his reports may
show no constructive suggestions in this field — but many on
production and layout. These, obviously, are the subjects to
which he has paid attention. Then we know, beyond doubt,
that his real interests lie here and we put him in that branch
of the work."

Irresistibly, in spite of ourselves, we are all drawn to what
is close to our inmost interests and impulses — interests of
which we ourselves are sometimes unaware.

Above all else, people give their attention to themselves and
to their own affairs: to their own wants and problems; to the
things that touch upon their own experience.

Also, of course, they attend to what is new.

The way in which able men use "what is new" in managing
others, forms in itself a special type of strategy.

Alexander Graham Bell Offers to Make a Piano Sing

Alexander Graham Bell, founder of the Bell Telephone system, is out to raise money.

He is at the home of a friend, a Mr. Hubbard of Cambridge, whom he hopes to interest in an invention on which he is working.

Does he begin by talking about the profit he expects to make or about his scientific ideas? Not Alexander Graham Bell! Before plunging into all this, Bell takes the trouble to set the stage. He is a salesman and business man as well as an inventor.

"He was playing the piano," writes MacKenzie, "stopped suddenly, and said to Mr. Hubbard, 'Do you know that if I depress the pedal and sing a note into this piano, that the piano will respond with the same note? That if I sing "do," the piano will return "do"?'

"Mr. Hubbard did not know it. Politely he put down his book and enquired further. Bell explained his theory of the harmonic or multiple telegraph.

"Nothing could be more typical of Bell's instinct for good theatre . . . He would have made a superb press agent. The incident resulted in an offer from Hubbard to share the expenses of Bell's experiments." [7]

Bell's plan of campaign is simple. Before telling his story, he takes the trouble to rouse the other man's curiosity. He uses showmanship.

Watch me make this piano sing!

By doing something different and "new," Bell rivets Hubbard's attention to himself and to his ideas. It is a powerful type of strategy — and yet, as many of us know, it is surrounded by pitfalls. How often we have seen elaborate stunts fall flat, produce no more than a shrug of the shoulders or a lift of the eyebrows! Most able men are good showmen simply because they observe one important precaution in employing what is "new."

We can easily get at the principle of it all by comparing this plan of Bell's with the unsuccessful report which Swope submitted to the governors of the penitentiary.

Swope's report, with its technical language, was very different and very "new." But it was a fizzle. It failed completely to hold the other fellow's attention.

The words Swope used were, of course, altogether *too* "new." They were not interesting. They were merely *unfamiliar* and bewildering. And this is the trouble also with many so-called stunts. They are merely queer and puzzling.

But Bell combined the "new" with the familiar: Hubbard's own piano was to perform tricks.

What is "new" catches our attention — a new sound, for instance, a new movement, a new word on a printed page. In fact, we attend only to things that are "new" in some respect. But the "new" does not *hold* our attention unless it is in part familiar, unless it touches on our own experience.

It is the new combined with the familiar that grips our attention most strongly, that rouses our active curiosity. And this is what we are offered by the able salesman, by the newspaper editor, by the successful public speaker. All those who must make a strong bid for our notice use showmanship.

Bell himself, we are told, took the trouble to follow this plan in his ordinary conversation. He was a fascinating talker because he made things dramatic.

It was through a clever bit of showmanship that Cyrus H. McCormick introduced his binder into England.

Among gaily painted competing machines at the great London agricultural show, the McCormick binder appeared rusty and dilapidated, drawn by sorry looking nags. The ship carrying it had been wrecked and McCormick had purposely left the machine much as it was when rescued.

Imagine the surprise and admiration of the crowd when this pitiful looking affair won the contest hands down! A nine days' wonder to be discussed by thousands of people! In the last act, as it were, McCormick had sprung a complete surprise.

In a similar manner, Charles Schwab astonished the British government during the Great War. He refused an enormous contract offered on the condition that he make delivery in *six* months. Schwab demanded and was allowed *eight* months. Then he calmly proceeded to beat his own delivery date.

Fred Reppert, known as "one of the greatest living auctioneers," once said that this same method was always used to make buyers feel that what they were offered was "dirt cheap." Reppert always brought out first of all the most expensive animals, the "tops," in order that the prices of the lower-grade stock might come as a pleasant surprise later on.

Like Bell with his singing piano, like McCormick with his rusty reaper, and Schwab with his war contract, Reppert gripped the other fellow's attention by doing something unexpected.

These men understood showmanship. They used what was "new" and different to astonish the other fellow and to arouse his curiosity.

But they were careful to *base* their approach on his *own experience, on his own personal interests*. They combined the "new" with the familiar.

The object of such men is not *merely to catch* the other fellow's attention. This, of course, is essential, but it is not enough. They want to *hold* his attention and *convince* him.

When we wish people to accept and act on a new idea, the first precaution is this: to present it in terms of *their* experience.

Amos Cummings Lands a Job in New York

Amos Cummings, perhaps the most famous managing editor New York ever saw, used this strategy to land his first job with a newspaper.

Newly arrived in New York at the age of eighteen, Cummings had the problem of selling himself to some entirely strange editor. With thousands of men out of work just at that time and all the newspapers besieged by job-hunters, this was no light undertaking.

The only experience Cummings had to offer was a few years of typesetting for a printer.

It was because of what Cummings had learned about Horace Greeley, owner of the *New York Tribune*, that he tried this paper first of all: Greeley, like Cummings himself, had started work as a printer's boy.

Cummings believed that Greeley would be favorably impressed with a lad whose early training matched his own.

Cummings was right. Greeley employed him.

This youth easily convinced Greeley that he was worth hiring. He sold himself to Greeley just as Carnegie sold his bridge to the directors: Cummings was able to express his ideas about himself in terms of Greeley's own personal experience.

As a rule this strategy is very easy. Let us suppose that we have seen a new dirigible and want to convince people that it is amazingly long. To the fellow across the street we say that it would reach three whole blocks, all the way from Elm Street to Lincoln Street. He has walked these blocks frequently and knows just how long they are. To a farmer we say that it is twice as long as his own pasture lot. To the New York man we say that its length equals the height of the new Chrysler Building on 42nd Street. We convince each man because we make contact with *his* special experience.

Most of the time people do not even understand what we are talking about unless we approach them in this way. They cannot, of course, grasp our point until they tie it up to their own experience. And if what we say does not tie up quickly and easily they are apt to ignore it altogether. They shrink from the mental effort of thinking it out for themselves. Most human beings have the habit of laziness.

For this reason able men often go to considerable trouble to speak *the other fellow's language* in presenting their ideas.

On a tour with three of his children, John D. Rockefeller, Jr., besieged by newspaper photographers, wishes to shield his offspring from publicity. Does he issue stern refusals? Not the son of clever old John D.! Young John D. wants to keep the good will of the press, make these reporters see things his way.

He talks to them, not as journalists — but as men, who like himself, are fathers or hope to be. He appeals to them as one father to another, reminds them that publicity is not desirable in the training of the very young. They agree, withdraw courteously.

Another interesting example of this simple yet far-reaching

strategy we find in the career of Charles W. Brown, the sea captain who made himself president of the Pittsburgh Plate Glass Company, one of the largest firms of its kind in the world.

In his early days on shore, establishing his own stained glass business in Minneapolis, Brown took a big contract away from the most important concerns in the field, merely by considering the special experience of the buyers.

The committee which was to award the contract was composed of Westerners. So Brown made his design "rugged" and "bold." Competing designs from the East were "exquisitely beautiful." But Brown got the order. He approached these buyers *through their own experience*.

By this same plan Evangeline Booth was able to send hardened convicts to their knees in tears after talking to them for only a few minutes.

"She would start with things the criminal did as a boy," says Waldo Warren, "by asking him questions about his mother, drawing him out about his own experiences. The convict could resist anything that came from the *outside*, but against ideas that came from *within himself* he was powerless." [8]

Our boyhood hero, the famous explorer, La Salle, met disaster after disaster because of hostile Indians, until he finally won over certain tribes by addressing them in their own language and in their own particular style of oratory. Only with the help of these Indians was La Salle finally able to make his historic trip to the Gulf of Mexico.

It was by a single remark, by using one of the other fellow's pet phrases at the right time, that Henry Thornton, American railway man, believes that he assured his success in England as general manager of the Great Eastern Railroad. On arriving he found himself "welcome as a frost in May." The Board of the railroad had stirred up resentment by announcing that no "Englishman competent to fill the place" could be found. But Henry Thornton, future head of the Canadian National Railways, future leader of a hundred thousand men, used strategy. Publicly he addressed these Englishmen in their own language, in words that "struck the English fancy." All that he wanted, he said, was a "sporting chance."

To Joseph Choate, for many years leader of the New York bar, whose place as a charming and forceful speaker perhaps has never been filled, this strategy provided the very foundation and framework of an address.

Speaking before a school of art devoted chiefly to pottery, Choate opened by calling himself "clay" in the hands of the presiding officer, proceeded to sketch the history of pottery back to the days of Babylon and Nineveh.

As chairman at a gathering of fly fishermen, he started by picturing himself as a "strange" fish that one of their officers had landed at the meeting, probably much to their discomfiture. Then he described the great work of the United States Fishery Commission in re-stocking rivers.

We hear him at an English school enumerating a long list of the very distinguished graduates of the school, pointing out England's advantages in education over America.

Invariably Choate's main theme, much of his message, most of his humor, centered directly on the other fellow's personal interests.

Al Smith, Democratic leader, is a master of this strategy. He carefully chooses his words and phrases, as well as his subject matter, in the light of his audience. What he says is always adapted to the language and habits of his hearers, whether he is speaking at a university or at an East-side political gathering in New York.

To talk in terms of the *experiences* of your audience, says Arthur Edward Phillips, author of *Effective Speaking*, is the foremost principle of the art.

"*The more the speaker brings his idea within the vivid experience of the listener*," writes Phillips, "*the more likely will he attain his end*." "I tell my friend a neighbor has bought a load of alfalfa. I am unintelligible. Perceiving it, I continue, 'Alfalfa is a kind of hay,' and at once a reasonably clear conception of alfalfa is formed. The unintelligible has been made intelligible by *coming into the listener's experience*. . . .

"When my friend entered his home the sky was cloudless. An hour later I come in and say there will be a storm. He contradicts me. I then tell him that heavy black clouds are rolling up from the west, that flashes of lightning can be seen and that the wind is increasing. He now agrees with me. What did I do? I gave him three facts that were like his own experience in respect to the conditions generally preceding a storm."

"Reference to experience, then, means coming *into the listener's life*." [9]

When you want to hold people's attention and convince them, be careful to approach them through their own personal experience and needs. Speak in their own language: not only in the actual words that they are accustomed to using, but also in language of their thoughts.

To make a strong bid for notice, try to arouse curiosity. Be unexpected and dramatic. You can do this by combining something "new" with what is already familiar to them.

CHAPTER V

LETTING THE OTHER FELLOW
DO THE TALKING

Dwight Morrow Captures a President
The "Richest Man in Boston" Gets His Start
Why Henry H. Rogers Likes to Hear Questions

DWIGHT W. MORROW, fledgling diplomat, spreads his untried wings.

Ex-law clerk, ex-partner of Pierpont Morgan, he has been made ambassador to Mexico by Calvin Coolidge.

Morrow has a difficult job: "a first-aid job," Bruce Barton calls it, "on that hitherto sorest thumb of Uncle Sam's hand across the seas and borders — Mexico."

And now comes his critical moment: his first call on President Calles.

Will Morrow make a good impression? Will he succeed in putting across himself and his country?

Morrow turns the trick. Tense Mexicans, anxious Americans relax.

"Next day," writes Barton, "President Calles said to a friend that here at last was an ambassador who talked his own language."

What has this amateur diplomat said to President Calles? What has been his strategy?

"Morrow had nothing to say about the weighty problems with which ambassadors are supposed to deal," says Barton. "He just passed back for more pancakes, praised the cooking, lit a cigar and asked the President to tell him about Mexico.

What were the hopes of the Administration for the country? What was the President trying to do? How did he view the future?" [1]

Morrow captured Calles by a method we all can use: *He let the other fellow do the talking.*

By encouraging Calles to explain his ideas and problems, by listening attentively, Morrow showed his respect for the other man's personal interests, raised his *ego*.

All highly successful men have taught themselves how to *listen*. It will be interesting to see what has been written about them on this point by those who have observed them closely.

"Without saying a single word, Mr. Schwab can flatter more than any man I ever met," says Merle Crowell. "Listening with him is an instinct as well as a rare charm. Whoever talks to him, be he day laborer or financier, faces a man who hearkens gravely, attentive, eye to eye, until the speaker is quite done." [2]

William Randolph Hearst, "for a man of large affairs and crowded appointments, . . . is the world's best listener. . . . When he . . . wishes to please, Hearst can be as winsome as a woman." [3]

That noted American statesman, John Hay, "was as good a listener as he was a talker, . . . His manner toward the conversation of others was the most winning form of compliment conceivable. Every person who spent a half hour or more with him was sure to go away not only charmed with Hay, but uncommonly well pleased with himself." [4]

And "Silent Cal" — how well we know it! — "was Northampton's champion listener: listened his way into all the offices the town would give him." [5]

"He is an unusually good listener," [6] an old friend wrote of Colonel House in his college days. And it was this knack of listening that played a large part in making House "Assistant President" to Woodrow Wilson, that enabled him to delight and impress Wilson at their first historic meeting at the Hotel Gotham in New York City.

Such leaders have learned to make a fine art of listening. They know that it is far more than mere silence. They not only feel a genuine interest in what people are saying, but even more, they take the trouble to *display* it. Yet many men ignore precautions of this sort even with the very people whom they are most anxious to impress and win over.

"Many young men who go to see important personages wonder why they fail to make a favorable impression," writes Isaac Marcosson, celebrated for his interviews with the great. "Usually they attach blame to prejudice or indifference. In reality they have . . . overlooked the real reason which is in themselves. They have not listened attentively. They have been so much concerned with what they are going to say next that they do not keep their ears open. . . . Big men have told me that they prefer good listeners to good talkers, but the ability to listen seems rarer than almost any other good trait."

"The highest compliment that you can pay anyone is to listen intently to him." [7]

To "listen intently" is not only in itself an easy way to charm people. But, in addition, it is one of the most effective methods of inducing people to talk.

The "Richest Man in Boston" Gets His Start

William Alfred Paine, late head of the famous investment banking house — Paine, Webber and Company — was known for years as "the richest man in Boston." But when, with a fellow bank clerk, he first founded this firm, they had between them only their hopes and three thousand dollars.

This ex-messenger boy, ex-clerk, had, to be sure, been reading extensively about banking. "But it had seemed presumptuous," he said, "that I, a thousand-dollar-a-year clerk, should actually set up as an adviser to men who had so much more money."

Then William Paine made a discovery. It came when he began to interview customers. He himself describes it:

"Once started, I completely lost my sense of embarrassment. I discovered that older men liked to talk to me about things in which they were interested." [8]

Paine found that he could make an impression upon his customers, just as Dwight Morrow impressed Calles: *by causing them to talk about their own special interests.* Able men attach great importance to this strategy.

Let us observe Nicholas Longworth, speaker of the House, receiving callers in his office. Duff Gilfond has sketched him in action:

"He chats with his visitor in low tones . . . More often he listens, . . . People always tell him things. They can't help it. He establishes points of contact with everybody." [9]

Of Peter McCall, one-time mayor of Philadelphia and a man of unusual charm, Governor Pennypacker says: "With timid visitors at his home he broached one topic of conversation after another until he discovered the subject in which they were interested and informed, and *then he sat and silently listened.*" [10]

"In conversing with a stranger, send out tentative lines, baited with suggestions. Let him catch and hold on to the line that pleases him most." [11] So Lillian Eichler comments on this strategy in her *Book of Conversation.*

This same plan also frequently offers us the most effective method of convincing people.

It was chiefly by making the *other fellow* talk, that T. E. Lawrence, "Uncrowned King of Arabia," added new Arab tribes to his "army" during the Great War. This young English captain, who "single-handed overthrew the Turkish Empire," has himself described how in meetings with the Arabs his talk was "directed to light trains of their buried thoughts," so that finally it was they who were urging upon him "the full intensity of their belief." [12]

What a simple plan it is: merely to keep ourselves in the background, to show a sincere interest in the other fellow, and to release in him a flow of talk and ideas!

Yet few of us have escaped taking at least one tumble by forgetting this very precaution. We have plunged into conversation about some topic that interested us and then have suddenly found ourselves floundering, with the other fellow looking bored.

It is by making contact with the other fellow's personal interests, by shifting the burden of the conversation to him, that we can most easily maintain our own poise, free ourselves from any trace of embarrassment, and put both him and ourselves at ease.   This is the whole secret of breaking the ice with strangers.   What a relief it often is when we finally launch others on a topic that really interests them!

Many people cause themselves endless trouble by neglecting this precaution altogether.   We all know them: They are the men and women who are forever chattering about themselves and their affairs.   If they are salesmen they lose our business because we cannot get a word in edgewise.   If they are acquaintances or friends, they frequently bore us beyond words. These people are seriously handicapped.   The real reason they talk so much about themselves is that they yield to a childish desire to attract notice, to feel important.

Still other people irritate us by forever parading *their* silly notions about our business, about our hobbies.   They feel they should deal with our interests instead of their own.   But they foolishly try to impress us with what *they* know, with what *they* think.

Leaders do not make this mistake.   Their purpose is to let the other fellow display *his* knowledge, to increase *his* sense of importance.

In the first chapter we watched the newspaper man, Paul Leach, win Herbert Hoover in this way by giving Hoover a chance to correct him.   When all else failed it was a *misstatement of fact* about Hoover's own pet subject, mining, that saved the interview.   Leach raised Hoover's *ego* by showing plainly that he knew *less* than Hoover and that he himself realized it.

Sometime when you are up against a man who just won't talk, see if you cannot easily put yourself across as Leach did. Try making a slight misstatement of fact about something on which the other man is unusually well posted.   One of the surest ways to win a man and to start him talking is to show sincere respect for his superior knowledge.

Why Henry H. Rogers Likes to Hear Questions

Henry H. Rogers, New York capitalist, is being interviewed by Isaac Marcosson.

"I had to ask him many questions," writes Marcosson, "so many in fact, that I expressed regret over it.

"Quick as a flash he came back:

"'If you did not ask questions it would mean that you were not interested.'

"Many men," continues Marcosson, "never get anywhere because they are afraid to ask questions. They think it irritates or annoys a big personage. But the reverse is true. . . .

"A reporter on a New York newspaper once went to interview a well known Wall Street banker about foreign exchange, which is one of the most complicated subjects in finance. After fifteen minutes of conversation the reporter grabbed his hat and started to leave, saying, 'Thanks very much. I understand perfectly.'

"Before he got to the door the banker called him back and said: 'Young man, you are a wonder. I have been in the banking business for forty years, but I do not know "all about" foreign exchange even yet.'" [13]

Men often neglect to ask questions merely because, like this reporter, they are foolishly satisfied with what they already know, or else because they shrink from revealing their ignorance.

Yet, as we all realize, questions of the right kind are one of the most effective methods of winning other people. Theodore Roosevelt literally pumped men dry with questions.

"Under Roosevelt," says Charles Seymour, "the White House opened its doors to everyone who could bring the President anything of interest, whether in the field of science, literature, politics, or sport, and the chief magistrate, no matter who his guest, instantly found a common ground for discussion." [14]

Roosevelt's astonishing success in fascinating other men has often been misunderstood. Because he was himself so amazingly well posted on many subjects, some people have supposed that he charmed others by displaying what *he knew* himself. But actually he won them by just the opposite method: by showing that he honestly admired *their* store of information in some special field. Whatever the subject might be, Roosevelt thrilled the other fellow with his eagerness to learn.

Several precautions are observed by able men in using questions to win people and this is the first one: to be certain *that the question actually displays respect for the other man's knowledge.*

It was because he neglected this one precaution that David McLain "lost twenty jobs." Actually McLain was hunting information about steel-making, pushing himself up from his start as a nine-year-old foundry boy to his present high place as an internationally recognized foundry expert. But at the start he asked questions badly. "I lost job after job," he says, "because, in the eyes of the foreman, I 'knew too much.'" [15]

How often a question displeases us merely because it *sounds* critical!

The day came when McLain saw his mistake and corrected it. He found a way to show respect for his boss and for what his boss knew. He asked a question and got a pleasant and complete reply. That day marked a milestone in his career.

The second essential precaution in asking questions is *to be sure that it displays genuine interest.*

"A young woman," Lillian Eichler tells us, "once asked the president of Princeton, Dr. McCosh, a question on moral philosophy . . . He turned abruptly and asked, 'Madam, are you asking for information or just to make conversation?'" [16]

Dr. McCosh was a trifle rough with the girl. But she deserved it. Her inquiry sounded insincere.

The third important precaution to observe in asking questions is to be reasonably sure that the other fellow will *enjoy* answering them. We all know and avoid the man who attempts to push us into the witness box about our private affairs.

"I hear that rents are going up in this neighborhood," he says. "What do you pay?"

"Is the membership large at this club?" he asks. "What are your dues?"

In short, this fellow is impertinent and a pest.

It is, of course, easy to avoid this pitfall, nor is it difficult to frame questions that are successful on all counts.

The chief problem in asking questions, as in making contacts with people by any method whatever, is usually to locate the right topic. What shall we do, for example, with strangers whose personal interests are a complete mystery? There are a number of useful formulas. Lillian Eichler describes some of them.

"Anyone," she says, "will talk with pleasure about his hobbies, so you might ask a man what he likes best to do with his spare time. Anyone likes to relate an experience in which he is the central figure, so you might ask a man who owns a car what was the closest he ever came to a serious accident. Anyone likes to voice his opinion, so you might ask a man what he thinks of the mysterious murder everyone is discussing." [17]

You will flatter nearly any man by asking his views about a subject of general interest on which he is apt to be well posted. This is a highly useful type of question in all dealings with other people, whether business or social.

But the one topic which will pry open even the most hopeless clam, the subject which every human being likes to discuss, is, fortunately, the easiest of all to handle: *other people*.

A well known advertising man has called people "the most interesting subject in the world." And this is almost true. We ourselves come first, then *other people*. Whether it is Herbert Hoover or Lindbergh who is mentioned, our boss or our next-door neighbor, we prick up our ears and think of things to say, when we hear a comment about people whom we know.

If you are ever again caught in one of those awkward bogs of silence, which we all dread, use this handy exit. Bring up the name of a person with whom the other person is likely to be familiar: a mutual friend, your hostess for the evening, or any outstanding personality such as a politician or author, business man or aviator, actor or athlete. Try, of course, to select the person who is closest to what you can guess about the other man's special interests.

The easiest way to influence people and to impress them favorably is to induce them to talk about their own affairs and problems, their own knowledge and opinions.

Show your interest in these things by the way in which you draw the other man out, by the kind of questions you ask and by your manner of listening. Make it a definite part of your program to listen attentively when others speak to you.

CHAPTER VI

THE KNACK OF GETTING CO-OPERATION

Hearst Gets His Own Way by Not Asking for It
How Colonel House Sold Ideas to Woodrow Wilson
Whitelaw Reid Hires an Unwilling Lieutenant

WILLIAM RANDOLPH HEARST is disappointed. The famous cartoonist, Thomas Nast, has done a poor job.

Already Hearst is on his way to become the potent publisher we know today with twenty-three newspapers and twelve magazines. But at the time he has only a single paper in San Francisco.

He has seized upon cartoonist Nast, who happens to be in town. He wants Nast to help him in his most important project: a crusade to force the trolley companies to put fenders on their street cars.

And Nast has fallen down.

How can Hearst get a really fine piece of work from the great cartoonist? This poor cartoon must be "killed." Nast must be induced to start all over again. But is it possible to do this without destroying Nast's enthusiasm?

"At dinner that night, . . . " writes Winkler, "Hearst praised the cartoon highly.

"'The cars have been maiming and killing a good many children, Mr. Nast,' he said. 'Sometimes I look at those cars and see not a man but a skeleton at the control. The skeleton, it seems to me, leers at the little children at play as they run thoughtlessly across the path of the approaching Juggernaut.'

"'By George, Mr. Hearst, that would make a wonderful

picture!' exclaimed Nast. 'Kill that other drawing. Let me work on this.'

"Nast was so excited that he labored half the night in his hotel room and next day brought in a graphic masterpiece of the cartoonist's art, a drawing that did much to force the street-car companies to capitulate. Hundreds of similar examples could be given of Hearst's gift of artful suggestion." [1]

So, without argument, Hearst induces Nast to "kill" his own work and to "sit up half the night" carrying out another man's idea. Nast is carried off his feet by a new thought which he believes to be his own!

By "artful suggestion" Hearst has implanted this idea in Nast's mind without letting him realize how it really got there.

It is a method that is frequently used. People put forth their greatest efforts when they are carrying out ideas which they can claim as their own. One of the best ways to get them to adopt a plan with enthusiasm is to give them credit for originating it. By this strategy, whether we are dealing with our boss or our office boy, we uphold the other fellow's *ego*, cause him to feel important.

Frederick Taylor, the great efficiency engineer, followed the deliberate course of "making it easy for his associates to think that the boldly original ideas he instilled in them were their own."

Taylor "saw that his *real* purpose was not to win credit for himself but *to get things done* . . . " says W. H. Leffingwell, one of his able followers. "The net result was to give Taylor the very valuable reputation of being a man of influence." [2]

As president of the United States, Abraham Lincoln in this way controlled a powerful politician whom President Grant, later on, found it altogether impossible to manage. Lincoln handled Charles Sumner by adroitly "playing upon" his vanity, "by making him believe that he suggested measures which the Administration had already determined on." [3]

We all know people who hate to admit that anyone else has given them even a suggestion. Very frequently, when all other approaches fail, their armor can be pierced by letting them take the credit for our own ideas.

How Colonel House Sold Ideas to Woodrow Wilson

Among the men who surrounded Woodrow Wilson as president, Colonel House was the only one who succeeded in exerting any real influence upon him.   While others made little or no headway, House repeatedly sold far-reaching plans to Wilson.   Arthur D. Howden Smith has given us House's own account of how he did it:

"'After I got to know the President,' House told me, 'I learned the best way to convert him to an idea was to plant it in his mind casually, but so as to interest him in it — so as to get him thinking about it on his own account.   The first time this worked it was an accident.   I had been visiting him at the White House, and urged a policy on him which he appeared to disapprove.   But several days later, at the dinner table, I was amazed to hear him trot out my suggestion as his own.'" [4]

House not only let Wilson himself believe that such ideas sprang from Wilson's own brain.   Even more he took pains to give Wilson full public credit for them.

In the Spring of 1914, for instance, Wilson "cautiously approved" the Colonel's plan for the "Great Adventure," House's brilliant effort to avert the World War.

But in 1915 House, writing to Wilson from Paris, refers to this plan as though it were Wilson's very own original idea. House describes in detail his talk with the French Minister for Foreign Affairs in which he attributed the entire project to Wilson's foresight and courage.

It was largely in this way that House established his tremendous hold not only over self-sufficient Woodrow Wilson but also over many other men.

A member of the Democratic National Committee during the successful campaign of 1912 has described how Colonel House, though holding no position of any kind at headquarters, came in the end to be recognized as "the biggest man in the works."

"Colonel House would come into an office and say a few words quietly, and after he had gone you would suddenly become seized by a good idea.   You would suggest that idea

to your friends or superiors and be congratulated for it . . .
But sometime as sure as shooting, . . . you would come to
an abrupt realization that that idea had been oozed into your
brain by Colonel House." [5]

Here we have the chief secret of that mysterious influence
which Colonel House exercised during the entire Wilson administration — "a power never before wielded by any man out of
office, a power greater than that of any political boss or cabinet
member." [6]   House was master of a device that will literally
move mountains.

Let us see how Leffingwell, the management engineer, once
outwitted one of those headstrong men whom we all encounter:
in this case a department head, who had shown himself to be
dead set against all changes.   Leffingwell wanted to persuade
this executive to install a new type of visible index.

"Strategy, . . . being called for," says Leffingwell, "I went
to see him with the index tucked under my arm and bearing in
my hand some papers relating to other matters about which I
professed to be in need of his opinion.   While we were discussing these matters, I once or twice shifted the index from under
one arm to the other, and at length he 'bit.'

"'What are you carrying?' he asked me."

"'Oh, that?' I replied carelessly, 'It's only a visible index.'"

"'Let me see it for a moment.'"

"'Oh, you won't want to see that,' I said, as I rose to go.
'It's for another department.   You don't need it in yours.'"

"'Anyway,' he said, 'I'd like to see it.'"

"With a show of reluctance I handed it to him, and as he
looked it over I explained its workings in a casual but none
the less thorough way.

"'Don't want it in my department!' he finally exclaimed.
'The deuce I don't!   *Why that's the very thing I have been looking
for!*'" [7]

So Leffingwell, by pretending to be opposed to his own idea,
skilfully "eased it across."

Yet Leffingwell himself, like all of us, got himself into trouble
by completely ignoring this very strategy.

He tells us how he was teased and snubbed by his wife when

he tried by direct methods to teach her time-saving and effort-saving methods in running her household. He finally succeeded only by letting his wife hook herself.

When, for instance, he wanted her to have the laundress try a better method of handling laundry, he mentioned very casually how a similar problem had been solved in office work and let his wife apply the principle for herself. "It worked beautifully," he says.

Many men find their ideas "frowned upon" at the office, Leffingwell believes, largely because they neglect this precaution in dealing with their own boss. "Before we decide that our boss is a wall-eyed, fossil-minded old codger," he observes, "let us consider whether we haven't had a faulty method of selling these ideas to him."

Leaders have discovered that attempting to get credit for ideas does not, as a rule, pay in the end. They are not concerned with the pleasure of the moment. What they are after is power: control over people. To carry out their plans, they are willing to sacrifice their vanity; glad to have the chance of giving the other man full credit for any and all ideas.

One executive, James H. Foster, founder of the Hydraulic Pressed Steel Company of Cleveland, even in introducing welfare plans among his laboring men, took pains at the start to have the "germ of the idea" implanted in the minds of a few workmen so that all of them started discussing it and considered it *their own* project by the time he was ready to act.

When Mark Hanna, America's most powerful political boss, was sweeping aside all opposition at the Republican Convention of '96, and putting the famous gold plank in the platform, he kept himself so successfully in the background that at the last moment the "gold men" of the platform committee came to him with a threat: Either support the gold plank or else we will oppose McKinley, your choice for president! So by causing these men to force his own idea upon him, Hanna insured their enthusiastic loyalty to it.

When you want people to adopt one of your ideas and act on it with whole-hearted interest, it is often wise to let them think that it is their own, and to give them full credit for originating it.

For the same purpose leaders use still another shrewd type of strategy which is very similar to this and which is perhaps even more familiar.

Whitelaw Reid Hires an Unwilling Lieutenant

Whitelaw Reid is stalking big game.

He is managing editor of the *New York Tribune* under Horace Greeley. And he is on a man hunt. He is trying to bring in one of those brilliant assistants who will help to make him famous, who will enable him to succeed Greeley as owner and publisher of this great paper.

Just now Reid's guns are trained on young John Hay, just returned from a diplomatic post in Madrid. Hay himself believes he is bound for Illinois to practice law.

Later on both men will in turn serve as ambassadors to Great Britain.

But at present all Reid's diplomatic wiles are focussed on one man, on the unsuspecting Hay.

How can he persuade this brilliant youth to abandon his plans and take a job with the *Tribune?*

Reid "took him to the Union League Club to dine. . . . " writes Sears.

"If he had other plans for his friend he was not likely to announce them then and there.

"He proposed an after-dinner stroll down to the *Tribune* office. Looking over the telegrams he found an important despatch. The foreign editor happened to be away and he turned to Hay and said,

"'Sit down and write a leader on this for to-morrow.'

"He could not well refuse.

"The article was good enough to pass with Horace Greeley, . . . Mr. Reid asked him to stay a week, a month, and then to be one of the editors.

"And so Mr. Hay was diverted from his home and law to New York and journalism." [8]

So Whitelaw Reid bagged his game, landed Hay on the *Tribune* staff.

Without revealing his purpose, he merely induced Hay to make a small contribution which was likely to turn out well.

How often we have roused the other fellow's interest in our plans by this same method: by inducing him to participate!

When we tempt people to do something easy, arrange a little triumph for them, we give them one of the strongest incentives to further effort along that same line. Here their *ego* has been raised. Here they have been stimulated by a sense of achievement. And here they are likely to make a further try for pleasant experiences.

"The very essence of all power to influence lies in the ability to get the other person to participate," says H. A. Overstreet in *Influencing Human Behavior*.[9]

All leaders know and use this strategy.

Peary, for instance, in preparing for his expeditions to the North Pole, brought nearly all the materials for his sledges north with him, but always he was careful to have each sledge built by that particular Eskimo who was to drive it.

Most of us know how Leonard Wood, after the Spanish War, transformed ravaged, fever-ridden Cuba into an independent modern state. Wood "wisely let the Cubans themselves help him as much as possible. He even sent young Cuban girls to the United States to be trained to teach, instead of bringing American teachers into the country."[10]

Often enough, leaders have gone to great trouble to employ this strategy. But ordinarily, as in the case of Whitelaw Reid when he bagged John Hay, it calls only for a little forethought, for just a bit of added precaution.

To rouse people's enthusiasm for your plans, induce them to participate in them. If possible arrange for them to begin by doing something which will be easy for them, yet which they will regard as a real achievement.

CHAPTER VII

STRATEGY THAT FEW CAN RESIST

How Samuel Vauclain Persuaded an Enemy to Help Him
McKinley Throws a Congressman into High Gear
Roosevelt Outwits the Bosses
Mark Hanna Wins Over a Street-Car Conductor

A SINGLE DETERMINED OLD IRISHWOMAN is holding up an important project of the great Baldwin Locomotive Works. She is completely blocking one of the pet plans of Samuel Vauclain — Vauclain, the future president of the company, who is now working his way up from the shops.

At Vauclain's suggestion, a site has been purchased by his company for a much-needed office building. More than one hundred tenants have been asked to move.

But, led by this one old Irishwoman, a group of them refuses to budge. Under her able direction they stand on their rights, unyielding as a stone wall.

"We had to have that new building in full operation in a short time," says Vauclain, "but many months would elapse before we could move those tenants by court action. We didn't want to oust them that way, anyway; it would make enemies. . . . I'd sold the Works management on that six-story building so the management gave me the job of moving the immovables."

And move them he does, speedily and in a surprising manner.

Vauclain's entire difficulty centers on this one warlike old Irishwoman. He finds her sitting on a shaded doorstep in an alley. She glares up at him.

"'What's ailing ye?'" she remarks spitefully.

He is wearing an "old straw hat, old shirt, with sleeves rolled up on a workman's arms."

He chaffs her on having stirred up trouble. He joins her on the shaded step.

"'It's a shame you sit here and do nothing,'" he remarks, "'when you, *with your personality*, could persuade your neighbors to move to other and much better houses.'"

And with these few words Vauclain wins. The old Irishwoman caves in.

"She became the busiest woman in Philadelphia," says Vauclain, "bossing her neighbors around like old shoes and promptly moving the whole colony at half the expense I'd anticipated." [1]

"''Tis glad I am to have sarved you,'" is her farewell to Vauclain when the job is finished.

So Vauclain manages this gallant but misguided old woman.

Actually Vauclain has done nothing that appears unusual. He has jollied her along — that is all.

And yet the force of his strategy is astonishing. In a few minutes he solves a very unpleasant and serious business problem, turns a spiteful mischief-maker into an enthusiastic ally.

Vauclain wins over this bitter opponent in the same way that Benjamin Franklin turned his chief enemy into a lifelong friend (p. 7): by raising her *ego*.

He modestly asks for her help, compliments her upon her personality, her strength as a leader.

He causes her to feel important and superior.

This is the most certain way to make people like us and to win their co-operation.

On the other hand, one of the most certain ways to make an enemy is to injure the other person's *ego*.

How many lesser men would have attempted to deal with such a woman by a show of authority, by blustering and threats perhaps! They would have failed completely. By trying to overawe her with their own importance, they would only have wounded her vanity.

Wounded vanity is, without question, one of the greatest

causes of all the trouble and all the hard feeling in the world.

Historians, for instance, believe now that Woodrow Wilson wrecked his career very largely by two clear-cut mistakes — mistakes that bruised the self-esteem of people whose help he needed.

In November of 1918, as the Armistice is being signed, Woodrow Wilson stands forth triumphant, a leader with the whole world at his feet. In his own country, Republicans have joined with Democrats to support him; on every continent, in every country, statesmen, populations wait tensely for his slightest word. Yet only a year later, Wilson lies at the foot of his pedestal, broken, discredited.

That his League of Nations and his Treaty of Versailles have been rejected by the Senate is perhaps the smaller part of his defeat. Other statesmen have seen their measure fail and, after all, Woodrow Wilson has won his place in history as founder of the League. The real disaster is more far-reaching: Personally and politically Wilson is completely crushed, overwhelmed by enemies whom he himself has created.

A few days before the Armistice, Wilson has already made his first blunder, has issued that fatal letter urging the electors to vote only for Democratic senators and congressmen. It is a direct slap at all the Republicans who have backed him loyally, and it is deadly ammunition for all those who are preparing to fight him. It definitely helps the Republicans to gain a majority in the Senate.

Shortly afterward comes the second mistake. In spite of urgent advice from his friends, Wilson appoints no senator and no great Republican like Root or Taft to the Peace Commission. Another slap at the Republicans! Also a slap at the Senate — that Senate which cherishes its prerogatives and which Wilson hopes will ratify his treaty.

In Paris, Wilson's Commission helps him settle the destiny of nations. But at home angry men are waiting. In the Senate, now, many of his own Democrats are opposed to him, and it is the Republicans who have control. There and throughout the country Wilson has stirred up a back-fire of antagonism that will destroy him.

On a large scale, with hundreds, thousands of men, Wilson has slipped into the one deadly blunder that all leaders try to avoid: He has wounded the other fellow's vanity.

His failure forms an interesting contrast with the successful diplomacy of Samuel Vauclain which we have just observed.

Wilson turns friends into enemies by *injuring* the *ego* of his friends.

Vauclain turns an enemy into a friend by *raising* the *ego* of his enemy.

It is very largely by making the other fellow feel important that great leaders gain and hold their power over men.

McKinley Throws a Famous Congressman into High Gear

"Years ago," says Blythe, "just before the Spanish War, I met a famous congressman on Pennsylvania Avenue, in Washington, just coming from the White House. He was stepping high. His hat was tilted a bit to the left. He twirled his stick jauntily and smiled genially.

"'Judge,' I said, 'you seem to be feeling fit this morning.'

"'I am, my boy, I am. I have just been over to the White House to see the President and he put his arm around my shoulder and said to me: "Bill, on you, above all men, I am depending for help to win this war." I've been opposing him some, but now I'm for him. He is depending on me.'

"And I passed on, marveling at the power McKinley had to make men his friends, none the less because I knew exactly how many others McKinley was depending on in the same manner and with the same results, to help him win the war." [2]

Few men have understood better than McKinley how to secure people's friendship and co-operation.

"He had a way of inviting one to a private conference," says Chauncey Depew, "and of impressing you with its confidential character and the trust he reposed in your advice and judgment which was most flattering." [3]

A newspaper reporter who applied this principle in an amusing and somewhat unscrupulous way has been described to the authors by Paul Leach of the *Chicago Daily News*.

"About five years ago," said Leach, "I knew a reporter who had remarkable success in getting good interviews with important people. He did it by working on their sympathies. Having pink cheeks and a cherubic, childlike appearance he would deliberately throw himself on the mercies of the person he wanted to interview and play the part of a cub reporter, half scared to death in the face of his first important assignment. Actually, although only twenty-five years old, he was a shrewd and experienced newspaper man with plenty of poise and confidence."

It is not by showing off our own importance, but rather by giving the other fellow a sense of importance that we draw him to us, arouse his interest in ourselves and our plans.

Because John Hay, the noted American statesman, observed this precaution with everyone he knew, Marcosson has called him "the greatest personality" he "ever met." Hay, says Marcosson, "invariably made an obscure person feel at home in his presence. When all is said and done this is the real measure of a man." [4]

Big calibre leaders have no patience with that childish type of man who tries to impress people by his air of importance or who pretends that his work is mysterious or difficult. "The stuffed shirt, the pretentious conference are going or gone," Walter S. Gifford, head of the American Telephone and Telegraph Company, recently observed in the course of an interview. Gifford himself is noted for making everything seem easy. This man, who runs the country's largest corporation, even says that his own job is not difficult!

The really successful man is too busy looking out for the other man's vanity to worry about his own.

Roosevelt Outwits the Bosses

Theodore Roosevelt was once asked to describe his method of handling the political bosses as governor of New York. Brander Matthews wanted to know how he was able to keep on good terms with them all and yet force through so many reforms which they violently disliked.

And Roosevelt explained his strategy. It was very simple in principle. But it was supported by a most ingenious device.

His plan, Roosevelt told Matthews, went into operation "whenever there was an office to be filled." His first move was to ask the bosses for "recommendations."

"At first," said Roosevelt, "they might propose a broken-down party hack, the sort of man who has to be 'taken care of.' I would tell them that to appoint such a man would not be good politics, as the public would not approve it.

"Then they would bring me the name of another party hack, a persistent officeholder, who, if he had nothing against him, had little in his favor. I would tell them that this man would not measure up to the expectations of the public, and I would ask them to see if they could not find someone more obviously fitted for the post.

"Their third suggestion would be a man who was almost good enough, but not quite.

"Then I would thank them, asking them to try once more, and their fourth suggestion would be acceptable; they would then name just the sort of man I should have picked out myself. Expressing my gratitude for their assistance, I would appoint this man — and I would let them take the credit for the appointment." [5]

It was by these tactics, Teddy explained, that he "kept on good terms" with the party leaders. "I would tell them," he said, "that I had done these things to please them and now it was their turn to do something to please me." And please him they did — by supporting such reforms as the Civil Service Bill and the Franchise Tax Bill.

So, with all his cards on the table, Roosevelt outwitted the bosses. So he ruled them by holding their good will.

Under very real difficulties, he used a form of strategy that some of us may neglect altogether. He took great pains always to *consult* the other fellow. He found a way to appoint whomever he pleased and yet to *show respect* for the advice and suggestions of the bosses.

We have all noticed how quickly other people warm up when we ask them for advice. This is one of the simplest methods of making them feel important.   But do we, like Roosevelt, take the trouble to offer this courtesy *regularly* to those whose co-operation we desire?   Do we look on it as a matter of strategy?

Many of us forget the *first* part of the homely saying which Teddy made famous: "*Speak softly* and carry a big stick: you will go far."

It was by speaking "softly" that Roosevelt set the stage for his "Big Stick," and made himself master of the State of New York.

One of the sure ways to win people's good will is to consult them on subjects in which they are interested.

By this strategy, an unknown boy, fresh from the country, once obtained interviews with the most powerful men in New York.

"I want to know how to make a million dollars" — it was with these words that youthful A. B. Farquhar addressed Jacob Astor after he had managed to get into that great man's office.

And Astor, both amused and pleased, not only talked to him but also helped him meet and interview such other notables as Hamilton Fish, A. T. Stewart and James Gordon Bennett.

In this escapade, we see at work that keen knowledge of human nature which helped make Farquhar a millionaire leader of industry.   The fundamentals of his strategy hold for all of us.   He used one of the best methods of making a new contact: These men were genuinely complimented to have their advice asked and their wisdom so warmly admired.

With all types of people, we find able men taking great care to request advice and suggestions.   It is, for instance, one of the most powerful methods by which they insure enthusiasm and loyalty in their subordinates.

Whenever possible the leader tries to let his plans actually come from his subordinates, tries to *adopt* and *act* on *their* idea rather than his own.

"Encourage even a greenhorn when he comes with a suggestion, even if it is a poor suggestion," [6] is one of the noted "maxims" that John Wanamaker set down to guide his own dealings with employees.

By many different methods we find able men causing other people to feel important.

Mark Hanna Wins Over a Street-Car Conductor

Let us observe Mark Hanna making a friend of one of the conductors on his Cleveland street railway.

Hanna, who regularly rode on the front platform of the cars and chatted with the motormen, knew nearly all of his men. But Peter Cox had never spoken to him until this particular day, not long after Hanna had met with an accident on a lake trip.

When Hanna boarded the car with the help of only a cane, Cox congratulated him on getting rid of his crutches. And this gave Hanna his opening.

He proceeded to tell Cox all about his mishap, "being as friendly," says Cox, "and going into as many details as he would in case I were a close business associate. . . . He always talked freely and confidentially to his men, no matter who they were." [7]

It was Hanna's own personal standing with such men as Peter Cox that very largely made his company so remarkably successful and carried it through twenty-five years without a strike. And here we see one of his ways of charming the Peter Coxes: He complimented them by offering unexpected confidences.

Personal confidences of this sort, as we all know, raise the other man's *ego*. Up to a certain point they flatter him, show him that he is important to us. Beyond this point, of course, when we pour out our story merely to ease our own mind, we are placing a burden on him — a burden which it is sometimes wise to let him assume, but which very definitely tests his friendship.

It is when we reveal things which are *unexpected*, when, like Hanna, we compliment people by our willingness to be frank with them and trust them, that we raise their *ego*. Leaders use this method very frequently.

On Charles Dawes' campaign trip to New England in 1924,

for example, his first move in handling a group of reporters, most of them strangers, was to tell them at great length, and with no request for secrecy, a series of humorous and highly confidential stories about his war experiences, making known in this way that he put complete faith in their honor and good judgment.

Another effective means of giving people a sense of importance is even simpler than this, yet it is very widely neglected: the hearty greeting.

A vivid close-up of Theodore Roosevelt in action has been given us by Bishop Lawrence — also, by way of contrast, a picture of Henry Cabot Lodge.

"When the two men stood side by side in a receiving line, the knowing ones would watch them," says Bishop Lawrence, "and note the almost forced smile with which Cabot greeted the shoemakers and farmers, shaking hands as warmly as his rather fastidious taste would allow him, and doing his best to brighten the occasion by a formal word or a shaft of wit. Theodore, beaming all over, would step forward, greet each stranger as a long-lost friend and lead every man, woman, and child to think he was the one whom the President would remember." [8]

Theodore Roosevelt's famous "dee-lighted" still echoes pleasantly in many memories.

How warmly we respond to the man who shows that he is genuinely glad to see us!

How it chills us, on the other hand, to be greeted in an off-hand, indifferent manner!

Yet do we not all of us frequently neglect to *show* our pleasure when we meet people?

Roosevelt did not make this mistake. Successful men of his type find in the cordial greeting an easy and certain method of making friends.

Samuel Vauclain discovered this early in his career. When he was still a young lathe operator, he was once asked to give a bond of $40,000. He retired abashed from the courtroom. But to his astonishment, a Jewish clothing merchant, named

Sheeline, whom he barely knew, offered to go his bond. Vauclain accepted, and asked him why he was willing to do it.
Sheeline replied that it was merely because Vauclain was one
of the few people in Altoona who had bothered to greet him
pleasantly on the street.

By whatever method we make people feel important, it all
boils down to this: *We show them that we like them and are genuinely interested in them.*

This, of course, is one of the messages that we flash to others
every time we smile. And as Walter Strong, publisher of the
Chicago Daily News, recently remarked to the authors, "a smile
often counts more than a thousand words a minute."

Nothing, nothing in the world, can take the place of a smile
in showing people that we like them and consider them important.

Commenting on the "magnetic" personality of the English
admiral, David Beatty, victor of Jutland, and on the devotion
which he inspired in his men, an American naval officer has
called his smile, "the smile that whipped the German navy." [9]

Not only by deliberate strategy, but even more perhaps by
many little things of this sort of which they themselves are
frequently quite unaware, leaders are constantly raising the
other man's *ego.*

*One of the sure ways to establish your influence over people is to
take pains to show that you consider them important.*

Sometimes, as in the case of Vauclain and the old Irishwoman, or Roosevelt and the bosses, you will do this as a
clear-cut method of winning over people who dislike you or
who are indifferent. But more often still, you will do it in
one of those many simple ways which are as natural as breath-
ing: by a cordial greeting, by a smile, or by just letting people
know that you like them and trust them.

CHAPTER VIII

TRADING PENNIES FOR DOLLARS

A Bookkeeper Makes a Deep Impression on John Patterson
An Office Boy Sells a Bond to a Bank President
One Little Thing Frank Munsey Never Forgot

A T A RECENT DINNER of business men in Chicago, the story
of a certain bookkeeper's surprisingly swift rise was told
to illustrate an important point in dealing with people.
At the age of only twenty-six, Stanley Allyn, the bookkeeper,
had become comptroller of the great National Cash Register
Company. At only thirty-five, he had been elected treasurer
— which position he holds today. Allyn's success hinged on a
seemingly trivial matter which others had ignored. He himself has given the facts to the authors.

When he was a mere youngster in the accounting department, John Patterson, founder of the business, expressed a
desire to see financial statements in a special form: in enormous figures, on sheets the size of double newspaper pages.
But his own accountants were not willing to give them to him.
They looked on Patterson's idea as outlandish and absurd.

Allyn, however, against the protests of his immediate superiors, prepared just such "absurd" reports and saw to it that
they reached Patterson.

Patterson sent for him to discuss the reports. And this event
was the real start of Allyn's career.

By meeting Patterson's wishes in this one, small matter,
Allyn gained his personal notice and liking. Suddenly he was

singled out from among all the other young men in that large organization. Now he had an opportunity to make known his very real abilities. His rapid climb to high office had begun.

Allyn won over and impressed the head of his company by giving him something that he wanted.

How many of us take the trouble to study the small wants of our superiors? How many of us keep our eyes, our thoughts, fixed upon them, shape our work to meet them?

It is through the other fellow's *wants* that we can influence him most deeply and most decisively.

His desires, his problems, his needs are the most active part of his personal interests. Above all else he gives his attention to these wants of his, whatever form they may take at the moment.

One of the most important of all facts to remember in handling people is that their wants are different.

Leaders take great pains to learn the other man's special wants even in matters that seem very trivial. These small wants offer an effective way of controlling him. By showing respect for them, they raise his *ego*, win both his attention and his good will.

By this strategy William Wrigley, Jr., in his early days as a salesman, easily handled a crusty wholesaler whom other salesmen dreaded. He got many orders from this man and won his lasting friendship merely because he took into account one fact about him which others had ignored. This merchant had a passion for starting to work early in the morning. So day after day Wrigley made a point of reaching the wholesale house ahead of him, getting there in the small hours of the morning — and then would greet him at the door of his office when he arrived. The wholesaler was delighted to have his hobby treated with such deference.

An Office Boy Sells a Bond to a Bank President

Anthony Dimock, office boy, stands waiting to speak to a bank president.

He hopes to sell him a bond.

This eighteen-year-old lad, fresh from Phillips Academy, son of a poor New England minister, is already making headway. Three years later, he will have to refuse an election to the New York Stock Exchange because of his youth. In his early thirties he will be a millionaire.

But at present, Dimock is running errands, doing odd jobs for a broker at $1.50 a week. His employer considers him a smart boy, has given him a chance to sell a railway bond.

And now this youth is waiting his turn to speak to the president of the City Bank of New York: Moses Taylor, Dimock knows, is interested in securities of this special railroad.

But what shall he say to this mighty gentleman?

"As I approached the desk," writes Dimock, "he said impatiently to a man beside him who was talking volubly: 'Come to the point, come to the point,' and a moment later dismissed him with a shake of his head and nodded to me to come forward. I placed the bond upon the desk before him, saying:

"'Ninety-seven.'

"Mr. Taylor looked quizzically at me and, drawing his check book toward him, asked:

"'What name?'

"'Mr. Blank.'

"When he had filled out the check he inquired:

"'What commission does Mr. Blank pay you?'

"'A quarter per cent.'

"'Tell him for me that it isn't enough, that I paid you one per cent and that if he doesn't do the same I will do it for him.'" [1]

Dimock has sold his bond. More important still, he has caught the bank president's personal attention, has laid the foundation for an important friendship.

By keeping his eyes and ears open, Dimock has spotted a small yet violent desire in this great banker: Taylor loves brevity with astonishing ardor; he despises words. Thereafter, in all his dealings with Taylor, Dimock "practiced laconicism and never used a redundant word." Taylor is delighted, flattered. He continues to buy from this young man, gives him active help.

How many other older men Dimock must have won by simple precautions of this sort!

Early in life Anthony Dimock saw the importance of *meeting the other fellow's wishes in small matters.*

One Little Thing Frank Munsey Never Forgot

In the biography of the late Frank A. Munsey, written by his associate, Erman Ridgway, we find a striking paragraph. It helps to explain how Munsey made himself a leader of men, how he lifted himself from humble beginnings to high place as publisher of the *New York Sun.*

"I lost the hearing of my right ear about twenty-five years ago," wrote Ridgway shortly before Munsey's death, "and never once afterwards, in the hundreds, the thousands of times that we were together, did the Chief fail to place himself on the side of my good ear. In his room, in the office, in the auto, on the street, at meals, everywhere and always he placed himself with a view to my comfort, did it so easily and so naturally that no one ever noticed it. I think that was wonderful." "He was unusually thoughtful for the comfort of his companions." [2]

Like all able men, Munsey was careful to respect the needs of his subordinates in little things.

Tact, courtesy, consideration — we have many different names for such small attentions. And it is through these very precautions, these small acts of thoughtful kindliness that able men inspire confidence and personal devotion.

Calvin Coolidge, as vice president, for example, carefully reversed one whole feature of the program when he was scheduled to speak at the dedication of the great government hospital at Tuskegee, Alabama. The program originally provided that the Governor of Alabama should board Coolidge's car at the Georgia-Alabama line. But Coolidge, mindful of the Governor's rank in his own state, insisted on going himself to the Governor's car to pay his respects.

And before this, when the committee first invited Coolidge to speak in place of President Harding, who had been forced to decline, Coolidge remembered that Harding had personally worked to establish this splendid hospital. He refused to thrust himself into the limelight, declined to accept until the committee called once more on Harding and were then able to assure Coolidge that Harding himself wished him to make the address.

Trifling points! Yet it is by just such little things that men win and hold friendships that make their lives successful.

"The Great Art, and the most necessary of all is the Art of Pleasing," wrote Lord Chesterfield, the English statesman who stands today as the one recognized expert of all time in this same art. "If . . ." he says, "you would rather . . . be loved than hated, remember to have that constant attention about you which flatters every man's little vanity, . . . if you were to laugh at a man for his aversion to a cat or cheese (which are common antipathies), or by inattention or negligence to let them come in his way where you could prevent it, he would in the first case think himself insulted and in the second slighted, and would remember both. Whereas your care to procure for him what he likes and to remove from him what he hates, . . . flatters his vanity, and makes him possibly more your friend than a more important service would have done." [3]

James Reeves, builder of the Reeves grocery chain of New York, believes that customers are chiefly won and held in this same way: by carefully organized courtesy.

"I know of nothing," he says, "that builds trade faster and holds it more firmly. . . .

"There are thousands of these little things. For instance, a mother sends a small child to the store with a list of purchases and the money to pay for them. Well, the wise clerk wraps up the change in paper so the youngster won't lose it on the way home." [4]

A well known Washington correspondent has told the authors how one small courtesy of this sort greatly helped some of the newspaper men who regularly interviewed Calvin Coolidge. The President was partial to those reporters who were never too busy with their own thoughts to find time for a hearty laugh at his little jokes, at his famous flashes of dry humor.

It is easy to neglect what the other fellow wants in such little things. And often this neglect is costly.

A young man in the office of John Gates, the steel magnate, once missed out on a job as branch manager even after it had already been offered to him and he himself was about to accept it, because he came to the final meeting without having "put on better clothes or slicked himself up as any man naturally would for such a momentous day. That was enough," says Owens, "Gates sent him away empty handed." [5]

This youth was no timber for an executive. He paid no attention to what his boss expected and desired in such a small matter as clothes.

"No book on business," says Wallace B. Donham, head of the Harvard business school, "effectively warns you that if the boss has a prejudice against men who wear red neckties it is your business to know it. Yet such little human elements are of great importance." [6]

Be on the alert to notice and remember the other fellow's wishes and preferences in small matters. By showing him that you have them in mind, by meeting them when practical, you make a deep impression on him and win both his friendship and his confidence.

CHAPTER IX

HOW TO MAKE PEOPLE SAY YES

*Joseph Day Sells Elbert Gary an Office Building
with Two Questions*

*Charles Schwab Closes One of the Biggest Deals
in the History of Business*

*Herbert Hoover Prods a Man in His Most
Sensitive Spot*

Eugene Stevens Calls a Bluff

*Henry Ford and Owen D. Young Put This
Precaution Ahead of All Others*

ELBERT GARY, head of United States Steel, sends for Joseph
Day, the man who is known in New York as the "greatest
real estate salesman . . . in the world."

"Joe," he says, "I think that the Steel Corporation ought
to have its own building."

Through the window of Gary's office the two men can look
down on the Hudson River with its crowded shipping and
piers. A stirring spectacle! And important to both of them.
The building he is to buy, says the steel master, must give
him either this same view, or else an outlook over the harbor.

"Keep your eye on possibilities."

Day spends weeks studying "possibilities," making maps,
charts, estimates. But actually none of these documents is
used. He sells Elbert Gary a building with two questions and
five minutes of silence.

From the start, of course, one of the "possibilities" is the very
building in which Gary's office and the offices of the Steel

66

Corporation are already located: the old Empire Building itself. From nowhere else is Gary's beloved view more inspiring. But Gary has seemed to favor a more modern building next door and some of the other officers, he has said, definitely want to buy it.

And there are other "possibilities" — altogether too many. Day wants to close this deal quickly.

So when Gary sends for him again, Day immediately suggests that the Steel Corporation stay where it is, buy the old Empire Building itself. The view from the building next door, Day points out, will soon be cut off by a new structure. But here in the Empire Building, Gary's outlook over the river will be safe for years to come.

This suggestion Gary promptly opposes. He begins to "debate the matter," to show that the old Empire Building will not do at all.

Day does not argue. He listens and thinks fast. What does Gary himself *really* want to do?

Right now apparently Gary is dead set against the Empire Building. And he is proving his case, like the lawyer he is.

But these criticisms he is making, these objections about the old-fashioned woodwork, for instance, are only minor points. And quite clearly they have started not with Gary himself but with the younger officials.

As Day listens, it suddenly comes to him that Gary is not showing his hand, that actually he would like very much to buy this very building which he is so vigorously attacking.

At length with no one to dispute his case *against* this building, Gary stops talking.

Both men sit for a moment looking out the window, their eyes on that familiar view which Gary loves so well.

Day himself has described his entire strategy from this point on:

"Without turning my eyes, I said very quietly:

"'Judge, where was your office when you first came to New York?'

"There was a little pause before he answered, 'Why — it was in this building.'

"I waited a minute. Then I said, 'Judge, where was the Steel Corporation formed?'

"There was another pause before he replied, 'Right here, in this very office where you and I are sitting now.'

"He spoke very slowly — and I said nothing more. Not a word! For five minutes and they seemed like fifteen — we sat there in absolute silence, gazing out of the window.

"Finally, with a half-defiant note in his voice, he said, 'Almost every one of my junior officers wants to leave this building, but it's our home. We were born here; we've grown up here; and here's where we're going to stay!'

"Inside half an hour the deal was closed." [1]

No high-pressure selling. No vast array of figures. A master salesman has been at work.

Day has staked everything on his hunch about what Gary really wants to do. Skilfully Day has stimulated this hidden want, sent it leaping to fulfillment. He is like a woodsman nursing a tiny flame, building a fire.

Day has put himself across because *he has taken the trouble to study Gary's wants.*

In Gary, Day has sensed something of which the steel master himself is only vaguely aware: a conflict of wants.

On the one hand, Gary wishes to leave the old Empire Building. On the other, he wishes to stay.

The reasons Gary wants to *stay* in the old Empire Building are very clear to us, though perhaps not to Gary himself: This old familiar building with its familiar view is a part of him; it reminds him of his early triumphs, sustains his *ego.*

The reasons Gary wants to *leave* are equally clear, at least to us: Feeling that his sentiment is difficult to explain and may expose him to ridicule, Gary fears the opposition of the younger officers.

It is by causing Gary to settle this conflict in a new way, that Day closes his big deal.

The only way to get people to do anything is to cause them to want to do it. Only by making contact with the other fellow's wants can we hold his attention. Only through these wants of his can we hope to influence him in any way whatever.

*Charles Schwab Closes One of the Biggest Deals in the
History of Business*

J. Pierpont Morgan has declined to buy the Carnegie Steel
Company.

Both Carnegie himself and Elbert Gary have tried to persuade Morgan to make this great purchase. But both have
failed. Carnegie himself has been repeatedly refused.

Now Carnegie has given to Charles Schwab, president of his
company, the job of handling Morgan. Schwab is to convince
this overlord of American finance that he has made a mistake.

And Schwab is most ingenious. He calls in confederates
and gets Morgan into a place where he has to listen without a
chance to say "No." Then he uses a very simple method that
is familiar to all of us.

"A number of New York bankers," writes Arthur Strawn,
"gave a dinner in his honor, and it was arranged that Morgan
should be present. Charlie spoke at the dinner. He painted
a picture of the future possibilities of the steel industry in such
glowing and overwhelming terms that his audience sat spellbound. Without naming any companies specifically and without seeming to address his remarks to Morgan, he showed that
a perfect industrial organization could be created by a merger
of all the companies — a merger which would promote efficiency, eliminate competition, and mint a fortune for its pro-
moters. His eloquence, flowing from the heart, was irresistible,
and when the dinner was finished, Morgan sought him out for
further questioning. Before they were through, Charlie had
sold the Carnegie works for $492,000,000. This transaction,
as everyone knows, led to the formation of the billion-dollar
United States Steel Corporation, with Judge Gary as chairman of the executive committee and Charlie himself as
President." [2]

So Charles Schwab closed one of the biggest deals in history
by stirring the imagination of the elder Pierpont Morgan, by
stimulating his desire for money.

Suppose we are trying to persuade a friend to go on a camp-
ing trip with us. "It's certainly wonderful up there in the

woods," we say, "paddling across those lakes under the open sky, sleeping on balsam boughs. Every meal's a banquet when you're really hungry and smell the smoke of the campfire, etc."

In order to rouse in our friend the desire to go with us, we literally take him on a trip by the power of our words.

And this was all that Schwab did.

He painted for Morgan a vivid picture of the future. Of a certainty, Morgan was counting his profits before he left the table.

It is by stimulating the wants that are favorable to us, that we can cause people to act as we desire.

Of this art, Napoleon was a master.

We see him, only twenty-five years old, a newly made general of France, taking command of the ragged, hungry soldiers of the Army of Italy, playing upon their need for food and clothes:

"Soldiers, you are half starved, half naked . . . I will lead you into the most fertile plains of the world. There you will find flourishing cities, teeming provinces." [3]

Later, in captured Milan, his words ring differently. Now he stimulates not the stomach but the *ego*. In glowing phrases, Napoleon portrays his men as makers of history, as heroes in their own home town: "You will return to your homes, and your neighbors will point you out to one another saying: 'He was with the army in Italy.'" [4]

"Half of what he achieves," says Emil Ludwig of Napoleon, during this Italian campaign, "is achieved by the power of words." [5]

Time and again we find Napoleon linking his projects to the desires of his men, weaving a spell about them.

Fighting under the Pyramids, they are again heroes of all time: "Soldiers," he says, "forty centuries are looking down on you." [6]

Before the disastrous capture of Moscow, glory once more awaits them, he announces, but also "abundant supplies, comfortable winter quarters, and the prospect of an early return to their homes." [7]

Herbert Hoover Prods a Man in His Most Sensitive Spot

Herbert Hoover once saved his Belgian relief work by stimulating in a German general a want which this general himself had completely forgotten to consider.

Infuriated by Allied newspaper attacks, the Germans were about to take revenge by kicking out the Commission for Relief in Belgium. Hoover rushed from London to the German Great Headquarters.

Here an eminent German soldier angrily informed him that the Commission must go. Hoover's men, he said, were nothing but "a set of Entente Spies." He raved about the "unfairness" of Allied newspaper criticisms of German war methods.

Hoover's arguments "moved the general not at all."

But at this critical moment Hoover got an idea.

Graphically and in detail, he pointed out to this all-powerful German the danger to his reputation as a soldier that lay in shutting out food from Belgium: He personally, the general with the decisive vote, would go down in history as "the butcher of a whole people."

The general blustered. But his rage cooled quickly. He told Hoover to come to see him "tomorrow morning."

Hoover had won. The Belgian relief remained on the job.

Above all else, this general valued his military record. Here was the core and center of his *ego*. Here was the great desire of his life. Yet he himself had apparently failed to consider it seriously in connection with Belgian relief.

Because Hoover stopped to think carefully about the other man's wants, he was able to locate this sensitive spot and to swing the balance his way.

The outstanding fact to remember in dealing with people is this: *their wants are different.*

The universal needs, such as the desire to uphold the *ego*, such as the hunger drive and the sex drive, are always there. But in each person they form a different pattern — a pattern that is constantly shifting and changing.

All the people we know, men, women, and children have, at any moment, special sets of wants and preference, just as distinct from other people's, just as definitely their own as their faces, their voices, or their bodies. No two people can be handled in exactly the same way.

"I've dealt with thousands upon thousands of men in my life," William Wrigley, Jr., recently remarked to the authors, "and the one thing that sticks out most clearly in my mind about them, is that they were all different."

Albert Brunker, the mining engineer who made himself at thirty president of the Liquid Carbonic Company, and a millionaire before he was forty, has stated this point very interestingly:

"You can no more get results," he says, "by treating everybody alike than you can feed the population by trying to make everybody eat ripe olives. People aren't built alike, to start with; and they are all trained differently.

"The result is that one man will respond in one way to a suggestion but another man may not respond that way at all. You've got to know which trigger to pull, and when."

To illustrate this point, Brunker has told about an employer who lost a good man simply because he pulled the wrong "trigger."

The subordinate, says Brunker, had "heard that another firm would be glad to hire him. He didn't care to make the change, but he thought he would go to the boss and talk things over.

"His employer told him that he had made remarkable progress, and ought to be contented for years to come. Now, the employer did not understand that young man's nature. The chap had youth, ambition, and ability. What encouragement was there for him in being told that he ought to be contented for years to come? He knew he *wouldn't* be. So he left and went to the other firm." [8]

This employer got one thing right: This young man really wanted to stay with the firm and he was not trying to hold up his boss for an immediate raise. But at this point the boss made a hurried guess and shot completely off the track.

He decided that the subordinate merely wanted a pat on the back, a little candy — and this is a very common desire indeed.

But he was wrong. This young man wished to know that

there was a future for him, an opportunity to develop. By going slowly, by feeling his way with questions, the employer could probably have uncovered this real want and found a way of satisfying it. But he did not take the trouble to do this — and he lost his man.

From a practical standpoint the first precaution in managing people is to discover what they really want, especially the exact nature of the most active wants which touch upon us and our plans.

Eugene Stevens Calls a Bluff

In his early days, Eugene Stevens, president of the Continental Illinois Bank of Chicago, sold bonds in Minneapolis. With a capital of only a thousand dollars, he had started his own investment banking business at the age of thirty.

Recently he described to the authors the strategy he once used in securing an important new customer. At a critical moment he made a shrewd guess as to just what the other man really wanted.

"He was an elderly man," said Mr. Stevens, "with big bushy eyebrows. I can remember to this day how he looked."

This bushy-browed gentleman was very successful, extremely rich. Stevens had obtained an interview but found it heavy going. "As I brought up one issue after another, he raised picayune objections. I was not getting anywhere with him.

"All of a sudden, I leaned forward across the desk and said to him: 'You know yourself that your objections are of no importance. They do not affect the value of these securities in any way. They have nothing to do with the fundamentals.'

"A beatific smile broke out on the other man's face.

"'That is right,' he replied.

"From that moment it was easy sailing," concluded Mr. Stevens. "I made an important sale."

Like two poker players, Stevens and his customer have faced each other across the table.

The older man's strategy is evident: He is sizing Stevens up, making foolish criticisms to see if Stevens actually knows bonds. It is a useful plan of testing people.

And Stevens? It is clear that he sees through the other man's device. But, even more than this, he senses the big want that lies behind it: the desire to safeguard money. This rich man wishes to know if Stevens' opinion about bonds can be relied upon. Stevens' abrupt reproof is the most direct route to the want that is at work in the other man.

Almost always these wants of the other fellow's require a little thought. Seldom can we rely, to any great extent, on what he himself tells us about them. Sometimes, like Gary, he does not even know himself just what they are and is neither able nor willing to describe them. Still more often, like this customer of Stevens, he simply does not care to give us the facts.

During the War, when the National Cash Register Company was turning out delicate and difficult jobs for the government, "Jack" Barringer, who has now succeeded Patterson as active head of the business, found that the work was seriously hampered by the constant coming and going of workers. Men were forever quitting.

Why? "More money" — they want "more money": so the employment manager explained the exodus.

But Barringer was not satisfied with this explanation.

Personally he went to talk to several hundred men who were waiting to draw their final pay; sent away all company employees except his own secretary and proceeded to ask searching questions of each man in turn. And suddenly a new world of wants opened up before him: working conditions that needed correction, serious complaints on many points.

He promised reforms, spoke of the War, of the government work. Many of the men got back on the job.

"When I analyzed the reasons given by the men as to why they were quitting," says Barringer, "I discovered that 'more money,' instead of being the chief reason, was fourth on the list." [9]

The demand for money had been with them largely a mask to disguise other wants which they did not care to discuss.

Sometimes it is best not even to mention such hidden wants, even while we are satisfying them.

By observing this precaution, Max Mason, former president of the University of Chicago, once secured a million-dollar endowment for this seat of learning.

A somewhat smaller gift, a half-million-dollar laboratory, had just been accepted.

Max Mason summoned his publicity man.

Next morning, the rich man, the giver of the laboratory, read his *Chicago Tribune*. On the third page he saw headlines about his princely gift. On the back page, among the photographs of important events, he found two that pictured *his* event, one of himself.

Within a few days, Max Mason received a second offering from the same man: this time a whole million dollars.

Mason had located the hidden desire in this man that prompted the first gift.

What this man really wanted, of course, was that balm to vanity, that joy of public recognition which every one, openly or secretly, longs for in some form or other.

But did Mason mention this motive? Far from it. This benefactor, both of them assumed, was aiding science, promoting education. And no doubt the rich giver was quite sincere in this. If at the same time he was promoting himself, he probably did not know it.

People's motives are always mixed. If the strongest motive is one of which they cannot be very proud, they tend to ignore it and to emphasize some other motive which reflects more credit upon themselves. Most of the time they are quite unaware of all this and fool themselves completely. Psychologists use a long word to describe this process. They call it "rationalization." All of us are constantly deceiving ourselves in this way.

Ordinarily it is not very difficult to find out what people want and how they want it. All that is necessary, as a rule, is simply to keep our mind on the other fellow's problems instead of on our own, to make a real business of studying his viewpoint. Yet time and again, we find ourselves forgetting completely even to take his wants into account.

Thomas Edison's first patent, for instance, was an utter

fizzle, because he neglected to check up on the needs of other people. He perfected an ingenious device which nobody wanted: a vote recorder for law-making bodies.

"That was a good solid lesson to me," [10] says Edison himself. Then and there he determined never again to start an invention without making certain that it met a real need.

Henry Ford and Owen D. Young Put This Precaution Ahead of All Others

"I am convinced by my own experience, and by that of others," says Henry Ford, "that if there is any one secret of success it lies in the ability to get the other person's point of view and see things from his angle as well as from your own." [11]

"The man who can put himself in the place of other men, who can understand the workings of their minds, need never worry about what the future has in store for him," [12] says Owen D. Young, head of the General Electric Company.

In these words Ford and Young sum up all the strategy of handling people that we have so far considered in this book. With the familiar phrase, "point of view," Ford has merely described those differences in people which we have already discussed: their special wants, problems and prejudices, their personal interests and experiences.

Only by approaching people through their own point of view can we hope to control them.

Yet this essential precaution is seldom very difficult. Often, indeed, it calls simply for a little care in choosing our words.

Have you heard the amusing story which Andrew Carnegie tells about his brother and good old Colonel Piper?

The Colonel, a partner in Carnegie's Keystone bridge works, was "exceedingly jealous" of the other Carnegie establishments such as the mills which supplied the bridge works with iron. Many disputes arose, says Carnegie, and at one time "Pipe" complained to Carnegie's brother about a contract which he claimed had not been copied correctly.

"The prices were 'net,' and nothing had been said about

'net' when the bargain was made. He wanted to know just what that word 'net' meant.

"'Well, Colonel,' my brother said, 'it means that nothing more is to be added.'

"'All right, Thomas,' said the Colonel, entirely satisfied.

"There is much in the way one puts things," concludes Carnegie. "'Nothing to be deducted' might have caused a dispute." [13]

Carnegie's brother merely appealed to what Colonel Piper wanted, in a way that "Pipe" could understand.

This little joke illustrates the one vital principle that underlies the use of words, whether written or spoken, to influence other people.

A distinguished New York lawyer, Martin Littleton, noted for his brilliance as a speaker, once covered this vital principle very clearly: "When we fail to interest or convince those with whom we come in contact or in dealings, it is usually because we have not considered the subject from their point of view." [14]

As all of us who have done any selling know, the success of an idea or plan depends not only upon the nature of the idea itself, but even more upon the manner in which it is presented to people.

One small suggestion along this line from Colonel House did much to help Woodrow Wilson swing the French government into line at the start of that brilliant campaign of personal selling in which he put across the League of Nations with the great powers of Europe. Fifteen minutes before Wilson's first meeting with Clemenceau, "Tiger of France," House came to him with a shrewd yet simple idea. He proposed that Wilson introduce the League of Nations by talking first about the freedom of the seas: the one thing clearly connected with the League which the French wanted at that time.

As it turned out, Clemenceau was favorably impressed — became in the end a staunch supporter of the League idea.

Woodrow Wilson sold his plan to Clemenceau by showing him how it satisfied one of his active wants, by gearing it up to his point of view.

The other man's point of view! Here is one of the keys to

all personal power. Yet time and again we fail to use it merely because we forget to stop and think.

Do we, for example, always pause before a meeting and review what we are going to say in order to see if our ideas are expressed in terms of the *other* man's interests, directed toward *his* most active wants? How many of us *regularly* take this precaution? Before making a report to a superior? Before an interview with a customer or prospect? Before a talk with an associate? Before a meeting with a subordinate?

A very able salesman, says Dean Donham of the Harvard business school, once made this significant remark: "I would rather walk the sidewalk in front of a man's office for two hours before an interview than to step into his office without a perfectly clear idea of what I am going to say and what he — from my knowledge of his interests and motives — is likely to answer." [15]

To influence people, appeal to their wants. Remember that the only way to get them to do a thing is to make them want to do it.

Remember also that people's wants are different, that everyone you meet has his own special set of desires and preferences. Certain universal needs are common to all of us, but they take a different form in each person.

Take pains to find out just what the other fellow's wants really are, especially those that touch upon you and your project. Deal with him in terms of these wants. Try to stimulate those that are favorable to you and to give them a new direction if necessary. Very often you can get results by modifying your plans to meet his wants.

Sometimes if the other fellow is not likely to be proud of the desire on which you are counting, it is wise to appeal to it indirectly, to spare him from having to admit it openly.

CHAPTER **X**

MORE DETECTIVE WORK

*A Bit of Napoleon's Strategy Produces
Results in New York*

*John Patterson Astonishes the Salesmanagers
of America*

How Walter Chrysler Tracks Down His Customers

The Making of a Merchant Prince

A SINGLE, CASUAL REMARK, made not long ago in New York, launched the biggest merger in the history of the advertising business.

In an offhand manner William H. Johns, president of George Batten Company, one day offered these few far-reaching words to Roy S. Durstine, vice president of Barton, Durstine and Osborn.

What Johns said was to set many wheels in motion. Yet he merely mentioned one of several facts which might mean that a merger between the two companies was not impossible. Durstine has described the incident to the authors:

"I noticed the other night," said Johns, "that your agency and mine have no clients whose interests are in conflict."

"What do you mean by that?" asked Durstine.

"None of your business," [1] replied Johns, smiling and walking away.

Nothing more was said for several weeks.

But meantime, the idea which Johns had planted in Durstine's mind began to sprout.

Did Johns really intend to suggest a merger? Durstine de-

termined to find out. Their next meeting saw the first of many
long discussions which gave birth to that impressive combina-
tion, Batten, Barton, Durstine and Osborn.

Johns employed familiar strategy — a device that Napoleon
once used years before. Johns opened negotiations by feeling
his way. He started with a comment which committed him
to nothing, which he could easily pass off later on with another
smile, yet which at the same time conveyed his idea to the
other man.

Obviously Johns had one object in mind: He wanted to
uncover the other fellow's point of view before he himself made any
real proposals.

Seldom can we foresee exactly how others will react to a
new idea. At best we can make a shrewd guess — no more —
and almost certainly we will go wrong somewhere along the
line. This risk able men try to avoid.

We see Napoleon at Erfurt with the Russian Czar, bringing
up in the same indirect way the idea which he had at that time
of getting a Russian princess as wife to share his new imperial
throne. Napoleon remarks to the Czar that he needs rest, a
home and children; that his present wife is ten years older
than he; and he apologizes for this frankness about the
"stirrings" of his heart.

There is a pause. " 'Hullo,' " says Napoleon, " 'I see it's
almost dinner time,' " and makes his departure.

"How prettily," observes Emil Ludwig, "he can introduce a
delicate topic just before dinner, so that he can slip away without having it discussed at this state." [2]

This same strategy Benjamin Franklin used in launching his
many plans in Philadelphia. In this way, with no official
power, he gave the city modern fire and police organizations,
founded the University of Pennsylvania and the American
Philosophical Society. In each case he would feel his way by
bringing up the idea at a club meeting, by publishing an
article in his newspaper, perhaps putting the plan aside for a
time if the response was weak. Slowly, carefully, Franklin
would start by uncovering the viewpoint of those whose support he desired.

During the negotiations that preceded the dramatic purchase of the old St. Paul and Pacific railroad, by which James J. Hill established his fortune, he made a formal offer to buy the road, which he knew would not be accepted. It was a deliberate feint. He did this partly to flatter the vanity of a certain man who represented the bondholders, but principally to get information about terms and prices in advance of his final offer.

This, too, was the purpose of that letter which George Washington sent to his brother at the time he was buying up, at bargain prices, the Kentucky land claims which American officers had received for services in the French and Indian War.

Washington wrote to his brother: "As you are situated in a good place for seeing many of the Officers at different times I should be glad if you would (in a joking way rather than in earnest, at first) see what value they set on their lands." [3]

When able men find themselves dealing with new people, or with a new problem, they make it a point to go slowly.

We have already watched Roosevelt at that decisive period in his life when he first loomed up at Albany, speaking "softly" to many people, feeling his way by asking for advice.

Al Smith's famous "submerged first three years" in the New York Assembly represent the same strategy. His leader, Tom Foley, has pointed out that Smith was cannily waiting until "he was sure of his ground," "thoroughly familiar" with his new surroundings before "he walked out" to become the "dominating figure." [4]

Time and again we find successful men taking great pains to learn the other man's wants and objections before they go into action.

When Lloyd George, British War premier, was conducting "ticklish negotiations" with the French, he "gave the impression," says Marcosson, "that he could not speak their language, and invariably carried a squad of interpreters with him." Thus, Lloyd George managed to pick up "a good many asides not intended for his ears." [5]

John Patterson used strategy of this kind in selling to a nation of retail merchants that famous cash register of his which people at the start regarded as a freak invention.

John Patterson Astonishes the Salesmanagers of America

To market his cash register, Patterson personally organized and trained a sales force which became the model and the envy of other manufacturers throughout the country.

And one of Patterson's most stubborn convictions was this: that his men should make no effort whatever to sell during their first few calls on a dealer.

"It is one of our fixed principles," he told Samuel Crowther, "that no talk about selling should be started until the agent knows all about the business of the man he expects to sell."

Every salesman, he said, was completely instructed "on how to go into a store and what to look for; to make a purchase and see how it is handled, to watch what is done with credit, C.O.D. and delivery sales, to talk with the clerks and to watch out vigilantly for some actual mistakes that involve or might involve a loss; to pick up from the owner or the clerks the policies and characteristics of the business, and also to sketch the layout of the store." [6]

Here is one of the famous Patterson methods which astonished American salesmanagers. And yet how simple it is! Patterson merely took care that his men should understand the real problems of every merchant; made certain that his cash register would always be presented in terms of the other man's actual needs.

Clay Hamlin, probably the world's most successful insurance salesman, uses a similar method. He calls it the "advance interview."

During this "advance interview," he gets the other man to do the talking. He himself is largely occupied with asking questions and listening.

"Learn to listen": This is one of the very few reminders on strategy which Clay Hamlin recently wrote down on his year's work plan — a schedule which called for a ten-million-dollar volume of business.

Simple enough, isn't it? Yet how many salesmen whom we have encountered are so anxious to tell *their* story that *we* cannot get a word in edgewise!

Listen and let the other fellow talk! We have already discussed this strategy as a means of winning his liking, of making
a good impression on him. But the same plan serves another
important purpose: There is no better way to learn all about
him, to form a clear picture of his motives, his intentions and
his character.

"The average man talks too much, especially if he has a
good command of language," said Elbert Gary in discussing the
strategy of trading and making a deal. *"A wise man keeps a
close mouth."*

"It is well to let the other man talk half the time — or more!
Each one is trying to 'size up' the other before naming figures,
or stating final conclusions. The experienced and wise man,
if he is a good listener, is able to determine with considerable
accuracy something of what is in the mind of the other man.

"One should carefully weigh every word that is uttered by
one's self," Gary continued, "and by the other person as well.
This will help him to form an intelligent opinion of the other's
integrity, and to judge the reliability of a statement that the
offer made is the 'last dollar' that will be paid or accepted as
the case may be." [7]

In John D. Rockefeller, the "habit of listening" is a prominent trait, says Edward T. Bedford, one of the "Old Guard"
who helped him build the Standard Oil Company: "He was
always glad to listen to anyone. He always encouraged his
partners to talk. We seldom knew what he was thinking, but
he always seemed to know what we were thinking." [8]

And of Marshall Field, self-made merchant prince of Chicago,
an executive who worked with him many years has observed:
"It was characteristic of him when he was trading, to start by
asking questions. He was a good listener and not given to
interruptions. He used very few words." [9]

That veteran salesman and advertising man, Henry T. Stanton, describes this strategy very concisely:

"When you are selling a man spend ninety per cent of your
time thinking about him and only ten per cent of your time
thinking about what you have to say." [10]

How Walter Chrysler Tracks Down His Customers

A few years ago a man who was once a railway shops employee at thirty cents an hour, staged one of the great business scoops of all time.

In 1924, the new Chrysler automobile swept into popular favor with a rush. Its success has now lifted its creator to his present position at the head of one of the largest automobile industries in the country.

How did Walter P. Chrysler plan this car that so swiftly captured the country?

He himself has described one simple formula, a device that anyone can use who deals with *groups* of people.

"It is a good thing," he says, "for those of us who are dependent upon the satisfaction of thousands of customers to *think of them sometimes as just one customer.* If we will picture to ourselves one ordinary man or woman and his or her thoughts about us as vital to our continued business well-being, the seriousness of satisfying the consumer will strike home.

"There is really no exaggeration in visualizing a business *as one man or woman.* That is what determines the fate of the business in due time — not, strictly speaking, the satisfaction of one person but the satisfaction of individual units." [11]

So Walter Chrysler, we may well assume, himself has studied the interests and wants of his buying public: He selects *one* typical man, *one* typical woman to keep before him. In terms of *their* viewpoint, "their vanities . . . their virtues, their habits," he plans his cars, reviews his manufacturing and selling policies.

Walter Chrysler knows that all who deal with groups, whether merchants or teachers, after-dinner speakers or ministers, bankers or writers, editors or manufacturers, have before them most of the time only a vague and shifting picture of the people they hope to influence. It is practically impossible for any of us to think clearly in terms of hundreds or of thousands of people. The result is that we are apt to be guided *not* by other people's wants and interests, but rather by our own. Without intending to do so, we ignore the very people whom we desire to lead.

Against this error, Chrysler sets up his simple landmark for all decisions: One *typical* man, one *typical* woman, to represent his public.

A successful advertising man in using the same sort of strategy puts photographs on his desk to represent typical people he is trying to sell: farmers who buy rubber boots, women who buy high-priced coffee, men who buy office supplies. Thus he keeps his mind focussed on the other fellow's problems and interests instead of his own.

Walter Strong, publisher of the famous *Chicago Daily News*, told the authors recently how he built up a "cross section" of his public. He divided his readers into four classes according to income and sent out ten men to talk to four thousand men and women representing these classes, to chat with each of them about what they read and liked in the *News*.

What these people said, analyzed and summarized, is a sort of a business bible for Strong. "We felt we were shooting in the dark about certain changes," he said. "If I published a paper to suit myself, it wouldn't go very far."

When Ferdinand Foch, Allied commander-in-chief during the World War, first graduated from military school, he made no effort to be sent to a gay garrison city as most of the other young officers were doing. On the contrary, he asked to be sent to the dull town of Tarbes. He had a definite object in view. Here Frenchmen of many racial types came for the horse market. Here he would be able to learn their "temperamental differences." This study of men he continued throughout his career. His "knowledge of different men's minds and the way they work . . ." says Laughlin, "his comprehension of many types of men, his ability to get along with them and to harmonize with them . . . meant almost as much to the world as his military genius." [12]

The same result was secured in a different way by Edwin Grozier, the reporter who made himself publisher and chief owner of the *Boston Post*. He once told how "night after night" as an editor in New York, he "used to go over among the swarming millions of the East and West sides of the city; . . . stroll about . . . and listen to the women gossiping on the doorsteps. . . . stop beside a group of men, and by a judicious use of . . . cigars . . . become one of the group." [13]

Similarly Adolph Zukor, ex-factory hand, now overlord of Paramount Pictures, used to stand night after night in the lobby of his theater to watch the people as they came out, to listen to their remarks, to study the expression of their faces.

Such successful men use many different methods to study the people whom they wish to influence.

Yet many men ignore precautions of this kind in dealing with that one most important person of all: their own employer. Wallace B. Donham, the well known Boston banker, now head of the Harvard business school, believes that this is one of the chief reasons that men so often fail to progress.

"'Business is full of young men who seem to have ability,'" he recently told Bruce Barton, "'who work hard; who believe in their companies and are eager to get on. Their industry and faithfulness carry them to a foreman's position or a chief clerkship. But there they stop. Why? Most often, I believe, it is because they approach every problem from the standpoint of the little part of the business with which they are familiar; not from the viewpoint of the business as a whole, and not from the employer's standpoint. They never imagine themselves behind the boss's desk and ask, "What is he trying to accomplish? What are the problems as he sees them? What would I be trying to do for this business if I had his responsibility?"'"

"The one thing that has helped me most in the many positions that I have filled," says Matthew C. Brush, ex-newsboy, now head of the American International Corporation, "is that I have always looked for things to do which my superior had been in the habit of doing. I tried to anticipate every move, every wish, to keep ahead of him in everything. I always got to the office ahead of him and had his desk ready, anticipating his plans for the day." "Once inside an office, keep thinking two laps ahead of your boss. Try to figure out what his next move will be, and show your brains by being ready for it." [14]

Yet even at that critical moment when they are asking for a raise, many men neglect completely to consider the viewpoint of their employer.

"'A man will say,'" continues Dean Donham, "'"I have been here so many years, and I think I should be doing better," or "My family has increased and I need more to live on"; or, "You are paying Jones so much a week more, and I don't see why I am not raised, too."'

"'All of this may appeal to the Boss's sympathy but not to his business sense.'" [15]

The men who give real thought to the employer's viewpoint, before they ask for a raise, can usually find many facts about themselves which make contact with *his* wants and interests.

Charles Schwab has pointed out a device which many leaders have used as a guiding principle in their early business careers. It is this: *to try to act at all times as though they themselves owned the business.*

The same strategy, of course, applies to getting a job. Yet most men forget all about it. This fact deeply impressed Earl B. Morgan, an industrial engineer who had received over five hundred thousand letters from people hunting work.

"The first mistake," he said, "that nearly everybody makes who is out of a job is to use his shoe leather instead of his brains. . . . Nearly all people — I don't care whether they are mechanics or coal shovelers or college professors or magazine writers — fail utterly to consider the *employer's side of the problem.*" [16]

The whole secret of controlling other people lies in this one precaution: to uncover the other man's point of view and keep it constantly in mind.

The Making of a Merchant Prince

"Bankruptcy within a few months was freely predicted," when John Wanamaker, at the age of twenty-three, opened his first store in Philadelphia at the corner of Sixth and Market Streets. Commencing work as a messenger boy at fourteen, he had saved barely enough to buy his stock of merchandise with the help of a partner. Wanamaker's capital was entirely inadequate. And the nation was on the verge of the Civil War.

Yet his success was dazzling. Wanamaker, as we all know,

became one of the few really notable merchants of America.

From the very beginning he made headway by breaking precedents by using fresh, untried methods. One after another he introduced innovations for which he was attacked, but which eventually changed the whole mercantile system of his day.

His strategy was simple: He merely determined to find *new* ways in which to satisfy the needs of his customers.

"The thought came to him," says Gibbons, "and never left him again . . . that he must *study the customer*." [17]

One price for all, a fixed figure on every article — this is one of the best known of the policies with which Wanamaker upset tradition in Philadelphia. Haggling had been the order of the day. But did customers really *like* it, *want* it? No, decided Wanamaker: They really wanted a fixed price.

Study the customer! That was the basis of Wanamaker's career. Even when his store becomes a vast labyrinth of departments, we find him, like Marshall Field of Chicago, making a complete tour every day, keeping in touch personally with customers and merchandise, hearing complaints.

Like many others who have gone far, Wanamaker took the trouble to *anticipate* other people's wants.

Dr. Charles Paterno of New York, starting with his brother on a capital less than $4000, made himself a millionaire real estate operator in just this way — largely as a result of listening to women's remarks about such things as doors, halls, and icebox handles. It was he who originated the idea of the modern apartment with its convenient floor plan and other improvements so different from those suites of the old days with their long gloomy halls and small living rooms. And it was he who eventually erected the building which broke all records for luxury and high rentals, the famous 270 Park Avenue, New York. From the day of his first venture, Dr. Paterno took one precaution: He personally rented all his apartments. Like Wanamaker, he studied the needs and tastes of his customers at first hand. So he was able to *keep ahead* of his public — to offer them what they themselves wanted before even they themselves were fully aware that they wanted it.

When Edward S. Evans was completely wiped out at the

age of thirty-six, home and furniture gone, sixteen thousand dollars in debt, he was glad to get a job as salesman at five dollars a day. But within a few months, he had laid the foundation of a business that saved the automobile industry $60,000,000 and quickly put him in the "big money" circle in Detroit. His job as salesman was with a mill owner who made wooden blocks to be used in shipping automobiles. Before long, Evans was able to put himself on a commission basis and make a little real money.

Then came his big moment: He decided to gamble his earnings in order to discover what the other fellow really wanted. Automobile manufacturers found these blocks useful, it seemed. But what was their whole problem in shipping automobiles? What else might they want which they were not getting?

Evans hired flat cars, an engine, a short stretch of track; bought old automobiles, samples of all loading equipment in use, samples of many different kinds of wood; borrowed instruments. For weeks there followed a bumping and crashing, a shunting and coupling; curves were taken at full speed; collisions were staged. . . .

He emerged finally, not only with a better block, but with a whole system by which automobiles could be loaded more securely, more cheaply, more quickly than ever before.

"I had something more to sell," says Evans, "than a block of wood." [18]

Today he is head of the Evans Auto Loading Company of Detroit, selling loading equipment to most of the leading automobile makers of the country.

Evans was not satisfied with giving others merely what they already wanted. He *anticipated* a whole set of *new* wants.

There are times when this strategy *and nothing else* makes a sale possible.

James H. Rand, Jr., today chairman of the board of Remington Rand, Inc., was headed for failure until he discovered this well known fact. He had broken with his father and with meager capital had set up in St. Louis a one-man business in competition with him. The going was hard. No one seemed to want his systems of office records.

Then one day Rand stopped trying to peddle his wares up and down the street. He decided to concentrate on large banks and study their routine, to uncover their real problems and try to turn up unsuspected weaknesses; finally to offer a complete *plan* based on what his products could do. He did this. And then at last he started making large sales.

Such men not only uncover the bright side of the picture, the wants and interests that are favorable to their plans; but also they gauge the wants and interests that run counter to their ideas. They try to foresee objections and resistance.

How frequently, after some setback, we realize that we have crashed into a hidden obstacle, have encountered unexpected opposition!

Julius Rosenwald, the wholesale dry goods clerk who has made himself the richest man in Chicago, uses a simple method of anticipating obstacles: He makes himself the other man's champion.

" 'I try to feel,' " he once said, " 'that I am always selling merchandise to myself. If the firm of Sears Roebuck had a counter I would stand on both sides of that counter.' " [19]

In pointing out the importance of this strategy, Owen D. Young gives Cecil Rhodes as his model:

"It is said," Young explains, "that Cecil Rhodes, the empire builder of South Africa, whenever his board of directors was formulating the terms of some important deal, would walk up and down the room, impersonating the other side and firing all possible objections to the terms proposed." [20]

A definite program for keeping in touch with such hidden resistance has been adopted by Isaac Kilbrick, "one of the biggest life insurance men in the East." He goes after the business of small policy-holders, even though it may not be profitable, simply because they are constantly raising objections and asking questions and thus force on his notice the concealed obstacles which he meets in other buyers. "The big man," he says, "asks few questions, but the questions are in the back of his mind just the same and need to be satisfied, even though unexpressed." [21]

Whether the other man reveals his objections or keeps them

hidden, we will fail — unless we take them into account. Always the one sound method is to figure them out *in advance*, if possible.

The essential precaution, observed by successful men is this: to learn as much as possible *ahead of time* about the other man's entire point of view. It is through the wants and interests which are *favorable* to their plans that they get action. But it is by preparing to handle those which are unfavorable that they succeed in dodging trouble.

In putting across your ideas and projects, try to uncover the other man's point of view before you take action. Find out all you possibly can. Keep in mind the various recognized methods of doing this.

Try, when possible, to anticipate people's wants, to meet them before they themselves mention them or perhaps before they even realize that they exist.

Make a point also of considering in advance the resistance that people may offer. Look upon their objections as wants and needs that run counter to your project. Take them into account in making all your plans. If possible, modify your proposals to satisfy them. In any event prepare yourself ahead of time to deal with them, whenever you can do so.

CHAPTER XI

THREE SUCCESSFUL SALESMEN AND THEIR ONE SECRET

Why These Eight Men Agreed to Sell
Herbert Hoover Puts Himself Across with Lloyd George

"WHAT IS THE CLEVEREST STROKE in dealing with people that you have ever observed?"

Thomas E. Donnelley, president of the Chicago printing firm, R. R. Donnelley and Sons Company, was recently asked this question by the authors.

He told them the story of Van Vlissingen and the eight land-owners.

J. H. Van Vlissingen, real-estate man, had been asked by Donnelley to buy a new plant site for the company at a certain figure. The property consisted of eight separate pieces, each owned by a different person.

Soon Van Vlissingen started coming in with options.

But the prices named were nearly twice what Donnelley was willing to pay. It was plain that Van Vlissingen had merely accepted the first figures demanded by the owners.

"What is the use of all this?" Van Vlissingen was asked. Nevertheless, he continued bringing in options at the same kind of high prices until he had all eight.

"Then," said Mr. Donnelley, "he called together all the owners at the Chicago Title and Trust Company. He assured them that the prices at which they had given the options were ridiculous. He pointed out that this was probably their only chance to sell. He told them the total amount which the company was willing to pay and suggested that they divide it up as they pleased.

"And this," Mr. Donnelley concluded, "was what happened. It was one of the cleverest bits of strategy that I have ever heard of."

Thus, without great trouble, without great delay, Van Vlissingen engineered a very difficult type of deal. He induced each one of eight different landowners to sell his property at a given time and at a stated price. He did it by using a well known principle of salesmanship.

With each owner at the start he concentrated on a single point: to avoid having any objections raised, to approach him in such a way as to be sure of getting the answer, "Yes."

To accomplish anything whatever, to make his final meeting possible, it was necessary first to draw each of the eight owners into negotiation, to have them all *coming his way*.

This method is vividly described by H. A. Overstreet in his book, *Influencing Human Behavior*. He calls it getting a "Yes-Response." "The more 'Yeses' we can, at the very outset, induce," says Overstreet, "the more likely we are to succeed in capturing the attention for our ultimate proposal." [1] This is, of course, the correct strategy, both in selling and in all deals that depend upon persuading people. The purpose of it is to make a quick contact with their interests and wants.

The book agent is used by Overstreet to illustrate the power of the "Yes-Response." Let us set such a salesman to work on our own account.

He appears on a doorstep, looms up before the "lady of the house" through the half-opened door.

"Wouldn't you like this handsome set of storybooks for the children?" he asks — if he isn't clever.

"No!" she says and probably slams the door in his face.

Now we will give our canvasser another chance.

"I understand, madam," he says, "that you have a son and a daughter at the Central School?"

"Why — yes." And this time, in spite of herself, she has started to come his way. He may not make a sale to this particular mother of two, but he has made a good beginning.

When any one answers "Yes" or thinks "Yes," he is drawn toward us. We have shown him that we are familiar with his point of view and his interests and that we *respect* them. He gives us his attention and warms up to us.

When he answers "No" or thinks "No," the opposite happens. We have shown ourselves ignorant or careless of his viewpoint. He is repelled.

Once people have said "No" to any of our proposals, it often seems to them a sort of surrender to agree later on. Their pride, their *ego* is at stake. Sometimes, if we cannot get a "Yes-Response" at the start, the best strategy is often simply to try to keep the other man from saying "No."

This, we will remember, was the method used by Charles Schwab (p. 69) when he sold the Carnegie Steel Company to Pierpont Morgan, after Elbert Gary and Carnegie had both failed. Schwab, we will recall, had a banquet arranged at which Morgan was a guest and he himself the principal speaker: Morgan had to listen to the whole story without a chance to say "No" and without any reason for even thinking "No."

Usually it is dangerous to muzzle the other man. Ordinarily it is wise to let him do *most* of the talking. But this is difficult if, like Morgan, he believes that he knows our proposition fully and has already decided against it.

Herbert Hoover Puts Himself Across with Lloyd George

By a similar method, Herbert Hoover once sold Lloyd George an important project: a plan connected with war-time finance in Belgium.

"Mr. Lloyd George read Hoover's memorandum," says Welliver, "decided that it couldn't be done and sent for Hoover to break the news to him.

"Hoover more than suspected what was coming, and decided to crowd matters. Instead of letting the Chancellor take the conversational initiative, Hoover seized it himself. Before the finance Minister had had a chance to spill his douche of ice water, Hoover launched into a careful statement of exactly what he wanted, why it was necessary, how it could be done. He wouldn't permit himself to be interrupted and there was nothing for the Welshman to do but listen. . . . Hoover knows when to talk and when to keep still, and he knew that this was an occasion for him to talk and the Chancellor to be silent. . . .

"While Hoover had talked, the Chancellor had been readjusting his views. When Hoover stopped, the Chancellor sat silent long enough to finish the process, and then in effect said: 'I sent for you to say that these things couldn't be done. I find that they can be done, and evidently ought to be; so I will make the necessary arrangements.'" [2]

Realizing that it would be impossible to extract a "Yes" from Lloyd George at the start, Hoover did the next best thing: He prevented him from saying "No."

Ordinarily such strong-arm tactics are not needed. As a rule, it is not difficult to get a "Yes-Response" at the start.

It is important, in doing this, to put *ourselves* in a "Yes" mood; to keep in the *back* of our mind what we know of the other fellow's objections, but to put in the *forefront* of our minds all that we know of his viewpoint which is favorable to us.

George Hopkins, founder of the Society of American Sales Executives, once pointed out that a good salesman is "emotional" and "will, when at his best, assume that the customer wants to buy. When he feels this way," said Hopkins, "he sells; when he makes preparations for failure, he fails." [3]

Our very confidence in the outcome helps to produce a "Yes" response. Feelings are contagious.

William E. Harmon, a highly successful real-estate developer, once discussed this strategy with James C. Dericux.

"The best salesman," said Harmon, "*leads* his prospect by talking in the affirmative. . . . Suppose, for instance, I want to sell a lot — and I've sold thousands of them personally. I go to the man with all facts about the value of the land, the value of owning a home, and the terms of payment.

"'Smith,' I say, 'you would like to own some land. You've been talking with your wife about a home, and both of you want one. Now, here's how you can get what you want.' And I go on advancing the same reasons to him that he and his wife have been using on themselves. In the end all I've got to do is have him sign the application blank.

"But if I said to him, 'Mr. Smith, you think you can't afford to buy a lot, don't you?' he would come back with something like this: 'I know I can't.' Then an argument would be on and his chances of winning would be even." [4]

The first step in persuading people to act as you wish, is to present your plans in such a way as to get a "Yes-Response" at the very start. Throughout your interview, but above all at the beginning of it, try to get as many "Yeses" as you possibly can.

CHAPTER XII

WINNING YOUR WAY AGAINST OPPOSITION

Edgar Bloom Runs Down a "Blue" Letter
John Hays Hammond Tells a Secret
How Henry Fletcher Made Himself Minister to Cuba
Salesmanship Is Not Argument

THE OLD FELLOW by the bar is in a rage, no doubt about it. Edgar Selden Bloom, youthful "trouble-chaser" for the New York Telephone Company is "wondering what to say."

One day he will arrive in the Western Electric Company as its president. Today, listening to the old chap curse, he is discovering strategy that will help him get there.

This irate hotel-keeper has written a "blue letter," a complaint "studded with profanity."

"When he heard I was from the Telephone Company," says Bloom, "the air became as blue as his letter."

To pacify this volcanic old chap is Bloom's particular job. By accident, he stumbles on the correct method — which he himself has explained.

"All at once, I decided to say nothing; he was saying enough. So I waited. Finally, he ran out of blue words. Then I talked a little. When I finished, he clapped me on the back and said: 'My boy, *you* are all right, but I don't care for the *blank-blank* company.'

"'Well,' I said, 'I can't go back unless you say that you are entirely satisfied with your service.'

"'All right,' he countered, 'I'll promise never to write the company another letter. Will that do?'

"He stuck to his word, and I learned an important lesson from that grievance: When a man wants to air a grievance, let him do it. He'll talk off most of his rancour." [1]

Nine times out of ten a grievance is exaggerated. Often it is imaginary. Almost always vanity plays a large part in it: Either the other fellow's *ego* has suffered or he merely wishes to give his grievance an airing.

No matter how bitter or how foolish his complaint, the surest way to quiet him is to follow the strategy of Edgar Bloom: to listen to him and to show that we understand his viewpoint; to sympathize with it, even though we are unable to agree with it.

Most people hate to admit that they are wrong, and it takes time for them even to realize that this could possibly be the case. Once they have taken a position, it is hard for them to retreat: Their *ego* is at stake. If we start by trying to prove that their attitude is unsound or silly, we do the one thing that will certainly egg them on to maintain it. But if we show that we respect their position and understand how they happened to get there, we make it easy for them to come down off their perch and agree with us.

And this same strategy offers one of the best methods of handling unexpected or difficult objections when we are selling or persuading.

"A good salesman should seek to restate his prospect's objections *even more forcibly than originally worded*," [2] say Borden and Busse in *How to Win an Argument*. By this move we not only gain the other man's liking and confidence, but we also weaken his defenses and steal his ammunition — which is especially useful if he is a stubborn chap. More important still, we gain time to figure out how his objections can be handled.

When we actually *come to grips* with an objection, it is always wise to *start* by dragging it into the open and listening to it.

John Patterson, even in a crisis, when he was preparing to force through a decision by threat of dismissal, when he had resolved to override all objections and had called together his unwilling superintendents and foremen to tell them that they must either make interchangeable parts or quit, nevertheless *started* by asking each man to state his opinion. He knew already that nearly all of these opinions would be unfavorable. But that did not matter, as Patterson himself later explained. "I always like," he said, "to have the other fellow bring up all the objections first." [3]

Nearly always, when we are *compelled to grapple with objections, this is the correct move.* If we are in a position to sweep them aside and intend to do so, it is the strongest possible bid for such co-operation as we can expect. If we must rely on persuasion and salesmanship to gain our ends, this strategy is, of course, still more important.

Charles L. Eidlitz, called the "Czar" of the New York electrical business, official peacemaker of the industry, has described how he deals with complaints and grievances:

"In bringing disputants together, I have found that what both sides usually crave most is *sympathy.* By sympathy I don't mean conceding that a man is right, but making him feel that you can understand how he came to take his position. Concede that his argument is worth listening to; and, if the other fellow has got his goat, do a little mourning with him for that lost animal.

"Whether it is an informal settlement or a formal arbitration proceeding, that is what I always do — listen. I encourage both sides to get everything off their chests that is there. I never try to shut a man off whether he is talking to the point or not. I never exclude any evidence, relevant or irrelevant.

"It is important not only to give both sides a fair deal, but to make them *feel* they have got it. At the close I invariably ask both sides whether they have anything more to say, and not until they admit they are through do I render my decision." [4]

It is very largely because all people with complaints "crave sympathy" above all else, that so many executives make it a point to be always accessible to any subordinate who has a grievance.

The famous "Sunday Court" established by General Goethals when he was building the Panama Canal, has been called "a master stroke of administration." There any one of the 30,000 men under his direction could air his complaints.

Samuel Vauclain, as president of the Baldwin Locomotive Works, considered that one of his chief jobs was to be "the recipient of inside kicks" and observed that he was "easily accessible to any employee of the Works." [5]

"My door is open to any and every man and woman and boy in the organization," [6] says Charles H. Sabin, chairman of the board of the Guaranty Trust Company of New York. And "Jack" Barringer, general manager of the National Cash Register Company, makes the same comment, adding that he takes time to see every worker who comes to him, "even if important business matters have to be held in abeyance." [7]

To be certain that all employees with a grievance could reach him promptly, Lord Northcliffe, the great British publisher, not only arranged that he could always be seen at a moment's notice either at his office or his London home, but also he worked out a plan which assured his entire force that a postcard bearing a complaint and sent to him at Printing House Square would be seen only by himself and his confidential secretary. When mails were heavy, he was always careful to read first of all any letters from his own subordinates.

The very fact that these leaders are always ready to hear complaints acts powerfully to keep imaginary grievances from becoming acute. Lord Northcliffe's scheme of the postcards had a "wholesome effect," yet "not half a dozen" such cards reached him "in the course of six months."

Able men always try to anticipate and prevent complaints and objections. But when these actually arise, their first precaution is to listen to them attentively, to show the other fellow that they understand and respect his point of view.

John Hays Hammond Tells a Secret

John Hays Hammond, long recognized as the "world's greatest mining engineer," is out after his first job. He has graduated from Yale, has studied three years at Freiberg, Germany. Now for a bit of work.

Hammond tackles Senator Hearst, father of William Randolph Hearst, "a foremost mine owner in the West."

And Hammond gets his job — with the aid of a little strategy.

"The Senator was a hard-headed, practical man," says B. C. Forbes, "and had had reason for being little enamoured of collar-and-cuff theoretical mining engineers.

"'The only objection I have to you is that you have been in Freiberg and have had your head filled with a lot of fool theories. I don't want any kid-glove engineers,' the brusque Senator told him.

"'If you promise not to tell my father, I will tell you something.' Hammond countered.

"The Senator promised.

"'I didn't learn a single thing in Germany!'

"'Come around and start work tomorrow,' clinched the Senator." [8]

Does Senator Hearst believe what Hammond says about his studies in Germany? It does not matter in the least.

What matters is that Hammond, in the face of a strong prejudice, has very easily got what he was after. He has used a well known form of strategy. Many business men speak of it as the "law of minor concessions."

We have already observed that the best way to deal with unexpected objections is to start by listening to them, by showing respect for the other fellow's point of view, even if we cannot agree with it.

But in many cases, it pays to go even further: Many objections can be handled best of all by conceding the point altogether.

In handling opposition, astute men make it a practice to *concede as much as possible*. About every point that comes up, they ask themselves: Can it be yielded without putting the main issue in danger?

Very often the point which the other man values most highly is the one that is actually the least important to us: For example, the prejudice that Hammond encountered in Senator

Hearst. In such cases what people usually want is merely to have their opinion respected, their *ego* sustained.

Not long ago Owen D. Young, chairman of the board of the General Electric Company, heard that one of his young executives was voicing complaints. This man, having participated in an unusually good piece of work, was now asserting that he had received no credit for it, but that all the glory had gone to Mr. Young himself. What Mr. Young did has been described to the authors by his assistant, Mr. Case. He wrote to the executive, simply conceding the point altogether. "When we are young," he said, "we find that we often fail to receive full credit for what we do. But when we grow older we find that we are frequently given more credit than we deserve."

Similarly Ivy Lee, America's foremost publicity adviser, who numbers among his clients Charles Schwab, both the Rockefellers, and many of the country's largest corporations, recently handled what appeared to be a difficult objection.

Lee was in England attempting to persuade Lady Astor to lay the cornerstone of the new Waldorf Astoria Hotel which is now (August, 1930) under construction on Park Avenue in New York City.

"No," said Lady Astor, "it is not dignified. All you want me to do is to advertise the hotel."

Then Lee gave her a surprise: "That is perfectly true," he said.

"However," he continued, "you yourself want certain things. You have ideas with which you wish to reach the public." [9] Then he went on to point out the opportunity which she would have through the nation-wide radio hook-up which was being arranged for the event. Also he explained to her that no statement was desired from her — but only her presence; and he emphasized the spirit of the occasion. These facts carried weight.

But what gave real force to Lee's persuasion was that unexpected concession at the start — that willingness to agree frankly with Lady Astor on an objection which she had advanced as basic and final.

In explaining the "adroit persuasiveness" of Lloyd George,

War prime minister of England, Spender says: "He . . . won his way often when everyone else thought that he had lost it. He knew when to sacrifice details in order to win principles." [10]

Sometimes it even pays to set the stage so that the other man can win a small victory; to arrange something harmless to which he can object — merely to give ourselves a safe chance to concede a point. For this purpose a Chicago advertising man once had a ridiculous red bow painted on a cat.

The cat appeared in a painting which was to be submitted for approval to a cranky executive of a large stove company. "Off with the red bow!" the stove-maker roared. Then, meeting no resistance, he subsided. He made no further criticism. For the first time on record, he actually praised a painting and "okayed" it without insisting on hurtful changes.

Whenever we can do so, the one best way to meet an objection is to agree to it. By yielding in the little things, we get our way in the big things. Sometimes it pays to withdraw altogether for the time being.

How Henry Fletcher Made Himself Minister to Cuba

When Theodore Roosevelt stepped into McKinley's shoes at the White House, Henry Fletcher "'decided to go up to Washington and see the Colonel.'"

Like many of Teddy's Rough Rider comrades of Spanish War days, Fletcher wanted to make sure that he would not be overlooked while the cake was being passed.

What happened at the White House he himself has recently described: "There stood 'my old Colonel,' smiling and grinning at me just exactly as he used to do in Santiago.

"'Well,' he said, throwing his arms around my shoulders, 'what do *you* want?'"

"Roosevelt," Fletcher continues, "was laughing when he asked that question; but I figured that the laugh might be covering up quite a bit of justifiable annoyance. Maybe I wasn't the only Rough Rider who had suddenly felt the urge to go into public life. . . . So I laughed too, and said I didn't want anything.

"'Impossible!' shouted the Colonel, with obvious relief. 'You're the only one of the lot. All the others are either in office or in jail.'

"I was satisfied with my visit. I knew I could have got a job right then and there. But I knew that I would stand better with T. R. in the end if I went away without asking any favors. So I went back to Chambersburg, bought a self-teaching Spanish dictionary, and began preparing myself for a diplomatic career.

"About a year later I read in the paper that the first American Legation was to be established in Havana. This was my chance. I knew Cuba. I knew Spanish. And I think I have already shown that I knew the Colonel. The rest was easy. I went up to Washington again, told him of my ambitions and my studies, and started on my second trip to Cuba with Theodore Roosevelt as my boss." [11]

So Henry Fletcher made himself minister to Cuba, opened his long and brilliant diplomatic career. So he sold himself to Theodore Roosevelt.

The moment Fletcher sensed hidden resistance in the other man, he retreated and bided his time.

Obstacles of this kind are often encountered: objections which arise merely because the moment is unfavorable. In the face of such resistance able men withdraw, whenever they can do so. In some cases, a minor concession of this sort is the only way in which to make a contact with the interests and wants that are favorable to us.

Isaac Kilbrick, star insurance salesman, tells how he wrote an important policy as a result of this precaution:

"One day I dropped into an office, and the man whom I approached replied with considerable gusto that I was the fifth insurance man who had called on him that morning. I told him in that case I felt sure he was in no humor to listen to me.

"'Well,' he said, 'you're the first salesman intelligent enough to realize it without being told.'" [12]

On the next visit to this man, Kilbrick closed a sale.

"I seldom do what the other fellow wants," says Henry Fletcher, "but I can often do what I want *his way*." [13] This sums up the whole strategy of minor concessions.

The chief purpose of such leaders is to induce the other fellow to come their way willingly, to make him glad to co-operate with them. Sometimes, of course, resistance must be met head-on. But they know that very little is accomplished, as a rule, by trampling roughshod over the other man's wants.

If the main point itself is directly at stake, if minor concessions and other devices cannot be used, they often try to delay the issue.

When Clemenceau had suggested Versailles as the place for the Peace Conference after the Great War and found that Lloyd George and Colonel House both favored Geneva, he "did not argue the matter" but permitted it to be "postponed for further discussion" — thus gaining time to organize the plan of action by which he won his point in the end.

Most people hate, above all else, to yield under pressure. The salesman who is after the name on the dotted line, in every interview must, to be sure, frequently exert such pressure without appearing to do so; and professional buyers in many cases expect it. But in dealing with average people, it is usually wise to give them time to readjust their viewpoint and thus save their pride. Often they themselves see later on that their objections are unsound or have been based upon misunderstanding.

Conan Doyle, creator of *Sherlock Holmes*, set up a seemingly ironclad obstacle when he first sold the dramatic rights of his stories: "There must be no love business in 'Sherlock Holmes,'" [14] he told Charles Frohman.

And Charles Frohman, "Napoleon of the Theatre," agreed to this condition — for the moment.

But on engaging William Gillette to build a play from these stories, Frohman said nothing to him about Doyle's condition. And Gillette, as many of us will remember, wove in the touch of romance that the American public demands.

A year later when Frohman and Gillette met Conan Doyle in England and Gillette read the manuscript for Doyle's approval, there was no comment whatever on the "love business." Doyle was delighted with the play.

Frohman had side-stepped an objection which became no

objection at all once the other man really understood the facts of the case. Yet had Frohman attempted to debate the question at the start, he would surely either have antagonized Doyle or else have lost his point — or both.

"Some problems settle themselves if let alone, just as some letters answer themselves if neglected," [15] says Brand Whitlock, ambassador to Belgium during the Great War.

One highly successful executive has a special drawer in which he puts those letters which he finds it very difficult to answer. From time to time he goes through the drawer and usually finds that most of the letters have answered themselves in one way or another.

Frequently the best way to settle a dispute is to avoid disputing.

Salesmanship Is Not Argument

A fact that all of us know — but sometimes forget — was once vigorously stated by William E. Harmon, of New York, whose companies had sold over $200,000,000 worth of real estate mostly to small buyers:

"'I'll tell you what salesmanship isn't,'" he said to James Derieux. "'It isn't argument. . . . An argument is a contest and you hate to lose a contest, don't you?'" [16]

Seldom is anything accomplished by forcing other people to *admit* that they are wrong. As a rule it is only inexperienced boys or men of small caliber who use this foolish method.

Most of the time, we find the really big man advancing an idea in that modest and unassuming manner which defers it to the other fellow's judgment and thus invites agreement. "The tactful, 'Don't you think' is usually far more effective than the blunt, 'I think,'" [17] says Leffingwell, the management engineer.

Benjamin Franklin, who brought so many thousands under his influence, learned this lesson when still a boy in Philadelphia. Like many other clever youngsters, he had prided himself on a cocksure, self-important way of making statements. One day an older man gave him the truth — right between the eyes.

"'Your opinions,'" he said, "'have a slap in them for every-one who differs with you. They have become so expensive that no one cares to hear them. Your friends find that they enjoy themselves better when you are not around,'" etc.[18]

Franklin, embryo leader of men, was down for the count. But he picked himself up and did some thinking.

Soon he adopted a quite different strategy, which he himself has described: "The habit of expressing myself in terms of modest diffidence; never using, when I advanced anything that may possibly be disputed, the words *certainly, undoubtedly,* or any others that give the air of positiveness to an opinion; but rather . . . *it appears to me,* or *I should think so,* . . . *or I should imagine it to be so;* or *it is so if I am not mistaken.*

"This habit," says Franklin, "I believe has been of great advantage to me when I have had occasion to inculcate my opinions, and persuade men into measures that I have been from time to time engaged in promoting. . . . The modest way in which I proposed my opinions procured me a readier hearing and less contradiction. . . .

"And to this habit (after my character of integrity) I think it principally owing that I had early so much weight with my fellow-citizens . . . for I was but a bad speaker, never elo-quent, subject to much hesitation in my choice of words, hardly correct in language, and yet I generally carried my points." [19]

There are times, of course, when the positive, dogmatic state-ment is useful to inspire others with confidence in us and in our plans. And, as we shall see, many successful leaders use it for this particular purpose.

There are also times when it is essential to argue: to engage the other fellow in debate, as a lawyer does in the courtroom, and to defeat him if possible. But the object here is to con-vince not the other man, but rather an audience.

Between two friends who both enjoy debating, an "argu-ment" may be both profitable and pleasant. Then it is really not an argument but a discussion. Woodrow Wilson, for in-stance, once spent an hour with Edward Bok asking him "ques-tion after question," forcing him to defend a certain opinion to which he himself seemed "diametrically opposed." At the end of the hour, Wilson astonished Bok by telling him he had changed his mind, that he had just been drawing him out and now saw the question from a different angle."

But it is doubtful if even this strategy can be counted on to promote cordiality.

After all, it is to be expected that other people will disagree with us in many things.   And what does it matter if they do?

Of Theodore Roosevelt, a newspaper man, who was not in accord with some of his policies, said:

"It was not necessary to agree with him to hold his friendship. 'My dear fellow,' he would say, 'it's bully of you — just bully — to come here and fight it out with me.   You're a trump and a fine fellow but on this we don't see it the same way.   We'll talk of something else.'

"Then would come a temptation to abandon your opinion and accept his." [20]

There are countless examples of this strategy.

At the first meeting between Clemenceau and Woodrow Wilson at the time of the Peace Conference, for instance, House reports that they were both careful not to "touch upon topics which would breed discussion."

Grover Cleveland, says Hugins, "was a good listener and when he was not sympathetic with his caller's views he listened to the point of painfulness, letting the other man do all the talking." [21]

And Parnell, the Irishman who made himself "one of the most powerful leaders in the history of English politics," followed this same plan in winning the support of Irish Americans on his trip to the United States.   Faced with many shades and degrees of opinion, "He did not talk much, but he listened a lot." [22]

At times, if we must express disapproval, it may be helpful to do what Colonel House in his diary speaks of doing time and again: to listen in such a way that our silence conveys disagreement.

Whatever tactics successful men adopt in controlling people, we find them first and foremost trying to avoid an argument. Their strategy is to influence others by appealing to their wants and to use caution in handling opposition.

When you encounter objections or resistance of any sort, ask yourself this question: "Can the point be conceded without risking my main purpose?" In bringing people around to your way of thinking, make as many "minor concessions" as you can. Sometimes, in yielding to such opposition, it even pays to withdraw completely for the time being.

If you are up against strong resistance to your main point, it is often wise to delay the issue. This gives the other man a chance to reconsider and provides you with an opportunity to reorganize your campaign.

If objections and complaints must be met head-on, try to get a "Yes-Response" at the outset. Draw people out and listen to what they have to say. Show them that you thoroughly understand the position which they have taken even if you cannot agree with them. Often it is wise to restate an objection with even more emphasis than the other man himself has given it.

Above all, remember that an argument is nearly always useless and often harmful. Try to induce people to accept your idea without forcing them to admit that they themselves have been in the wrong.

Under ordinary conditions, advance your ideas in the modest way that invites agreement — not in the positive manner that provokes opposition.

To steer clear of idle argument, avoid topics likely to cause a dispute. Try to listen silently when others attempt to force ideas upon you to which you cannot agree.

In dealing with subordinates, make it easy for the man with a complaint to see you and let it be known that you are ready and glad to listen to him.

CHAPTER XIII

HOW TO AVOID MAKING ENEMIES

Colonel House Gives Bryan a Pat — and a Shove
Disraeli Purposely Makes Dull Speeches
Why George Putnam Delivered Another Man's Speech

COLONEL HOUSE is handing William Jennings Bryan some bad news.
He is shattering one of Bryan's pet hopes. It is January of 1915, the second year of the Great War.

Bryan, secretary of state, is not to be permitted to go to Europe as American peace emissary. For this difficult post House himself has been chosen by the President. And to House has fallen the equally delicate job of breaking the news to Bryan.

House is to pluck Bryan's tail feathers — and make him like it. In his diary, House describes this ticklish interview with Bryan:

"He was distinctly disappointed when he heard I was to go to Europe as the peace emissary. He said he had planned to do this himself. . . .

"I replied that the President thought it would be unwise for anyone to do this officially, and that his going would attract a great deal of attention and people would wonder why he was there. . . .

"He was generous enough to say that, if he did not go in an official way, I was the one best fitted to go in an unofficial way. . . ."[1]

How dexterously — how easily House salves the wounds of the Great Commoner!

He would "attract a great deal of attention": With these words, House pours balm on Bryan's vanity. The idea about an *un*official emissary is, of course, ingenious. It will do much to save Bryan's self-esteem, good old clumsy Bryan who has to be kept at home. But the Colonel's master stroke at the moment is that glimpse which he gives Bryan of his own importance, that picture of himself attracting "a great deal of attention."

House rounds this risky corner by strategy: He safeguards the other fellow's *ego* by making him feel superior. Quite easily and pleasantly, House pushes Bryan further back on the shelf. With one gesture he gives him both a shove and a pat.

The real danger of breaking bad news is clearly recognized by men like House: It lies not so much in the news itself, but rather in the way it is presented.

Most people do not realize it, but the downfall of another person nearly always raises their *ego*. They cannot prevent this. But if they let the other man suspect, even for an instant, that they are pleased with his misfortune, he will hate them for it.

When able men are forced to break bad news or to thwart other people's desires, they take great pains to spare them humiliation.

Henry Ford, for example, has a regular system of handling the man whose request he must refuse. To soften the blow and to save the other man's pride, he regularly refers him to one of his executives "indicating just how he would have the man and his request handled." Sometimes he even uses a private code, giving the applicant a note to present. If in this note the word "see" is correctly spelled, s-e-e, the executive knows that the request is to be granted. But if it is misspelled, s-e-a, his job is to let the other fellow down as easily as possible.

A simpler, more direct method was used on many occasions by both William McKinley as president, and by Marshall Field. When they were forced to disappoint a man, they started by showing him a special mark of respect: They would invite him to have lunch or dinner with them.

Of William McKinley, Olcott says that he "was obliged to

say 'no' many thousand times, but he did it so graciously that the disappointed applicant almost invariably remained a friend." [2]

To break bad news in a pleasant way often calls for only a little care in choosing our words.

You may have heard the well known story which George Hopkins once used to illustrate this point:

"A shoe salesman told a woman trying on pumps, 'Madam, one of your feet is *larger* than the other.'

"In the next shoe shop the salesman said, 'Madam, one of your feet is *smaller* than the other.'

"And she bought.

"The second man was a salesman; the first was not." [3]

John R. Todd, head of a large New York firm of contracting engineers, tells of a young employee named White who has made himself master of this strategy: "I have known him to take a disagreeable message," says Todd, "into the private office of the most cranky man in New York and make a fast friend of that man before he had left." [4]

When you must break bad news or disappoint the other fellow be careful to shield his vanity — if you value his good will.

Disraeli Purposely Makes His Speeches Dull

He is jeered into silence, publicly humiliated.

He is a brilliant orator — but they will not listen to him. His maiden speech is a complete failure.

Before many years have passed, this pale, slender little Jew will be master of them all.

But just now, young Disraeli, with his "white waistcoat, covered with gold chains," is the butt of the British House of Commons.

"Some day you shall hear me," he says before he sits down.

And very soon he goes into action to make good his prophecy.

Disraeli's plan is simple, but unusual. He starts delivering *dull* speeches. He reasons "imperfectly," offers details, quotes "figures, dates, calculations."

For several months he deliberately masks his genius.

Then suddenly he emerges from his disguise. Once more he offers these British M. P.'s a brilliant speech.

And this time they "hear" him, are pleased and impressed. Disraeli is on his way to become prime minister of England, one of the few great European statesmen of his day.

So Disraeli won the British House of Commons by being dull. Why this strategy worked is very clear.

At first sight these solid Britishers disliked him. His reputation for showy brilliance had preceded him. Also his clothes were too gaudy, too ornate. Thumbs down on this cocky lad! He has no respect for our goodly traditions! He thinks he is clever!

Wounded vanity rising from a hundred hearts struck Disraeli down. And Disraeli saw a great light.

By those dull speeches of his he disarmed opposition. They were in line with tradition: like countless others heard every week by that dignified body. They said quite plainly: "I really do not feel that I am exceptionally clever — certainly no more clever than you."

So Disraeli soothed the other fellow's *ego* by sacrificing his own.

The chief trouble that most people have in managing others is this: They are too deeply interested in convincing themselves that they are superior and important persons, too much occupied in upholding their own *ego* to think much about anyone else's.

Time and again we all of us defeat our own purposes by wounding the other fellow's vanity, without intending to do so. There is a striking example of this in the story about a pupil of W. L. Tomlins which one of his friends recently told the authors.

Tomlins, long known as the dean of American choral directors, was trying to give pointers to a young woman who was a personal friend. But she was making it difficult for him.

One day Tomlins went to Waldo Warren, the man who has given us the story.

"She could get a great deal out of me," Tomlins said to Warren; "I could help her. I could perhaps save her five years of work. But she is always trying to prove to me that she already knows what I tell her. I feel clogged when I talk to her. See if you can get it over to her."

Warren spoke to the girl. She changed her tactics. The results, Warren reports, were remarkable.

Without realizing it this girl had been trying to show off. Like Disraeli, at the time of his first speech, she had been airing her own *ego* at the expense of the other fellow's.

Many are the employers who make this mistake with their subordinates. Many are the hopeful young men who make it with their own boss.

A young man who lost his job through errors of this sort in dealing with his boss, has been described by Dr. David Mitchell, well known consulting psychologist. "'On a number of occasions, . . .'" says Mitchell, "'when questions of policy had come up, he had bluntly told his chief that he was dead wrong. *He did not know he had done this* — people usually don't.'" [5]

There is a genuine thrill in feeling more clever, more skilful or better equipped in some respect than the people around us. But the true leader goes after a greater, more permanent thrill — the thrill of power. He lets the other fellow do the strutting while he himself sits in the background and pulls the strings. He takes care to shelter the vanity of even his humblest followers.

Frederick Taylor, the great efficiency engineer, went so far in subordinating his own *ego* that he even avoided using the word "I" in talking to his subordinates.

To protect the other man from a sense of inferiority is the first precaution in all types of leadership.

Of Lincoln, at the time of his victory in the famous Douglas debate, Sandburg has written: "He did not profess to know anything. He said wonderfully witty things but never from a desire to be witty."[6]

Charles E. Carpenter, a well known Philadelphia manufacturer, noted for his brilliance as a speaker at banquets, found in this strategy "the main reason" for his success.

"People," he once said, "are not at all interested in having you prove to them by your line of talk that you are the possessor of super-intelligence or are even uncommonly clever. . . .

"Public speakers who can't learn this elementary fact are always trying out new stuff that they think will enable them to shine. They really are aiming to please themselves, not their audiences." [7]

The small man often lets his hearers feel that he is clever and that they are dumb — but not the real leader who sweeps people off their feet. His strategy is to make his *listeners* feel clever.

John Hay, our noted statesman and diplomat, followed this same plan in talking to individuals. He "said his good things," writes Bishop, "as though he owed his inspiration to the listener and never exhibited a shadow of consciousness of his own brilliancy." [8] In this he was like Madame Récamier, the French conversational genius who "always made the person with whom she was talking, and not herself, seem clever."

Take care to safeguard the self-esteem of all people with whom you wish to maintain friendly relations. Protect them from your own desire to feel superior and important. Remember that this desire is always at work within yourself, whether you realize it or not.

Why George Putnam Delivered Another Man's Speech

George Haven Putnam, head of the famous publishing house, G. P. Putnam's Sons, once deliberately stole the speech which another man was about to deliver. In fact, he purposely had his own place on the program changed so that he could do this.

Originally, Putnam was to have delivered the closing address. But he persuaded the presiding officer to give this honor to the famous minister, Dr. Henry van Dyke. Thereupon Putnam proceeded to cut the ground from under van Dyke's feet.

What a scurvy trick it seems! Actually it was a carefully worked out bit of strategy — one of many dexterous moves in a big undertaking. And Putnam knew his man: van Dyke would take this joke good-naturedly.

It was a long and difficult campaign in which Putnam was engaged at that time. Working through many agencies, he was leading the publishers in their successful fight for international copyrights. It was in behalf of this cause that both he and Dr. van Dyke were speaking that night. Putnam was entirely familiar with van Dyke's material and it was good. But this was not why he stole it. Not at all. He stole van Dyke's speech because he wanted van Dyke to cover certain points that were still more important: Those vital business issues which he himself had been discussing for so long.

"I utilized my time," says Putnam, "to deliver Dr. van Dyke's sermon. When his turn came, he had, as he stated, no other course open to him than to devote his time to the consideration of the business side of the question, largely appropriated, as he frankly admitted, from the arguments and statements he had heard from Mr. Putnam." [9]

In other words, by a deft maneuver, Putnam himself stepped into the background and shoved van Dyke into first place as standard bearer of the cause.

An important principle of leadership is illustrated by this amusing incident. Always people are prone to suspect a leader of seeking personal glory and prominence. And the minute this happens, they are likely to grow indifferent or else actively hostile. For this reason, true leaders often try to advance their project from behind the scenes.

We find that master organizer, Benjamin Franklin, working in just this way when, as an obscure youth of twenty-five, he founded the Philadelphia city library and later when he established the academy which has become the University of Pennsylvania. In both cases he kept himself "out of sight" as much as possible. The library he brought forward as a scheme of "a number of friends" who had asked him to present it to "lovers of reading." His academy he presented as an aim not of his own but of a group of "public-spirited gentlemen."

Franklin himself points out "the impropriety of presenting one's self as the proposer of any useful object, that might be supposed to raise one's reputation in the smallest degree above that of one's neighbors, when one has need of their assistance to accomplish that project. . . . The present little sacrifice of your vanity," he says, "will afterwards be amply repaid." [10]

Always the able man makes the cause he serves more important than his own personal interests.

Of Edward H. Harriman, the great railway builder, Nelson O'Shaughnessy, who was with him during his last illness, has said: "I was conscious . . . of that great power of his of commanding the allegiance of those with whom he came into contact, a power proceeding not less from his unfailing recognition and appreciation of ability in any form, than from the conviction with which he inspired those around him that *his aims were beyond the personal and broader than the interests of any one individual.*" [11]

It was in this spirit that Joseph Pulitzer, builder and publisher of the *New York World*, instructed his editors to ignore his own wishes if in a moment of stress he should issue orders which were out of keeping with the policies of the paper.

And we find Gustavus Swift, founder of Swift and Company, raising the wages of a night watchman who, not knowing him by sight, steadfastly refused him admission to his own plant.

Small men are likely to put their own convenience, their own whims and vanity, ahead of everything else at any given moment. But the true leader holds up the common cause as something bigger than anything which he himself may do or say.

The man whose authority is shaky, or who has to settle knotty questions without any real authority, can adopt no better strategy than this. Many a young executive has solved his problems in dealing with difficult people merely by setting up broad policies as a guide for all decisions. Once he takes the trouble to formulate such policies and get them approved by higher authority, his troubles tend to disappear.

When you are acting as leader in an enterprise, or inducing others to carry out your plans, keep yourself in the background whenever possible. Make it clear that you consider the project in hand far more important than yourself.

Often it is wise to have other people voice your own ideas.

In dealing with subordinates or followers be careful to put your own established policies ahead of your personal views at the moment.

CHAPTER XIV

A SURE WAY TO WIN PEOPLE'S GOOD WILL

Woodrow Wilson Springs a Joke on Himself

Thomas Beck Turns a Brickbat into a Bouquet

Rockefeller, Carnegie and Schwab All Agree on This

ALL OF US AT TIMES face the problem of breaking the ice with a group of people. Perhaps we come as strangers among strangers; or perhaps we have a new idea to present to people whom we already know.

Frequently we overlook one helpful bit of strategy which many able men have used with remarkable results.

Shortly after Woodrow Wilson had been elected governor of New Jersey he was introduced at a dinner of the New York Southern Society as a "future President of the United States." For him it was a big moment.

"'I find myself,'" said Wilson after a few opening words, "'in one respect (I hope in only one respect), resembling certain persons I heard of in a story that was repeated to me the other day. A friend of mine was in Canada with a fishing-party, and one member of the party was imprudent enough to sample some whiskey that was called "Squirrel" whiskey. It was understood that it was called "Squirrel" whiskey because it made those who drank it inclined to climb a tree.

"'This gentleman imbibed too much of this dangerous liquid, and the consequence was that when he went to the train to go with the rest of the company, he took a train bound south instead of a train bound north.

"'Wishing to recover him, his companions telegraphed the

conductor of the south-bound train: "Send short man named Johnson back for the north-bound train. He is intoxicated."

"'Presently they got a reply from the conductor: "Further particulars needed. There are thirteen men on the train who don't know either their name or their destination."

"'Now, I am sure that I know my name, but I am not so sure as your presiding officer that I know my destination.'" [1]

The audience chuckled. Wilson had told another of those funny stories for which he was famous.

His hearers warmed up, relaxed pleasantly. With that laugh he had won them.

But it is probable that few of those who laughed at Wilson's story understood just what had really happened to them.

First of all, of course, the jokes at which people laugh most certainly and most vigorously are those that are on the speaker.

But Wilson's strategy went far deeper than just getting a laugh. Actually he was employing one of the most powerful methods of winning people's good will and support, of disarming hostility. He was raising the other fellow's *ego* at the expense of his own.

How often we hear the successful man cracking jokes about himself or criticizing himself when he first makes contact with a group of people! He charms and delights them by making them feel superior to him — for the moment, at least.

In Washington, Vice President Charles G. Dawes captivated many, extended his personal power and turned his thankless job into a post of real influence by various types of strategy — one of which was to make frequent "speeches about the infinite jest there is in being a Vice President."

And Bishop Fiske, astonished to find that one of his sermons had held his hearers spellbound as seldom before, later discovered the explanation in one simple fact: He had accidentally opened by discussing "certain clerical shortcomings"; had observed that the "smug professionalism" of the clergy kept many a man from attending church; had admitted that the words of the divine did "not always ring true," and often smacked of "pious cant," also that the clergy's "immunity from friendly criticism had been disastrous."

The good Bishop captured his hearers by aiming criticism at himself.

It was in this spirit that Booker T. Washington, famous negro leader, sensing bitterness against him in a certain audience, started his address and made it successful by telling "a chicken stealing story, at the expense of his own race."

And just so, General Pershing, in those trying, futile days on the Mexican border, joined heartily in the laugh, when in the presence of newspaper men, a red-shirted scout glanced up and remarked: "As I figure it, General, . . . we've got Villa entirely surrounded — on one side." [2]

Albert Lasker, former chairman of the United States Shipping Board, millionaire advertising man, is said to have begun his presentation to a hostile board of directors with these words: "Gentlemen, I am an advertising man and a Jew — so you had better watch me closely." [3]

And Robert Maynard Hutchins, that astonishing executive who was recently made president of the University of Chicago at the age of thirty, emphasized two special points in his first statement to the press — two points which surely helped to smooth the path in his new and difficult undertaking: how little a man of thirty could really be supposed to know and how much he expected to depend on the guidance of the acting president, who was to become his assistant.

This powerful type of strategy is seldom used by the "small" man. He is too anxious to assert his own importance, to turn the laugh on someone else, or to prove that he himself is exceptionally clever and competent.

But the genuinely able leader, as we have already observed, takes the long view. His purpose is to control others, to establish his influence over them. And one of his methods is to let the *other fellow* do the strutting.

A successful salesmanager, Archibald McLachlan, once pointed out that men and women are only "kids grown up." And here perhaps is the true keynote of leadership. The big man tends to look on all the people he deals with as grown-up children. He is interested not in his own feelings at any moment but in what he can cause *them* to feel.

A joke on yourself or criticism of yourself is often an effective means of gaining attention and good will and of disarming hostility.

Thomas Beck Turns a Brickbat into a Bouquet

Not many years ago a salesmanager received a grossly insulting letter from one of his own salesmen.

The salesman observed that he neither liked nor respected his boss, that he considered him a poor salesmanager and that he wished his assistant manager might have the job instead. In every way it was a "hot" letter, an astonishing letter.

But the really surprising point is not the letter itself — but rather what this executive did with it.

The salesmanager was Thomas H. Beck, today the publisher of *Collier's Weekly*. His assistant, so dear to the salesman, was Bruce Barton.

This letter was actually addressed to Barton — not to Beck. It was not intended for Beck's eyes at all. But these two men had the custom of opening each other's business letters and Barton happened to be away at the time.

After reading the warlike letter, Beck took it straight into the office of his employer, Joseph P. Knapp, owner of *Collier's Weekly* and of other things too numerous to mention.

"Look what a good salesmanager I am," he said to Mr. Knapp. "I pick such a good assistant that my own men think he is better than I." [4]

Not a trace of jealousy in Beck, no wounded vanity — only pride at this evidence that his lieutenant was an able man.

So Thomas Beck turned a brickbat into a bouquet. Highly successful men are doing this sort of thing constantly. It is one of the "secrets" that enables them so often to enlist and direct subordinates who are in many respects even abler and more clever than themselves.

The "small" man, without realizing just why perhaps, is apt to be jealous of brilliant subordinates. Actually it is because he has his values twisted. Above all else he prizes his own sense of importance, wishes to feel day in and day out that he, and he alone, is the whole works. But the really big man sees straight.   He values results more than his own vanity.

Andrew Carnegie, for instance, always explained his amazing success by saying that he had surrounded himself with men who knew more than he did.

And Abraham Lincoln selected for his cabinet not only strong men who were hard to handle, but even more, in two cases at least, men who regarded him personally with contempt. Edwin M. Stanton, his competent secretary of war, who early succeeded Cameron, had habitually referred to Lincoln as the "original gorilla" and had attributed the disaster at Bull Run to the "imbecility of his administration." Salmon P. Chase, Lincoln's effective secretary of the treasury, was known at the start to dislike him and to be actively plotting against him.

Lincoln, regardless of his feelings, chose the men most capable of handling these all-important jobs.   At the same time, knowing his own weaknesses, he chose men who were able to offset them.

The "small" man not only cannot endure strong, unruly men around him.   But also he even finds it difficult to delegate responsibility.   Usually he says that he can get no really capable assistants.   This may be true in part.   But actually he does not want them.   Perhaps without being aware of it, he is nursing the idea that he alone is able to do things as they should be done.   Whether or not he understands the truth of it, he is, in fact, setting his own *ego* above results.

It is now believed that Germany lost the first battle of the Marne and perhaps the whole World War because Emperor William II in the old days of his glory had wanted no dominant figure near the top except himself.   He preferred men who bowed gracefully in his presence — and this apparently was exactly what he had got in his Chief of Staff at the outset of the war.   Von Moltke, it now appears, lacked the moral courage to carry out in full the bold plan of invasion as originally laid out by the General Staff — a plan which might well have brought immediate victory: to weaken the left wing of the German army advancing upon Alsace-Lorraine to the point of grave danger and to send the right wing with overwhelming force down upon the French before Paris.

William II's own grandfather, the first German emperor, William I, was a man quite different from his unfortunate offspring. For years, William I put up with overbearing, insolent Bismarck as chancellor, because he saw that Bismarck alone was strong enough and clever enough to transform provincial Prussia and divided Germany into a unified world power.

In discussing the reason why men fail or succeed, Edward Decker, president of the Northwestern National Bank of Minneapolis, makes this interesting comment:

"'One of the things I like to see, . . . is a man at the head of a business with a lot of strong men around him. If a man will not select strong assistants, possibly for fear they may displace him or not do as he says, he is not a big enough man to be at the head of a big business. Strong men will not always do just as they are told, to be sure. But it is not easy to run a business today with a convention of parrots. In a vigorous, growing organization, a great many fairly important decisions have to be left to men in subordinate positions. You can't have a healthy big business in any other way.'" [5]

Because the true leader takes trouble to see values as they are, he finds it easy to sacrifice his own vanity. And this is one of the chief reasons that we find him surrounded by able assistants, and possessed of powerful and helpful friends.

We all know men, often fairly successful men, who fail to get along with people who are more important than themselves. These men dislike looking up. They prefer looking down. They may enjoy being "seen" with persons of note but they tend to choose as bosom friends men whom they can patronize a little. Thus they cut themselves off from the very people who could help them the most.

Hudson Maxim, the great inventor and manufacturer, has put the whole idea in a nutshell:

"There are two kinds of consideration people seek to achieve from others, admiration and love. Now the way you want to conduct yourself is to let admiration go hang and get people to love you. Whenever people admire, they envy, and envy makes enemies." [6]

Be ready to sacrifice your vanity in choosing assistants and friends and in your contact with them. Try to find subordinates abler than yourself along certain lines — even if they themselves realize it. Choose friends whom you can admire and look up to.

One of the sure ways to shine is to be willing to let others outshine you.

Rockefeller, Carnegie and Schwab All Agree on This

"The real test of business greatness," says Charles Schwab, "is giving opportunity to others. Many business men fail in this because they are thinking only of personal glory." [7]

When John D. Rockefeller, testifying before a legislative committee, was asked to what he attributed his success he replied: "To others." [8]

"'No man,'" observes Andrew Carnegie, "'will make a great business who wants to do it all himself or to get all the credit for doing it.'" [9]

Of E. H. Harriman, the famous railroad builder, after that tremendous engineering triumph by which the whole Imperial Valley of California was rescued from certain destruction by flood, Kennan has written:

"If Mr. Harriman, personally, had been asked who finally controlled the Colorado River and saved the Imperial Valley, he undoubtedly would have replied: 'Epes Randolph, H. T. Cory, Thomas J. Hind, C. K. Clarke, and their associates.' But these gentlemen have publicly said that the driving power behind their work — the one thing that made it successful — was the invincible determination of their chief." [10]

The true leader, as we know, is not forever seeking the limelight. He gives it to others. At the least, he shares it. That is how he inspires his subordinates with enthusiasm and loyalty.

This is familiar strategy. Yet how often it is ignored! How many men even yield to the temptation to seize credit for themselves at the expense of their own subordinates!

"A typical case" of this sort was once described by Melville Wilkinson, prominent St. Louis executive. "I'm thinking now," he said to Rex Stuart, "of an executive who was always bringing new ideas to the managerial conferences of a store with which I was . . . connected. He paraded them proudly. He fought for them boldly. And we adopted a good many of them because they were essentially sound. This man seemed to be succeeding in his effort to create an impression.

"Presently I discovered that he was getting nearly all these ideas from subordinates, to whom he failed to give a word of credit. The people under him learned the same thing and resented it. The morale of his department which had been excellent began to crumble. It was a bad mess all round.

"Now suppose this executive had said to us: 'Yesterday, I heard Bill Jones make a suggestion that I think is a corker. I'm passing it along.' Why Bill Jones and all the other workers under him would have been tickled to death that he was 'boosting them to the boss,' and they would have worked their heads off. I would have congratulated myself that I had a department head who could inspire his people to think up things for the good of the business. And everyone would have been happy." [11]

This department head defeated himself by letting his *ego* run away with him. What a different picture we see when we consider the man who builds a strong organization and achieves a lasting success, no matter what his line of work may be!

"He was utterly devoid of vanity," says Thomas L. Masson in describing his chief, John A. Mitchell, founder and publisher of the weekly magazine, *Life*. "He encouraged everyone to feel his own importance, while always keeping himself in the background. The result was that, when he died, everybody in the office believed himself alone competent to run a paper that, actually, only one man had really run — although nobody, during his lifetime, was quite aware of this."

"I remember once his telling one of our advertising managers, not only how important the entire advertising department was, but how important *he* was. Afterwards I chided him on this and remarked that without the editorial end the advertising would be nowhere. Mitchell replied that, from the advertising man's point of view he was right and that he ought to be made to feel that way." [12]

Sometimes we find a leader even surrendering the very title of leadership to another man, because he recognizes in himself a handicap which can, at the time, be best offset by this method. Disraeli, the English statesman, for instance, when on his way to become prime minister, put another man at the head of the party of which he was actual leader and served him loyally as lieutenant until his death, because he realized that this other man was personally more popular than himself.

Not only does the true leader give his followers full credit — and more — for all that they do. In addition, he shoulders the blame for their mistakes.

No leader perhaps has ever inspired greater devotion in his men than Robert E. Lee, the Confederate commander-in-chief during the Civil War, who is today considered as standing among the few truly great soldiers in the history of the world. And this loyalty of his followers, military critics now believe, rested very largely upon one trait in Lee: He publicly placed the blame for all reverses on himself alone.

Yet few men, as a distinguished British general has pointed out, have had more opportunities to shift the blame to others. In Lee's early campaign in Virginia, for instance, when subordinate generals let victory slip away from them by failing to attack as he had ordered, he made no mention of it and wrote to President Davis: "But for the rainstorm, I have no doubt it would have succeeded." [13] And then, in silence, Lee faced the storm of popular criticism which descended upon him.

At the second battle of Bull Run, when Longstreet allowed the chance for a crushing victory to slip by because he attacked not as instructed by Lee, but a whole day later, there were no reproaches even, from his commander-in-chief.

At Gettysburg, once more it was Longstreet who failed Lee, who made defeat certain by setting his judgment against Lee's and twice delaying the attack. Yet this was what Lee had to say to his own generals and to Davis: "All this has been my fault." "No blame can be attached to the army for its failure — I alone am to blame." [14]

Lee's victorious opponent, Ulysses S. Grant, followed this plan with his subordinates — this strategy which is at once so noble and so shrewd. Grenville M. Dodge, a subordinate general, has written this of Grant:

"He absolutely sunk himself to give to others honor and praise to which he, himself, was entitled. No officer served under him who did not understand this. I was a young man and given much larger commands than my rank entitled me to. General Grant never failed to encourage me by giving me credit for whatever I did, or tried to do. If I failed he assumed the responsibility; if I succeeded he recommended me for promotion. He always looked at the intention of those who served under him, as well as to their acts. If they failed in intention, he dropped them so quickly and efficiently that the whole country could see and hear their fall." [15]

The leader expects much from his subordinates. But while they serve him, he stands like a rock between them and censure from others. He asserts his authority by making himself, and himself alone, responsible for all their actions good or bad. They are his "grown-up children."

He shines by letting others outshine him. He is well served because he sacrifices his vanity.

Of Grant, Andrew Carnegie has said, "I noticed that he was never tired of praising his subordinates in the war. He spoke of them as a fond father speaks of his children." [16]

To inspire enthusiasm and loyalty in subordinates, share the limelight with them. For their successes, give them even more credit than is due to them. For their mistakes, be ready to shoulder the blame.

CHAPTER XV

SIZING UP THE OTHER FELLOW

*How Abraham Lincoln Handled Clever
People in a Special Way*

Henry Clay Frick Sizes Up This Man as a Peacock

Why Woodrow Wilson Hated to Say "Yes"

*How Herbert Hoover Put Himself Across
with His First Boss*

AMONG THE THINGS everyone remembers about Abraham
Lincoln are his famous stories — those homely yarns
which he was forever spinning.

Part of his strategy in using them is widely understood: He
told these stories not only because he loved a laugh but, even
more, to make his points clear.

But one feature of Lincoln's strategy is seldom mentioned:
He did not use these stories with every one.

He found, says Conwell, that "astute minds, capable of
grasping the meaning of facts without illustration, sometimes
resented" the illustrations.[1]

Lincoln took care to gauge the other man before springing
one of his stories. With most people he found them valuable.
But with those who were unusually clever, he adopted other
methods.

Successful men, as we have seen, handle each person *differently*. Already we have discussed certain points which they
take into account: the other man's special interests, his wants,
his problems. Now we come to the really basic points of difference in people: their capacity to think and to do, the traits
of their character.

To decide whether the other fellow is clever or stupid is usually simple enough. But even this small fact about him is often of far-reaching importance in controlling him. On this simple point about another man, Newton D. Baker, former secretary of war, once based his entire plan in an important law case.

As a prominent Cleveland attorney, Baker had come to Chicago to represent the McCormick family in the Circuit Court of Cook County.

And here his strategy commanded the admiration of the other lawyers present: not so much his legal tactics, which were, as a matter of fact, brilliant; but rather his personal strategy in dealing with the central figure, the judge.

Baker had discovered that this pillar of justice was a bit dumb. Many skilful lawyers had failed in his court merely because they had confused him.

But not Baker. He posted himself in advance on his man.

"Ordinarily in a case of this type, a lawyer like Baker would make many points of law and cite many different cases," says a well known Chicago attorney who watched Baker in action. "Before this judge, however, Mr. Baker made only two points of law and cited very few cases indeed. He said now that he had made these points he would not return to them. But actually he did. He carried them through his entire presentation and ended up with these same points.

"The judge beamed, followed everything that Mr. Baker said, understood perfectly, was much interested." [2]

Baker had sized up his man.

The traits of character which set people apart are, of course, many in number. Some, such as honesty, courage, loyalty, good nature, etc., are frequently discussed. But others, less frequently mentioned, are perhaps even more important in handling people. Let us consider a few of the hidden traits for which skilful leaders are on the lookout and see how they turn them to their advantage.

Tom Johnson, for instance, famous mayor and city-builder of Cleveland, once got results by treating a grown man just as though he were a child.

War had broken out in Cleveland over a certain franchise — a franchise which Johnson greatly desired to have granted for the good of the public. But strong interests were fighting it.

That night at the council meeting, the measure would either be passed or defeated once and for all.

Now Councilman Kohl had come to him with a big piece of news: He had been offered a bribe. Here at last Johnson saw his chance to win.

Victory was certain if Kohl could be persuaded to take the bribe and flaunt it later at the council meeting. How could his nerve be screwed up to the right pitch?

Johnson knew his man. He dared Kohl to act:

"'If you were a really game man, I would suggest a line of action. But I don't think you would carry it out, so there's no use in my advising you.'

"This appealed to his vanity," says Johnson, "and he begged me to advise him. He said he would do anything I suggested except go to jail, and he'd even do that if I would promise to protect him." [3]

Kohl had swallowed the bait, hook, line and sinker.

Later that day "a dramatic scene occurred in the Council Chamber." At the critical moment Kohl threw on the table in front of Johnson the bills which he had accepted. The indignant council passed the ordinance "without a dissenting vote."

Councilman Kohl came through. Why? For one reason only: *Johnson understood his character.* He treated him like a small boy afraid to jump.

We all know such men who will rise to a dare. Many mature people resent an approach of this type. But a few are still childish in this respect. One of the surest ways to get them to do something is to dare them to do it in some way or other.

Back of this trait of character lies one of the most interesting and useful facts about human nature:

The great majority of all the people with whom we deal have an inferiority feeling: To some extent, large or small, they are uneasy about their ego.

The man who will take a dare usually has a strong sense of inferiority and has formed the habit of compensating for it in this childish fashion. He likes to show off by undertaking bold or unusual deeds. It is worth while to be on the lookout for this trait in the people whom we wish to influence.

Equally useful is this fact: that nearly everybody we know will accept a challenge if it is of the right kind. If we are dared to fight a vicious lion with bare fists, we will not think of accepting the challenge. Why? Because we have not the slightest doubt that the lion is more than a match for us.

A challenge will not make a man do the thing he is sure he cannot do and which he has no desire to do. Nor will it make him do a thing which he is calmly certain he *can* do.

If, on the other hand, he has, like most men, an inferiority feeling, if he is sensitive because he feels he may not be able to do a thing, if he would secretly like to do it, a challenge will stimulate him to try.

Theodore Roosevelt, for instance, is known to have taken a dare at least once in his life.

Just back from Cuba, the "hero of San Juan Hill" had been picked by Thomas Collier Platt for governor of New York.

The great political boss was preparing to present Roosevelt, the Rough Rider, to the Republican state convention.

Suddenly Platt and Roosevelt struck a snag. Roosevelt's opponents had got hold of the fact that he had "sworn off his taxes" in New York while assistant secretary of the navy — that he was no longer a legal resident of the state.

"At this juncture," says Platt, "Mr. Roosevelt took me aside and said, with a trepidation I had never before and have never since, seen him display: 'I cannot remain in this fight; I must withdraw from the race.' His desire to withdraw was made apparent to everyone in the room."

Platt urged Roosevelt to trust him to find a way out. Then he played his trump card.

"I said with brutal frankness: 'Is the hero of San Juan Hill a coward?'

"He replied with his customary vehemence; 'No, I am not a coward.'" [4]

So Platt won the hand. Roosevelt was rescued by famous lawyers, became governor of New York.

Platt got his way with Roosevelt because he understood his character.

Roosevelt's undoubted personal courage was not that of the stolid Russian peasant. Neither was it a sham. It was an achievement. Roosevelt, as a sickly boy, had struggled manfully against both ill health and timidity. He himself has told by what method he conquered fear. But he could not allow himself ever to doubt his own courage. On this point he would take a dare.

In nearly all of us there are such points about which we are a little uncertain, on which we have a sense of inferiority and are anxious to prove our own worth. In these matters we are vain and are likely to be influenced by a dare. Almost every man has pet vanities of this sort.

One of the important things to understand about other people is the nature and the degree of their vanity.

The strong man is vain usually on only a few points.

But some men, as we know, are vain about almost everything.

Henry Clay Frick Sizes Up This Man as a Peacock

Early in his career Henry Clay Frick was able to sweep an obstacle from his path merely because he took the trouble to size up a man of this type and to handle him correctly.

The future prince of steel and coke was on his way to "make a million" before he was thirty. He had started by sleeping for two years on the counter of a country store, working for his board and keep.

Now he was earning all of eight dollars a week as clerk in the big emporium of Macrum and Carlisle. Among twenty salesmen, all competing for high records, Henry Clay Frick was the latest recruit.

Soon his name was appearing at the head of the sales list. And this in itself is remarkable. But still more remarkable is the fact that he managed at the same time to win the good will and friendship of all the men whom he outstripped.

At the center of Frick's problem was a salesman named Blair who had many supporters. Not only had he "long been recognized as the leading salesman" but also he "claimed the privilege of serving the best customers" — a prerogative which "was conceded by all the other clerks."

It was this man's special privilege that Frick proceeded to challenge and to smash — without making a single enemy.

Frick succeeded for just one reason: He handled this man and his allies in the right way. He sized up Blair as being vain — as a strutter and a peacock.

What Blair chiefly wanted, Frick decided, was to have his own importance recognized. And this was simple.

Although Frick's success "'was gall and wormwood to Blair' and 'general unpleasantness' ensued for a time, Clay was so considerate of Blair's feelings and so tactful and good-natured that after a while he won them all and made them like him in spite of themselves." [5]

Here we see a master of men at work. Suppose Frick had attempted to handle Blair by treating him rough. How different the outcome would have been!

The vain man is after the glory of the moment — and little else. He upholds his *ego* by strutting and showing off. He will usually overlook a defeat altogether if we only save his precious vanity. His sense of inferiority is deep-seated: He cannot resist praise and flattery.

Such men fall into various childish habits of compensating. Vanity is one. Bragging is another. Boasting usually shows an especial weakness in the things boasted about.

Sometimes an inferiority feeling may be skilfully concealed — yet actually so deep-seated as to render a man almost worthless in any responsible position.

Not long ago a bond salesman looking for work was up before Charles Schweppe, head of Lee Higginson and Company's Chicago office.

The only point against this salesman was that he had moved about a great deal from one job to another. But he had offered excellent reasons for these changes and had already sold himself to one of the junior executives.

Now in his narrow office, Schweppe gave this young executive a surprise. He turned to the hopeful salesman, spoke coldly, harshly.

"Well, what do you think *you* could do for Lee Higginson?"
The salesman was confused. He made some weak reply.
Soon the interview was ended. The salesman was out for good.

"I had a hunch he had no nerve," said Schweppe later.[6]

This young man was self-possessed, plausible, persuasive, but he went to pieces in the face of a real obstacle. He was no salesman. Schweppe suspected this and devised a test to check his hunch.

Nearly all of us know at least one or two persons like this salesman. They usually have a strong inferiority feeling which they try to cover up by a pretense of superiority.

Such people often radiate confidence. They are frequently convincing and impressive talkers. While things go well their false air of superiority gains them, especially from strangers, a respect and admiration not justified by their abilities. Too often they break when stress comes.

Senator James Couzens, millionaire ex-partner of Henry Ford, describes a blunder made by him once with a man who apparently belonged to this class.

"The worst failure I ever hired," writes Couzens, "was an elderly man who had the gift of speech. He made me forget all of my principles and hired himself to me. He was a flat failure. His glibness had been trained exclusively to getting jobs — not to doing anything after he got them." [7]

Couzen's "elderly man" fooled the automobile manufacturer completely. Schweppe's bond salesman, on the other hand, was brought up short by a test which revealed his weakness.

It is very helpful indeed to understand the various ways in which a feeling of inferiority operates. A young salesman who was on the road to failure was once turned into a valuable executive by Melville Wilkinson, president and chief owner of a big St. Louis department store, because Wilkinson took the trouble to get at the root of the other man's problem.

The salesman was about to be discharged. He was " 'forever

WALTER P. CHRYSLER, one-time grocery chore boy, founder and head of Chrysler Motors. ∞ He tells how he studies his customers (p. 84)

P. & A.

U. & U.

JOHN H. PATTERSON, founder of the National Cash Register Company. ∞ He astonished American sales managers (p. 82)

ADOLPH ZUKOR, ex-factory hand, now overlord of Paramount Pictures. ∞ He found out what people really wanted (p. 86)

P. & A.

JAMES J. HILL, the St. Paul shipping clerk who created the Great Northern Railway; called the "Empire Builder." ∞ He used strategy to gather information (p. 81)

U. & U.

U. & U.

JOHN WANAMAKER, self-made merchant prince of Philadelphia. ∞ What he discovered about people (p. 87)

P. & A.

DAVID LLOYD GEORGE, War Premier of Great Britain; son of a needy Welsh school teacher. ∞ He pretends he cannot speak French (p. 81) antagonizing both his customers and his companions.'" Wilkinson found that this youth felt deeply dejected because no one seemed to like him. He also discovered that he was "'crazy to make good.'"

"'That evening,'" says Wilkinson, "'I went to the silk department where he had charge of about fifteen feet of stock, and showed him just how it should be arranged. At the same time I talked to him about salesmanship and tact, and let him know that I believed in him.'"

The next morning Wilkinson stopped casually before his section of the shelves, called the department manager's attention to the skilful arrangement of the stock, made a big point of it.

"'This harmless little subterfuge,'" continues Wilkinson, "'was all that boy needed to touch the spark. It changed the attitude of everyone in the department toward him and gave him new courage.'" [8]

Soon this near failure became a department head and was on the road to higher office. Here is one of the many reasons that Melville Wilkinson became known as "one of the ablest leaders and developers of men and women in the mercantile world of America."

To Wilkinson it was clear why the salesman was antagonizing people. The young man's haughty, quarrelsome manner was his way of compensating for a sense of inferiority. Wilkinson built up his self-confidence by showing faith in him and staging a little triumph for him. He developed in him the *habit of success*, substituted it for the habit of haughtiness. Wilkinson's strategy worked because the man was young and because there was really good stuff in him. Wilkinson simply provided him with a better method of compensating.

The man who is puffed up, who is haughty and conceited or disagreeable is, in most cases, compensating. It is all *camouflage*. What he really needs is not harsh treatment but rather praise and encouragement.

Sometimes, of course, the man with the swelled head is that less usual type: the grown-up spoiled child with a true and permanent sense of *superiority*.

Brunker tells how Mike Murphy, famous Yale coach, won a

track meet largely by handling a man of this sort in the right way.

The contest had been close and it was evident that one of the Yale sprinters had to place in the 220-yard dash, if Yale were to win. Shortly before, this same man had won second place in another race by a narrow margin.

"In spite of that close call," says Brunker, "the Yale man came in all puffed up. He wouldn't take a rubdown; said he didn't need it to beat that bunch. I'll never forget how Mike looked at him, turned a little white and then let fly at him with all the force of his extraordinary vocabulary. He called him more kinds of unpleasant things than you would have supposed there were in the world. I never saw a man called so completely. Mike sent him out to the last race white-hot with rage and he won. His winning settled the cup question." [9]

Murphy's method was extreme. But this spoiled child type of man, who honestly believes himself the lord of the universe, frequently needs to be brought down to earth with a thump.

Sometimes the man with such a superiority feeling hides his swelled head under a false modesty.

Lawrence A. Downs, president of the Illinois Central Railroad, describes one such man "whom it was dangerous to praise, because he puffed up and went to pieces under it." [10]

But men of this type are in the minority.

It is safe to assume that the majority of men who appear to us to be puffed up actually feel inferior.

Why Woodrow Wilson Hated to Say "Yes"

Another trait worth watching for in men, was discovered by Colonel House in Woodrow Wilson.

"When Colonel House put a project before President Wilson, he did not expect affirmative commendation," says Seymour. "He evidently took the President's silence for consent, for, as he once said, 'If the President did not object, I knew that it was safe to go ahead, for he rarely agreed in words; while if he disagreed, he always expressed himself.' With House the opposite was true." [11]

Now why did Woodrow Wilson hate to say "Yes?" When we recall how House used to ease ideas into Wilson's mind (p. 45), the answer is clear.

Wilson compensated for *his* sense of inferiority in a childish fashion that is fairly common: He pretended, even to himself, that *his own mind*, his own knowledge, were all-sufficient. In most cases, he would not admit that he needed suggestions from any one.

When he did hear something good which required his assent, he apparently found it difficult even to say "Yes." He merely said nothing.

We all know such men and women who are fortified against other people's suggestions. Psychologists have a special name for them. They call them "negativistic": people who are "negative," who like to say "No" and think "No."

When such people are exceedingly clever and cultured, like Wilson, we say they have "analytical" minds. Otherwise we say they are just plain "ornery."

We have watched Leffingwell, the industrial expert, selling a new idea, a visible card index to an executive of this type (p. 46). He gets the other man to notice it, tells him that it will be of *no use* in *his* department, then lets him discover it for himself. The executive falls in love with that card index because he thinks it is *his* idea. He is gleeful over proving that Leffingwell is wrong.

George Hopkins, founder of the Society of American Sales Executives, has told how a salesman should handle this kind of a man. He also mentioned some other interesting types:

"Each sales prospect presents a different kind of human problem and only the congenital dub will treat all alike. A good salesman will sell the close trader on how to make more money with less effort; he will sell the purse-proud fellow on how big a man he is; he will rush the snap-judgment buyer through to a conclusion; *but he will not try to sell the analytically-minded prospect at all — he will just give him the information in the form best suited and look in the next day for the order.*" [12]

Herbert Hoover got his first real start as an engineer by observing that his boss was not this sort of man at all. He sized up his employer as being big enough to welcome criticism even from a subordinate.   And he staked much on his opinion.

How Herbert Hoover Put Himself Across with His First Boss

Herbert Hoover is busy pounding a typewriter.

The serious face above the keys is not the chubby visage we know today.   It is less of a circle, more of an oval.   Hoover is twenty-one years old.

And he is very glad indeed to have this job.

Until recently he has been swinging a pick in a mine.

His diploma from Stanford University, his training as an engineer, have not helped him much — as yet.   But at least he is working *for* an engineer; in fact, for the greatest mining engineer in the West: Louis Janin of San Francisco.

Now Hoover is copying important papers.   Inexpertly his blue-gray eyes shift back and forth from the papers to the keys, from the keys to the papers.

But he sees far more than keys, far more than papers.   The words he is typing open vistas.   He is back again on vacation from college, working in Grass Valley.

This mining country about which he is writing — he knows it well.   There in Grass Valley he himself helped make discoveries which have never been published.

Pound, pound, peck, peck — suddenly Hoover stops.

It is all wrong.   What he is copying is not true.

The famous lawyer who has consulted Janin, the great Janin himself — they were both wrong.   What shall he do?

He goes to Janin; tells him what he believes.

"Of course," says Wade, "the mining engineer was at first angry at his typist for daring to question his opinions.   But he let him explain why he thought as he did; and as he listened, interest took the place of anger.   Not only this — he took young Hoover with him to the lawyer's office to talk over the matter with him." [13]

"The outcome of it all was that the papers were altered in the way the typist believed necessary, and the youth who had pointed out the mistake gave up typewriting at forty-five dollars a month to be sent to examine mines, not only in California but in other states in the West."

Hoover is on his way up. Two years later he will be chief engineer of an important mining company in Australia. Janin himself will recommend him for this high office.

Hoover has won Janin.

He has sized up his man.

Janin is one of those rare creatures: a genuinely big man with little or no sense of inferiority. He has the trait which was frequently noted in Pierpont Morgan, the elder, and in other leaders of that caliber. Janin is sincerely modest about what he knows, ready to learn from others.

Able men like Hoover take great care to form estimates of all the people with whom they deal. This strategy is one of the chief sources of their power.

It is not enough to know that men *do* things, we must know *why* they do them if we are going to control the situation.

In gauging one important trait of character, Frank W. Frueauff, former executive head of the Cities Service Company, used to watch closely to see whether men came to him *with* decisions or *for* decisions. He once made this pointed comment:

"A man representing one of our companies comes in and says: 'Do you want to do so and so?' He is trying to use *my* head. Another man comes in and says: 'I think we ought to do so and so!' He has been using his own head. You can tell a good deal about a man by the type of letter he has been sending in, and by the kind of reports he has made." [14]

Frueauff is on the lookout for a decisive trait: the habit of welcoming and seeking responsibility.

T. Coleman du Pont has summed up this whole point very clearly: "'Of course,'" he says, "'not all men are capable of filling positions which carry the responsibility of making important decisions. Some men can work wonderfully for other people; they are ideal tools or implements, when guided by others, but they lack initiative, originality, self-courage. They are capable, faithful, valuable followers but not leaders.'" [15]

Most men, as a matter of fact, shrink from added responsibility.

The strong man has largely conquered this tendency by learning the joy of achievement. He welcomes the chance to meet difficulties, to take on new responsibilities. He sustains his *ego* by acquiring a sense of power. He has the *habit of success*.

People of the clinging-vine type, so familiar to all of us, try to sustain their *egos* by making other people help them, by remaining at the center of the stage like a helpless baby. They have the *habit of laziness*.

The strong man is at one extreme; the clinging vine at the other. Most people are somewhere in between.

It is helpful to gauge these two traits in the other fellow. They form an important index to his true nature and to the sort of work for which he is fitted.

In sizing up the other fellow, consider these points:

Has he the habit of compensating for a sense of inferiority —

  By rising to a dare?

  By strutting: Is he a peacock — vain about almost everything?
  By boasting?

  By putting up a false front of confidence?

  By being haughty and superior or quarrelsome?

  By responding unfavorably to suggestions: Is he "negativistic?"
    Or is he a really big man who welcomes suggestions, criticisms?

Has he a pet vanity?   If so, what is it?

If he has a swelled head, is he, as usual, covering up a sense of inferiority?   Or is he that rare type, the grown-up spoiled child, with a genuine superiority feeling, who must at times be handled roughly, and whom it is dangerous to praise?

Does he shirk responsibility or does he seek it?

Is he clever or stupid?

To get results it is important to remember that people must be treated differently in the light of their character and of their capacity.

CHAPTER XVI

THINGS TO LOOK FOR IN
JUDGING PEOPLE

Marshall Field Inquires about a Mule

Lyman Gage Picks a Vice President

Harriman Sizes Up His General Manager

Colonel House Captures an Emperor

*A Small Town Dealer Earns a Profit of
$340,000 for One Customer*

ARK O. PRENTISS, New York business man, once told how Marshall Field contrived a test to gauge his memory.

As a youth Prentiss applied for a job with the famous Chicago merchant, who at that time personally interviewed all applicants.

"I have never seen a man," said Prentiss years later, "who asked so many questions. Mr. Field found out that I had worked in a mine as mule boy, and I'm damned if he didn't ask me the name of the mule!" [1]

So Marshall Field angled for clues in sizing up strangers.

Many are the ingenious tests which leaders have employed to gauge the character and ability of other people. A few of these tests we have already noted in the preceding chapter. And we shall observe more of them in this chapter.

Let us first, however, consider more closely just what kind of evidence the leader uses in forming his estimates of other men, just what it is that he looks on as a clue.

It was through a mere straw in the wind that Alvaro Obregon of Mexico correctly sized up the man whom he later had to outwit to save his own life.

We remember Obregon as the one-armed president of Mexico who was assassinated in 1928, as one of the few genuine statesmen of that unhappy country.

Now we see him as the soldier, the revolutionary general. For the first time Obregon is meeting Carranza, his First Chief. When Carranza leaves, he is asked what he thinks of him.

Obregon's answer is given in full by Dillon:

"'I have seen too little of him,' he replied, 'to have a judgment. But I can give you my impression about his qualities as a commander. He is a great man for little things, and a small one for great ones. The individual trees would hinder him from seeing the forest as a whole. And he is persistent and dogmatic to boot.'

"'That is an interesting estimate,' remarked de la Huerta, 'but I am curious to know on what you base it.'

"'It is partly intuitive and partly founded on a number of mere trifles which, like straws that show the direction of the wind, give me an indication of the man's specific quality. I will give you one instance. During our conversation with him this evening, he stopped short twice or thrice and went outside to see whether his horse had been properly fed and looked after. Now, we know that he has a man to see to his horse, and if the man were worth his salt, there was no need of the chief looking after him. This is but one case. There were others. And they seem to indicate that he has a bent for details, and that his mind is irresistibly attracted to particular circumstances in lieu of taking in the whole!'" [2]

How well this estimate of Carranza serves Obregon in the end! Forced later to choose between flight and a visit to the capital at Carranza's invitation, he goes to Mexico City, walks into what his friends call a "death trap." But he knows his man. He realizes that some petty, foolish trap will be sprung and is prepared to deal with it. He foresees the plot to fasten treason upon him and escapes at the right time with popular anger focussed on his enemy.

Straws in the wind, tell-tale trifles! Here is one secret of that skill in estimating character which we observe in able men. Their skill has often been called uncanny, often attributed to intuition. But actually these leaders are merely careful to watch for bits of evidence which others ignore.

They rely on the only sure clues that exist to a man's character: "What he *does* and *has done*," [3] to quote Professor Kingsbury. They take more trouble than most of us to observe how men behave in given situations.

When we discover what holds a man's attention and what he neglects, what makes him angry or glad or sorry, what frightens him, what rouses his pride or tickles his humor, we begin to see him as he is. We find out what we really want to know: how he is probably going to feel and act under certain circumstances.

If Smith gets himself into trouble, will his fears master him? Will he try to shift the blame to us and lie out of it? Or will his sense of honor cause him to shoulder the blame and to shield others?

There can be no certainty of what Smith will do. But we find a *clue*, at least in what he has felt and done in the past under similar conditions.

Like all of us, Smith has formed habits of feeling and acting which largely control him. These habits of his we call traits of character. And they are revealing themselves constantly: in all his actions, in his posture, in the *changing* expression of his face, in the things he says, in his tone of voice.

Even when people take no apparent action, they usually betray their real feelings in some way.

One banker, well known to the authors, almost always yawns or pretends to yawn when he is annoyed or angered. Another executive almost invariably laughs or smiles under these conditions. Still another man usually puts his hands in his pockets when upset.

A business man who lost hand after hand in a poker game was recently described by Wallace B. Donham, head of the Harvard business school.

"I was playing poker with five bankers the other night,"

this man told Donham. "One of them raised me every time he had a better hand than I and never even called me when I had him beaten. After the game I asked him how he did it. 'Oh,' he said, 'I noticed that every time you had a good hand your Adam's apple moved up and down.'" [4]

Because many men play a part and conceal their real nature and emotions, the most reliable clues are often those that are secured without their knowledge.

Lyman Gage Picks a Vice President

A cashier from Minneapolis drops in to see Lyman J. Gage, new president of the First National Bank of Chicago.

The call takes an unexpected turn.

James B. Forgan, the cashier, has come merely to pay his respects. Gage is the big city banker who handles the principal Chicago account of Forgan's own bank.

But this important and busy man, it soon appears, is disposed to chat, to prolong the meeting.

"In conversation with me," Forgan writes later, "Mr. Gage entered into most minute inquiry as to my career from boyhood up to that time and especially as to my banking experience. This struck me as rather odd." [5]

Forgan is puzzled. Still mystified, he returns to Minneapolis.

Then shortly after, Gage shows his hand. He offers to make Forgan a vice president of the First National. Forgan accepts.

Six years later when Gage himself enters McKinley's cabinet, the cashier from Minneapolis succeeds him as president of this bank; becomes one of the leading bankers of the country.

Gage has picked an unusual lieutenant. And it is no accident. He created a chance to study Forgan *when Forgan did not realize he was being observed.* Without revealing his purpose, Gage drew him into conversation, asked questions, listened and watched.

It is what a man does and says when he is off his guard that furnishes the most reliable clues to his character. Successful men frequently use Gage's strategy.

George Westinghouse, for instance, invited a man whom he was considering for high office to visit at his home, found there was "no business in him."

Albert Brunker, the engineer who made himself a millionaire leader of industry, believes that one of the best ways to size up a man is to play tennis or golf with him.

Frank Davis, western production manager of the Penn Mutual Life Insurance Company, who owes his rise to early success in selecting and training salesmen, was forever hiring clerks whom he noticed in stores, and chance acquaintances picked up in hotels and on trains. He studied these men when they were off their guard. He drew them out and uncovered clues to their real character.

Thomas Scott, later president of the Pennsylvania Railroad, selected as his clerk and assistant a tow-headed young telegraph operator whom he had long watched at work. It was Andrew Carnegie.

Charles A. Coffin, former head of the General Electric Company, observed ability in a lawyer who had been making things difficult for him and employed him as his own vice president and chief counsel. It was Owen D. Young. John Gates, the steel man, in a similar way chose a lawyer to put through a merger for him. It was Elbert Gary.

Such men take the trouble to study the other fellow when he does not know he is being watched. They set up many safeguards against error in forming their final judgments.

"I don't believe much in trusting too much to first impressions." [6] So Frederick D. Underwood summed it all up when he was president of the Erie Railroad.

Always there are many false clues in what we first notice about a man's outward appearance.

When Edwin Stanton first caught sight of General Ulysses Grant and his staff, he looked them all over one after another. On seeing General Grant he said to himself, "Well, I do not know which is General Grant, but there is one that cannot be." [7] Yet it was he.

"John D. Archbold, who ruled the destinies of the old Standard Oil trust for years was as unprepossessing," says

Isaac Marcosson, "as one of his secretaries, and apparently as self-effacing." [8]

A gaunt, awkward, small-town attorney, who had come to Cincinnati on the McCormick reaper case, was once snubbed and ignored by his illustrious fellow lawyers from the East. He was Abraham Lincoln.

All of us are constantly being deceived by such first impressions.

Among the most misleading of all false clues are the fixed features of the face: the shape of the other man's chin or nose, the space between his eyes, the placing of his ears, etc. That such features can be counted on to reveal character is an ancient and popular myth which has been completely exploded by science.

From this superstition successful men have long been free. They realize that a "weak" chin does not indicate a weak character, nor close-set eyes a mean spirit.

It is in a man's face, of course, that we look for the *changing* expressions which reveal his emotions. But few, very few, are the fixed clues to character which can be found there. Such as they are Professor Kingsbury has recently described them:

"One experimenter," he says "has proved that the ability to gaze firmly and unwaveringly into the examiner's eyes is highly indicative of a strong, forceful personality, while a vacillating gaze is equally indicative of a weak, non-aggressive disposition."

"A man who has smiled so long that his face has adopted the habit is likely to be judged a cheerful individual.

"The person who has for years been practising the habits of scowling, clenching his teeth, and thrusting out his lower jaw, until his face has 'grown that way,' is equally likely to be judged pugnacious or disagreeable. . . .

"These are really *behavior* traits, the after-effects of long-exercised facial muscle habits, which are, in turn, the direct expression of character and disposition. It is they who lead us to remark of a man, often with great accuracy, 'His meanness just naturally shows in his face,' or 'You can tell by looking at him that he is honest and kind.'" [9]

These clues are things that men *do*, or traces of the things they *have done*.

They are among the very few points in a man's face which can help us at all in forming a correct first impression.

It is chiefly the smart aleck young salesman or hotel clerk with the knowing eye, who prides himself on his swift judgments of people. But the true leader is cautious.

William Wallace Atterbury, president of the Pennsylvania Railroad, even in dealing with his own subordinates, invariably checks his estimate of them. "Personally," he says, "I would not think of elevating a man to a responsible post on this railroad without first consulting my associates . . . They might know more of my candidate than I did." [10]

Men like Atterbury are chiefly interested not in *swift* judgments of strangers but rather in *accurate* judgments of those whom they have an opportunity to observe.

We find the great leader whenever possible either developing executive timber from among his own employees or else hiring men whom he has had a chance to watch in action.

Andrew Carnegie's partners, for example, nearly all began with him as workmen. "He took 43 young men, all poor," says Casson, "and made them millionaires." [11]

It is the boast of the heads of many of our greatest companies that they have never gone outside their own organization to fill an executive position.

What the able man wants in order to judge people is definite bits of evidence which can be *counted on* to give a *true* picture of their character and their capacity.

Harriman Sizes Up His General Manager

Edward H. Harriman, master builder of railroads, is sizing up a subordinate. President now of the Southern Pacific, he is forming his estimate of Julius Kruttschnitt, the general manager whom he has inherited.

Week after week telegrams come pouring in on Kruttschnitt, "Sheaves of telegrams," says Kruttschnitt, "many of them on the most trivial matters."

Just how competent is Kruttschnitt? How well does he know the great system under his charge? How patient is he, how good-natured? How sound is his judgment? Harriman will read the answers to these questions in the replies to his telegrams.

"The friends with whom I talked," writes Kruttschnitt, "predicted that for some time Mr. Harriman would adopt his own peculiar method — that he would test my temperament, familiarity with details, and ability — and he would test it to the breaking point!" "I was told that he either trusted a man completely or not at all; . . . Unless he could trust a man implicitly he would soon replace him with one he *could* trust. . . .

"After less than a year's experience with Mr. Harriman, I had the satisfaction of being told by him on more than one occasion not to waste my time offering explanations . . . not asked for, also not to refer many matters to him. He told me to settle things according to my own judgment." [12]

Julius Kruttschnitt has been approved. He will succeed Harriman as head of the Southern Pacific.

So, by devising tests, Harriman studied his subordinates.

A number of tests, some of them exceedingly interesting, which are used in the Pennsylvania Railroad organization have been described by President William Wallace Atterbury. He tells how one of his locomotive engineers, who seemed to have possibilities, was tried out for promotion. He was asked to solve a problem for which "the division staff already had a solution." He did well, was further tested and was then raised to an executive position.

"We are constantly testing men," says Atterbury. "A foreman takes a 'vacation' in order that his assistant may be in charge during his absence. A superintendent has subordinates solve problems that he himself has already solved. Promising men are made 'acting' this or that to see how they act under responsibility. Often they go back to their old jobs to remain there for months before promotion comes; often they go back to them permanently, tested but found wanting. But the process goes on." [13]

One unusual test was regularly used by E. W. Scripps, the

great publisher. And in the case of Roy Howard, at least, it yielded most valuable clues.

Dapper little Howard, slated for an executive job on one of Scripps' newspapers, had been sent out to see the old man at his California ranch.

What Scripps discovered about him at that first meeting in 1907 launched Howard on the career which has made him active head and part owner of the Scripps-Howard newspaper chain of today.

"The giant boss in high boots," says Bruce Barton, "looked down at this immaculate live-wire about whom he heard so many stories, . . . In a minute they were in the midst of the first of more than several hundred battles; the big man trying to terrify the little one, or make him lose his temper, or trap him into some fool remark; and Howard side-stepping, shifting his guard, and giving him back as good as he got.

"Scripps loved a verbal battle. He took great pleasure in advancing an argument which he himself knew as fallacious, in order to test the intelligence and independence of his subordinates." [14]

"'He was a great character,'" Howard himself recently told Earl Reeves, "'and I was very fond of him; and I think he liked me. But he had no use for any man he could walk on. If I did not agree with him I told him so, and we fought the question out, hammer and tongs, until we understood one another. That was his way of testing a man.'" [15]

This particular test devised by Scripps is a bit crude. But tests of this general nature are frequently used.

Alfred H. Smith, late president of the New York Central Lines, for instance, often asked a man if he were satisfied with a result which he himself knew to be unsatisfactory. "'If he says he is satisfied,'" said Smith, "'then I know he is not of the right calibre. If he says, "I have been doing the best I could, but wish I could have done better," then the thing to do is to get behind him and give him all the help possible.'" [16]

Tests which may be applied in the course of an ordinary interview have been described by J. C. Penney, founder and builder of the famous chain of Penney stores, in an article which he wrote after talking to "at least five thousand applicants for jobs," in a single year.

"One time when it pays to watch a man," he writes, "is when you ask for his references. If you do it suddenly and catch him off his guard, a man who has nothing to conceal answers without hesitation that he has worked for So-and-So. When men hesitate and look embarrassed it is time to begin wondering why they do not speak up at once. We often find that such men have been discharged for reasons which they know would influence us unfavorably."

"One of the first tests to which I put an applicant is to make our offer just as unattractive as possible. I tell him baldly that he will have long, hard hours of work. I describe the dull little towns in which he may have to live. I emphasize the small salary on which he must start. I make everything *except* the ultimate goal of a partnership, as little tempting as possible. If the man is the kind that thinks through to the end, sees what he wants to gain, and is willing to pay the price for it, I'll find it out then and there. Men often smile when I have painted the dreary prospect in drab colors and say, 'You can't frighten me. I want that job!' And if they are that kind, then we want them."

"Sometimes they hem and haw and say, 'Well, of course, I have my wife to consider. I don't know how she'd feel about living in a little town.'"

"If they flinch at the picture I draw, they are not for us." [17]

Able men are constantly on the lookout for such clues to character. Tests are one way of getting them. But many men not only neglect to use such tests; even more, they do not usually bother even to examine the clues which are constantly coming to their notice.

Anyone can easily increase his power to influence others by simply taking a little added care in observing them.

Colonel House Captures an Emperor

A slender little American stands talking to an emperor on the terrace of his palace.

Ten feet away, an ambassador and a distinguished statesman

JULIUS ROSENWALD, head of Sears, Roebuck, once a wholesale dry goods clerk, now the richest man in Chicago and a noted philanthropist. ∞ ∞ He stands on both sides of the counter at the same time (p. 90).

CHARLES H. SABIN, chairman of the board of the Guaranty Trust of New York, uses the overlapping grip. ∞ His office door is always open (p. 100)

FERDINAND FOCH, late Marshal of France, Allied Commander-in-chief during the World War, leaves the White House after a call on President Harding. ∞ How he taught himself to understand his men (p. 85)

EDGAR S. BLOOM, president of Western Electric Company. ∽ How he handled complaints as a youthful "trouble chaser" (p. 97)

U. & U.

Keystone

Acme

CHARLES FROHMAN, late "Czar" of the theatre, who started work as a clerk in his father's New York cigar store. ∽ He sidesteps an objection (p. 105)

JOHN HAYS HAMMOND, of Washington, known as the world's greatest mining engineer. ∽ He lands his first job by a bit of strategy (p. 100) are waiting impatiently. Will this interview never end? What has come over the Emperor?

A prince appears on the terrace, approaches the two men who are so earnestly engaged with each other. The Empress has sent him to break up the interview. But he sees the absorbed, animated look on the face of his royal father. He withdraws.

The Empress herself comes out on the terrace, hesitates, then departs. The Grand Chamberlain, despatched by the Empress, interrupts and is curtly dismissed by his master.

William II, German emperor, is fascinated. He wants to talk to Colonel House. Everything else can go hang.

Soon all Berlin will be agog, wondering what these two men have said to each other — and why.

It is House who finally closes the conversation. He stops talking, is "very quiet." Then the Emperor and this amazing American say good-bye. Colonel House is rushed to his special train.

The exact message which House gave William of Germany on that June day at Potsdam, has not been disclosed. But this does not matter. We know that House was in Europe on his "Great Adventure," trying to avert that terrible war which exploded on a heedless world two months later.

What matters to us just now is not the message itself, but *how* this message was delivered.

By what strategy did Colonel House hold the Emperor spellbound? The answer to this question is known in full detail.

Before that memorable meeting, House *studied his man.*

Months ahead of time, when House was still in the United States only hoping for a chance to meet the Emperor, "he read everything worth while about the German ruler," says Arthur D. Howden Smith, "and he talked with every person in this country who knew the Kaiser at all well . . . Before he left New York he was familiar with Wilhelm II's personality, his tastes, fads, habits, hobbies, pet policies and beliefs, his personal aversions and preferences, the public men and rulers of other countries he liked or disliked." [18]

House was able to gear his every word, his every action to the

man he wanted to win. He understood *all* the points of difference which set him apart from others:

The traits of his character, his capacities —

The things he wanted: his problems and his prejudices —

His special interests, his achievements and his hobbies.

It is no wonder that the German was swept off his feet. He
yielded to Colonel House's strategy, to his "personality," as
hundreds of other men had yielded before him — in the same
way and for the same reason.

It was by this same strategy that Theodore Gary engineered
the notable deal which started him on the road to riches and
fame.

A Small-Town Dealer Earns a Profit of $340,000 for One Customer

In the little town of Macon, Missouri, six-foot Theodore
Gary, with his fiery red mustache, is asked to sell some mining
property.

One day he will be the head of companies doing a yearly
business in nine figures and supplying eighty per cent of the
world's automatic telephone equipment.

But just now young Gary is a small-town dealer in real
estate and bonds.

In the chance to sell this mining property he sees one of the
big opportunities of his life.

It takes Gary two years to dispose of the mines. But he sells
them for $400,000, just $340,000 more than they cost originally. And at the same time he forms the friendships and
contacts which make possible his career.

This youth from the sticks meets the most powerful business
leaders of his state and of the country. He interviews such
railroad giants as Harriman, Hill, and Huntington.

Some of these men will later become his associates in business. Soon he will be able to deal with thirty banks, many of
them as a result of meeting the officials while working on this
mine deal.

How does Gary accomplish these wonders?

"From various sources," says Dutton, "he gathered data concerning each of these men as an individual. He wanted to know their habits, views, idiosyncracies, hobbies, and even the names of some of the books they read. He bought these books and digested them. He took the expressed opinions of the men on important matters of the day, against them formed his own opinions, which were not always in agreement. In short, when he met these men who were able to buy the mines, he wanted to meet them on their own ground, prepared to talk their language and to deal in their terms." [19]

This youthful country dealer won over one important stranger after another by following the method of Colonel House. *He posted himself in advance on all outstanding points about each separate man.*

Sometimes before an important interview with a stranger, it will pay us to make a thorough study of him ahead of time, just as it paid House and Gary.

But even without such advance study, it is possible to gather many clues even at a first meeting. All that is needed is close observation of details.

Louis J. Fohr, head of a large and rapidly growing insurance agency in Chicago, collects and interprets such clues according to a regular program.

"When Mr. Fohr enters a man's office," one of his star salesmen, Durand Allen, recently told the authors, "he makes a practice of systematically noticing certain points in the office and about the man himself: the pictures on the wall or the desk to get a line on the man's family, his interests and hobbies; the state of the top of his desk to get a line on his importance in his company and his methods of work; all small objects in the office to form an estimate of his character, interests, income, habits, etc."

It is more important still and far easier to make a detailed study of the people with whom we deal day in and day out.

We find a striking example of this point in the career of Charles M. Schwab, the stake driver who has made himself a steel magnate — the leader who "in his fifty years in the Kingdom of Steel never had a strike" and who "never lost a good man." [20]

"Perhaps Mr. Schwab's methods of getting results," says Stockbridge, "are best explained by saying that he works with men as his instruments as other business men work with dollars."

He knows the "form of stimulus that will work most effectively in any particular case . . . how to appeal to individuals, to read men's characters, appraise their relative values and deal with each particular man in the way to which he will respond with greatest alacrity." [21]

To gain such knowledge of the people around us is not difficult. It is largely a matter of precaution — of *using* the facts which we already possess about them and the facts which are constantly coming to our notice, of listening and asking questions at the right time.

How well we know this! And yet — ! Let us be honest with ourselves. Do we always take the trouble to *understand* the people we wish to influence? Are we careful to treat each person *differently?*

Most of us are careless about this strategy even in contact with our customers and our boss, let alone with those who must take orders from us. Yet this precaution is the very gateway to power and riches.

In dealing with people whom you wish to control or influence, consider all the points of difference that set them apart from others: the traits of their characters, their capacity, their special problems, wants and interests. Plan to treat each person differently in the light of his own nature and viewpoint.

Be on the lookout for clues that reveal traits of character and ability. Be on the alert for tell-tale trifles. Try to understand what trait lies back of actions that are unusual, even if they seem trivial. And above all, be sure to make use of every bit of information about people which you already possess.

Remember that the only safe clues to character are things people do or have done when they are off their guard. Watch their actions and the changing expression of their faces.

To gather clues it is often wise to make special arrangements to test people in some way or to study them when they do not know they are being observed.

Discount your first impressions. They are likely to be unsound. Most people attempt, in some degree, large or small, to conceal their real nature and their feelings. Also the fixed features of the face are never a reliable clue to character. This ancient theory has been completely exploded.

Before an interview with a man who is very important to you, particularly a stranger, it often pays to make a detailed study of him, by talking to people who know him and by reading whatever you can find in print written either about him or by him.

CHAPTER XVII

A SIMPLE WAY TO DEVELOP PERSONALITY*

Why Dwight Morrow Was Chosen as a Morgan Partner
"We Are All Salesmen," Says Charles Schwab

NOT LONG AGO Dwight Morrow astonished the entire country by giving up a "million dollar a year job" with J. P. Morgan and Company to become ambassador to Mexico.

What lies back of the spectacular rise of this one-time law clerk?

In large measure, Dwight Morrow's success is explained by a comment which his friends have recently made about him.

"Those who know him best," Clinton Gilbert tells us, have thrown light on that one biggest event in his life when he first emerged as a national business figure, as partner in the mighty banking house of Morgan. [1]

J. P. Morgan, we are informed, selected Morrow for this high post not so much because of his "reputation in the world of finance" but rather because of his "personality."

Personality! A magic word!

When Frank A. Vanderlip was president of the National City Bank of New York, he pointed out the one quality for which he looked first in hiring a $25,000 a year man: It was "personality."

---

* So many false claims about the development of personality are made by charlatans and pseudo-psychologists who advertise alluringly, that a word of warning against them is pertinent. On personality and vocational problems it is best to seek reliable and competent counsel. *The Psychological Corporation*, Grand Central Terminal Building, New York City, is an organization of psychologists of recognized scientific standing to which inquiries may be safely addressed. It has authorized representatives in many cities who are prepared to render consultation service.

Walter S. Gifford, the one-time pay-roll clerk, who has made himself president of the American Telephone and Telegraph Company, recently told the authors that he considered "personality" to be one of the few really important factors in success. "No one can say exactly what it is," he said, "and it cannot carry a man far unless he has the sound underlying qualities. But there can be no question but what personality plays a big part in all achievement."

Upon "personality" such men as Morgan, Vanderlip and Gifford have set high value. They recognize that *one of the greatest assets a man can have is the power to win the liking of others and inspire personal devotion.*

What are the facts about personality? How can it be developed?

Part of the answer we find in those words of Charles Schwab on this subject which we have already noted: "We are all salesmen, every day of our lives. We are selling our ideas, our plans, our energies, our enthusiasm to those with whom we come in contact." [2]

Personality, after all, is only the sum total of the effect we have on other people. If we succeed in selling ourselves, if other people like us and our plans, we may be said to have a good personality.

"Some people," a well known salesmanager once remarked, "are born with compelling personalities which they exert naturally and without effort. But others of us have to try consciously to gain the attention and liking of people. . . . We conceive a method of doing it; we study that method and practice it . . . And that method of developing good opinion is what we call personality." [3]

It is by using sound methods to win the other fellow's liking and co-operation, such methods as we have discussed in this book, that able men develop personality. And we can do the same.

But this is not all.

What is it about certain people whom we meet occasionally that attracts us and pleases us almost at the first glance? That makes us at once feel kindly toward them? What does Charles

Schwab mean when he speaks of "that indefinable charm that gives to men what perfume gives to flowers?"

Something very simple indeed, something which we can all cultivate in ourselves, lies back of the "indefinable charm" which these people possess.

It may be the light in their eyes that we notice, or their smile; the whole expression of their face perhaps, or their bearing. But actually these things, taken together, convey a single message: *They like their fellow human beings and are genuinely interested in them.* Without our realizing it, our *ego* is raised just by being near them.

What really charms and delights us in these people is a sort of inner warmth which they radiate. Theodore Roosevelt with "his genius in personal contacts" offers, as we have observed (p. 11), a striking example of it.

Here is an important key to personality and to charm: to *feel* a genuine interest in others.

Some men and women clearly lack this interest in people. And usually the reason is obvious: they have not been very successful in their contacts. They are indifferent about people just as a poor bridge-player is lukewarm about bridge, or a dub golfer about golf. These men and women need, most of all, to learn the game.

It is our failures in dealing with people that rob us of poise, that lessen our interest in them, that dwarf and warp that "indefinable charm." It is our successes that nourish it.

Few of us can *force* ourselves to feel a deeper interest in people. But all of us can *build up* this interest. The method is simple: to take a little added care in dealing with them and to employ sound methods.

As we acquire the habit of success in contact with others, our interest in them will grow naturally — and with it our poise and self-confidence. It will become easy to keep our minds on the other fellow instead of on ourselves.

And with this increasing sympathy for people, will come also a quicker insight into their real wants and emotions. As Henry Ford has observed, "The best way to understand human nature is to be friendly toward people." [4]

The methods of influencing others as explained in this book will do more than just help us meet our everyday problems as they arise. They will strengthen that sincere interest in others which we already feel. They will intensify that inner warmth from which personal charm arises and which alone can make our strategy effective.

With all people whom you wish to influence, whose loyalty and co-operation you desire, make it a point to deserve and gain their personal esteem.

To develop "personality," poise and self-confidence, use the strategy by which leaders have influenced others — particularly those methods by which they have won their affection.

Personal charm arises chiefly from a feeling of deep and sincere interest in other people and a genuine liking for them. By acquiring the habit of success in dealing with people, you strengthen your interest in them and with it your power to charm them.

CHAPTER XVIII

MAKING MEN GLAD TO WORK

*Leonard Wood Teaches His Privates a Joke
on the General*

Why Steinmetz Was Called the "Supreme Court"

A Man in Dress Clothes Emerges from a Manhole

A PRIVATE FAILS to salute his commanding General. Walking along with a girl, he pretends not to see him, stoops down to tie his shoe lace as General Wood's car approaches.

He is one of twenty odd thousand drafted men in training at Camp Funston in the fall of 1917. To build soldiers out of these raw recruits is the task of General Wood.

Does he sternly reproach this slack and ignorant rookie who will not salute? Not Leonard Wood. He uses strategy. The story of it is widely known.

"The General stopped the car," said Hagedorn, "and called the soldier to him.

"'You saw me, didn't you?'

"The man shuffled about uneasily.

"'Yes, sir,' he said.

"'But in order to avoid saluting me,' the General went on, 'you pretended to tie your shoe-string. That was it, wasn't it?'

"Reluctantly the man admitted that that was it.

"'Now I'll tell you what I would have done if I'd been in your place,' the General remarked. 'I'd have said to my girl. "Now watch me make the old man take my salute!" Get the point?'

"The soldier saluted. 'Yes, sir,' he said, grinning.

"The General answered the salute with marked precision, and drove on." [1]

To make these untrained boys proud to be soldiers Leonard Wood uses a device which many of us would scorn. He teaches them a joke on himself. They can force the "old man" to salute, he points out, by saluting themselves.

Like all successful leaders, Wood won the devotion and co-operation of his men by making them feel that they and their jobs were important.

"'Why are the men so fond of Wood?' one of the staff officers was asked.

"'I'll tell you why,' was the answer. 'Because Bill Smith in the rear rank thinks that as far as the General is concerned he is the whole Division.'" [2]

All of us, whether executives or not, deal with people who must take orders from us. Most of us have noticed what new interest they show when we give them a sense of pride in what they are doing.

Frederick Taylor, founder of efficiency engineering, led his subordinates to believe "that what they did was the important thing or the whole thing." [3]

"The average man," Samuel Vauclain points out, "can be led readily if you have his respect and if you show him that you respect him for some kind of ability." [4]

Of Edgar Selden Bloom, president of the Western Electric Company, an employee has said that he makes men feel that he expects much of them, but also that what they *can* do is important.

Charles Woodward, noted management expert and strike preventer, once told of an executive who was utterly unable to correct a serious trouble until, by a simple yet ingenious device, he gave each of the employees concerned a sense of personal importance in solving the problem.

He was a paper-mill manager, "worried by the excessive moisture in his product."

"He tried in every way," said Woodward, "to discover the cause and apply a remedy, but failed.

"So he sent a daily statement to each employee giving the percentage of moisture in the paper he had turned out on the preceding day. There was an immediate improvement. . . .

"The big idea in this instance is that the boss informed his employees about something that may not have been their business, for they were under orders, but he decided to try it, with the result indicated." [5]

A special plan to give younger employees pride in their work was frequently used by Stanley Resor, president of the J. Walter Thompson Company. He made a point of introducing them to important persons. One of the authors recalls vividly the glow of enthusiasm that came when, as a cub copy-writer, he was presented by Mr. Resor to well known men who had dealings with the firm. Horatio Nelson, England's greatest naval commander, followed this same plan with his young midshipmen.

Even office boys in the employ of Daniel Guggenheim, the copper magnate, are given a sense of dignity and importance: "'Boys,'" says Guggenheim, "'must be treated with just as much consideration as anyone else in the whole organization. If a boy comes with a message from others, or on any other duty, he must not be kept waiting, for his time is just as valuable to him as mine is to me.'" [6]

Why Steinmetz Was Called the "Supreme Court"

Steinmetz, "wizard" of the General Electric Company, had failed hopelessly as an executive.

For several years his whole department had been going "brilliantly from bad to worse." It was a mess.

What could be done? Steinmetz was invaluable. And Steinmetz was highly sensitive.

The officers of the General Electric Company used strategy. Steinmetz was given two titles, one official and one unofficial. At the same time he was gently separated from his department.

The "Supreme Court" was what his subordinates called him.

"'That's what Steinmetz ought to be,'" said one high official to another, "'a scientific Supreme Court.'" [7]

Informally, they recognized this title. Formally they gave him the title of consulting engineer of the General Electric Company — the "Supreme Court" in actual fact — but merely a new name for work which he was already doing.

Happily Steinmetz continued to evolve electrical marvels. And without him the calculating department began to function once more. So the officers of the company easily solved their problem — by giving titles.

Titles are a dazzling form of public praise. Few men there are who can resist them. Few *egos* but what are uplifted by them. They stimulate men to renewed efforts. They rouse loyalty and enthusiasm.

Samuel Gompers, founder of thirty different trade unions, builder of the American Federation of Labor and its president for nearly forty years, found his work difficult at the start. Labor was largely disorganized. He had no money. He received little co-operation.

One day he devised a scheme. He created "official commissions" to be bestowed as an honor upon labor men who were willing to act as organizers. Some eighty of such "commissioners" were appointed in one year. Membership in the A. F. L. started mounting.

Few leaders have understood the value of titles more clearly than Napoleon. Few have known better than he how deeply men long for such tinsel. To weld supporters to his new imperial throne, Napoleon scattered titles and honors with a lavish hand. He created the Legion of Honor and at once distributed crosses to over 1500 officers and men; revived the rank of Marshal of France and conferred this dignity on eighteen generals; dubbed his main body of troops the "Grand Army."

Even if they are empty, titles often do their work. When Emory Storrs, Chicago lawyer, demanded a cabinet position, President Arthur was up against a tough problem. This man was a political power who could not be offended; but also he was an "eccentric genius" utterly unsafe in any important post. Arthur appointed him a "roving diplomat" with lots of glory but nothing much to do. Off to Europe pranced Storrs, perfectly happy. He had a title.

An ex-bundle boy from America, Harry Gordon Selfridge, founded what is today one of England's largest stores. He inspired his English salespeople with loyalty by always calling them "members of the staff" instead of "shop assistants" in the English manner. "This," he says, "increased their interest in their work enormously." [8]

In that remarkable department store in Newark, N. J. created largely by Louis Bamberger, the word "employee" is never used. Every subordinate is known as a "co-worker."

Many industrial executives establish titles and honors for their most successful workers. In this spirit Charles Schwab created "the diamond cross of Bethlehem"; bestowed it on worthy assistants as Emperor William once bestowed the Iron Cross of Germany. Over one hundred men in the Bethlehem Steel Corporation are members of this "Pin Society" of Schwab's. The "diamond cross" is recognized as a token of distinguished service which is to be sought after and worn with pride.

A Man in Dress Clothes Emerges from a Manhole

An executive of the New York Telephone Company once stopped "in amazement at the corner of Forty-second Street and Broadway." [9]

He saw a man in dress clothes emerging from a manhole in the middle of the street.

It was Burch Foraker, head of the Bell telephone system in New York City.

On his way home from the theater this cold January night, Foraker had descended into the manhole on the business of his firm.

Was there a crisis? Was he worried over some grave difficulty? Nothing of the sort.

He had merely remembered that "a couple of his cable splicers" were working down in the manhole on a hurry-up job. He had just "dropped in on 'em to have a little chat."

Today Foraker is known as the "man of ten thousand friends." He is one of the foremost telephone executives of the country, president of the Michigan Bell Telephone Company.

This story of the dress clothes and the manhole is typical of many that are told of Burch Foraker. This dropping in at odd hours was a hobby of his.

He was forever visiting his men at their work in the spirit of comradeship. It was his way of showing that he considered *their jobs important.*

Nearly all great executives use this strategy in some form or other. Without lowering their dignity or permitting undue familiarity, they display a genuine interest in their subordinates.

John Wanamaker, for instance, year after year made daily tours of his great store. "He would stop and chat with stock boy, department manager, saleswoman. He would ask for members of the family, inquire about recent home happenings, give a word of advice on personal or business matters." [10]

The one most dangerous policy with subordinates is to ignore them. Workers and executives who are neglected, come to feel that what they are doing is unimportant. Unknown to them, their pride suffers and with it their interest. *All of us do better work when we are being watched or feel that we are being watched.*

The boss who can visit his subordinates at work in such a way as to make this a *pleasant event* for them, is using highly effective strategy.

It is important to remember that a visit which would please a day laborer might to a highly paid department head in some cases seem like spying or butting in. *The viewpoint of the man or woman concerned is the essential thing. The visit must please them in order to produce results.*

One of the authors remembers very well the visits of his boss when he was a junior executive in an advertising agency.

James W. Young, the boss, was and is one of the outstanding leaders in the world of advertising: a man who has been able to retire from active work in his early forties, honorary vice president now, of the J. Walter Thompson Company.

And like Burch Foraker, Mr. Young had a habit of dropping in on his subordinates in a spirit of friendliness. He would come strolling into an office with a cheery look in his eye, chat a bit, ask a few questions, perhaps make a useful suggestion. With many members of the organization, his visits left a sense of freshened vigor, of renewed enthusiasm.

Few things rouse the pride of subordinates so keenly as a sense of comradeship with their employer.

Of Herbert Hoover, William Hard says: "The men who have been his aides in his multitudinous enterprises have not remained merely his 'staff.' They have become . . . his 'gang.'" [11]

To rouse enthusiasm and loyalty in subordinates, and to win their liking, give them a sense of pride in their work. Show them that you personally respect their ability and consider them and their jobs important.

Display genuine interest in them and what they are doing. Try to build up a friendly comradeship with them. Visit them at their work in this spirit. Remember that this can be done without encouraging undue familiarity.

Titles and badges of honor are often a valuable means of stimulating and sustaining the pride of subordinates.

CHAPTER XIX

TUNING IN ON PEOPLE

*How Owen D. Young Explains His Own Rise to
High Office*

Marshall Field Promotes a Bundle Wrapper

NOT LONG AFTER becoming active head of the General
Electric Company, Owen D. Young was asked by
B. C. Forbes to "uncover some of the definite factors"
that led to his selection for this high place.

Young told Forbes that he would find an answer in the remarks that two other officers of the General Electric Company
had recently made. Forbes discovered that Gerard Swope,
the new president, had said this to Young:

"The thing that impresses me most . . . is your capacity to
make the other fellow's problems your own. When you sit
down and advise me about a thing I have got to act on, I somehow feel that you are taking as deep an interest in it as I am."
And Albert G. Davis, one of the vice presidents, had made this
comment to Young: "This promotion has come to you because,
among other things, you have a positively uncanny interest in
the individual man. Thus every man in the company feels
that you and he know each other through and through."[1]

In the statements of these two men, Owen Young, one-time
farm boy, one-time lawyer, finds an explanation of his own
amazing rise. Yet what a simple point it is that they mention:
his "capacity to make the other fellow's problems" his own!

Young merely takes the trouble to show people that he
understands their point of view.

It is something we all can easily do. But how often we neglect to do it! How frequently we understand people, sympathize with them, yet fail to let them know about it!

Able men are careful to *make known* their sympathy, in dealing with those whose co-operation they desire. It is one of the surest means of winning good will and loyalty. "I like to get the other man's point of view so well," says Young, "that I can restate it even better than he can."

An interesting story about Victor Lawson, late owner and publisher of the *Chicago Daily News*, was recently told the authors by his successor, Walter Strong.

To appreciate it, we must remember that it happened back in the days when hard drinking was a common vice among newspaper men and that Lawson himself was an absolute teetotaler, a stern enemy of liquor in all its forms.

One of Lawson's lieutenants, an important executive, had been ill, away from work for six months.

On his return, he found that nasty stories about himself had been whispered through the office: He was a drunkard, it was said, and drunkenness had caused his sickness.

These rumors, he believed, had started with a particular man who wanted his job.

It was a gloomy welcome for this executive, fresh from his sick bed. For this much was true: He did drink. And he knew Lawson's opinions.

Finally he invited Lawson to take lunch with him.

"He tried to repeat the rumors to Lawson," said Strong, "and explained that while he drank, he was fortunately never overcome by liquor. He continued to talk and because Lawson said nothing he eventually became embarrassed.

"Lawson finally noticed this and said, 'Is that all?' He turned to the waiter and said, 'Bring me a bottle of Mumm's Champagne and two glasses.'

"When the glasses were filled, he raised his and said, 'Your health, John.'"

Merely to show a subordinate that he fully *understood* his worries, this man of iron character violated his own strongest convictions.

Al Smith, the democratic leader, has a special means of showing people that he understands their viewpoint. It is described by Ida Tarbell, who has studied him closely.

When Smith has listened to a request or a suggestion, he himself *restates* it before giving his decision. Whether this decision is "Yes" or "No" he wishes to make known beyond all doubt that he sympathizes. To demonstrate that he has fully grasped the other person's desire, he takes the trouble to put it into his own words.

A remarkable clerk once waited on one of the authors. He appeared to be simply a middle-aged man with a rather square face engaged in selling theater tickets at one of McBride's offices in New York.

It was back in the days when orchestra seats at $9.00 and $10.00 apiece were a novelty, when the $2.50 ticket was still a fresh and fond memory.

The author, paying a stiff price for seats, made an experiment. He commented regretfully to this clerk on the golden age of cheap tickets, on the misfortune of rising prices.

Imagine his surprise when the clerk behind the counter entered into the idea, expressed his own regret!

An astonishing clerk! For it was largely because of these same high prices that McBride's ticket agency was prospering.

"Who is that man who waited on me — the one with the iron gray hair?" the author asked another salesman on his way out.

"That? Why that's Mr. McBride!"

And so the mystery was solved. This was the executive who was making McBride's a national institution, building a business whose yearly volume was soon to run into millions of dollars. This was a real salesman and a real leader of men. Therefore, quite naturally, he took the trouble to show others that he understood their viewpoint. Therefore, he expressed sympathy with his customers, even when he could not agree with them.

Marshall Field Promotes a Bundle Wrapper

Marshall Field, merchant prince of Chicago, is waylaid by a very minor employee; by a boy who wraps bundles in the wholesale department.

This lad wants a chance to do more important work. Three times he has made this request of his immediate boss; three times he has been refused.

Now he puts it up to Field himself. Field investigates.

"Why don't you advance him?" Field asks the boy's boss, manager of the cotton goods department.

"I don't want to change him," replies the manager. "The other bundle wrapper I had was no good. I had trouble with him. Selfridge is a good bundle wrapper, and I want him to stay on the job." [2]

Field points out that this is all wrong. He sees to it that the boy, Selfridge, is given an opportunity.

And here we observe a far-reaching principle of leadership.

It is interesting, of course, that this boy, Harry Gordon Selfridge, became a partner in the firm before he was thirty, and that he later founded the world-famous London department store, Selfridge and Company, Ltd. But this is not the point.

It is in Marshall Field himself and in the department head that we find our point.

The man who three times said "No" to Selfridge is today, after more than thirty years, still working at his same minor job.

But Marshall Field has left behind him one of America's great business organizations.

Field promoted Selfridge partly, of course, because he wanted to develop likely boys. But it went deeper than this: It was *Field's way of showing that he placed the welfare of his employees above the immediate needs of his business.*

The "small" man often holds back his subordinates merely because it is convenient to do so. But the big man helps them to get ahead just as rapidly as their real ability permits. This is one of the ways in which he displays his sympathy for their viewpoint, one of the ways in which he inspires them to give their best to his enterprise.

The "small" man, moreover, is likely to keep his subordinates down because he fears to lose them. But the big man, as we have seen, develops able assistants very largely by sharing the limelight with them. These men he wants to keep with him. It is they who make possible his success. But he does not, like Selfridge's boss in the cotton goods department, try to block their progress merely because they are useful to him.

"When a man can better himself by leaving," says Samuel Vauclain, chairman of the board of the Baldwin Locomotive Works "we say goodbye and wish him well." [3]

Dr. Frank Billings, "dean of Chicago physicians," has told the authors how P. D. Armour, creator of Armour and Company, followed this plan. Armour "discovered" and trained many executives who in the end left him with his entire good will: such men as John Cudahy, founder of the Cudahy Packing Company, and John C. Black, later an organizer and president of the Continental National Bank of Chicago.

This same strategy, at once shrewd and high-minded, is attributed by friends and former associates to Dr. Billings himself. All physicians are anxious, of course, to surround themselves with competent and loyal assistants. But many of them kill enthusiasm because they are short-sighted: They keep the youthful medico who aids them severely in the background. But not Dr. Billings. Far from it. He has not only given his assistants full credit with the patients for all their work, but even more he has urged them to set up in practice for themselves when the right time came. So he has developed many outstanding physicians. And so he has inspired with devotion all the young men who have assisted him.

One of the most pleasant and effective ways to draw people to you is to show them that you sympathize with their problems. It is not enough just to feel such sympathy. The important thing is to let them know about it.

This is particularly important with subordinates. Make it plain to them that their welfare and success are matters of personal concern to you.

CHAPTER XX

RIGHT AND WRONG METHODS OF PRAISING PEOPLE

George Haven Putnam Saves the Day with a Compliment

Roosevelt Disliked "Incense Swingers"

John D. Rockefeller Praises a Man Who Failed

GEORGE HAVEN PUTNAM once achieved surprising results with a simple form of strategy.

As head of the famous publishing house, G. P. Putnam's Sons, he had rushed to Washington to appear before a Congressional committee in support of a bill which was highly important to him and to other publishers.

And he was in a tight corner. His lawyer had failed him at the last moment. He stood alone among clever men who hoped to block the bill.

Most serious of all, Culbertson, chairman of the committee, was known to be opposed to the measure.

Yet it was through Culbertson himself that Putnam saved the day. He induced him, as a matter of fair play, to recommend that the bill should be reported to the House.

Putnam did not change the other man's views in the least. But he did something more important still:

By a very simple device, he gained Culbertson's personal esteem.

Throughout the hearing he addressed Culbertson as "your honor" and spoke of his committee as "your honorable body . . . sitting here in the capacity of a court."

Putnam treated Culbertson the politician as an impartial judge, set him up on a pedestal. He won by a compliment.

All of us know the value of a compliment of the right sort. It is an effective way of raising the other fellow's *ego*, of gaining his good will and co-operation.

The great leader is almost always a master of this strategy.

Theodore Roosevelt, for instance, had the ability, we are told by Seymour, "to find exactly the right compliment for the right person." [1]

And of Abraham Lincoln's use of compliments, Sandburg says: "Picking a man's point of pride or interest and then saying something that was true and that pleased the man in connection with the pride or interest, was an act of his every day."

"'A drop of honey,'" Lincoln himself once observed, "'catches more flies than a gallon of gall.'" [2]

All the men and women we meet, no matter how important, no matter how humble, enjoy the *right kind* of compliment. It gives them an increased sense of power, of achievement and of self-confidence. It offers an effective way to influence them.

We have all, of course, seen compliments and flattery fall flat, arouse suspicion or even disgust. But the art of complimenting rests on very simple precautions.

To compliment successfully it is only necessary to keep in mind a few of those points of difference in people which we have already discussed.

The peacock, the very vain man with a strong, underlying sense of inferiority, enjoys flattery on almost any point, as we have observed (p. 133). He likes it laid on with a trowel.

But most people truly appreciate compliments only on certain matters. The subjects, for example, on which John D. Rockefeller and Andrew Carnegie have been found open to praise are described by Fred Kelly, a well known newspaper man.

The oil king is "immensely pleased," says Kelly, when he is commended "for his little household economies." Also he "likes to hear what a power for good he is in his Church or Sunday School." [3] He became "cordial immediately" when Kelly offered him a compliment on a talk which he had made to his group of Sunday School children.

And Andrew Carnegie, the steel master, was easily led to

answer questions which he "would not ordinarily have listened to," by a reporter who flattered him on a speech he had made and told him how "helpful and inspirational" he had found it.

To have praised Carnegie or Rockefeller on their skill as business leaders would have been useless. The compliments would have struck them as insincere or foolish.

But household economies and speeches! These were subjects of a very different sort. These were their pet vanities.

Nearly all men, as we have already noted (p. 132), have such pet vanities — matters about which they are a little uncertain, yet in which they would like to shine and be approved. When they are praised on one of these points the compliment clicks.

It was this kind of compliment, of course, which George Putnam paid Culbertson when he called him "your honor" and referred to his committee as a court of justice.

"Men have various subjects in which they may excel, or at least would be thought to excel," says Lord Chesterfield, "and though they love to hear justice done to them where they know they excel, yet they are most and best flattered upon those points where they wish to excel and yet are doubtful whether they do or not."

One man who was known to be remarkably able, Sir Robert Walpole, was, Chesterfield points out, "little open to flattery upon that head, for he was in no doubt himself about it." But this man fancied himself as quite a rascal with the ladies, wished "to be thought to have a polite and happy turn" in this direction. And on this score he was wide open to flattery. "It was his favorite and frequent subject of conversation which proved . . . that it was his prevailing weakness."

And here we are given a key to the other fellow's pet vanity.

"*You will easily discover every man's prevailing vanity,*" says Chesterfield, "*by observing his favorite topic of conversation; for every man talks most of what he has most a mind to be thought to excel in. Touch him but there, and you touch him to the quick.*" [4]

Fred Kelly tells how he profited by locating the pet vanities of two very different types of men.

"Once," he says, "I wished to talk to the late Chief Justice Fuller at the close of a speech he had made before a western college. I realized that it was of no use to say anything to him about his oratory, because public speaking was to him an old story. But I did say to him:

"'Mr. Justice, I didn't suppose a man on the Supreme Court could be so human.'

"At once he gave me a smile which came right from his heart. The old chap liked to be regarded as a human being.

"A lot of men like to hear just the opposite. Many a man likes to be looked upon as a mere intellectual machine. In doing business with a man once, I insisted on having everything in writing.

"'Because,' I told him, 'you are so cold-blooded and shrewd that I want to know just exactly where we stand.'

"At that he fairly beamed all over. It was his ambition to be thought cold and shrewd in business matters." [5]

With nearly all women, even the homeliest, Lord Chesterfield tells us, personal charm is a pet vanity and on this they may always be complimented. Only the "undoubted, unconscious, uncontested beauty" is absolutely certain of her charms and she is to be flattered upon her mental powers, about which she may feel doubt.

Roosevelt Disliked "Incense Swingers"

Theodore Roosevelt's military aide, Archie Butt, has made a pointed and useful comment on the subject of compliments and flattery.

Certain people who dealt with Roosevelt apparently felt that he could do no wrong. Butt called them "incense swingers" — the type who were forever murmuring "perfectly wonderful. Isn't it marvellous? How extraordinary!"

Now Archie Butt was a great admirer of Roosevelt. Yet he made a determined effort not to become such an "incense swinger." And few people were more successful than he in gaining Teddy's affection and esteem.

Really big men do not like constant flattery and admiration. Least of all Theodore Roosevelt, who scorned the "yes man" and was forever welcoming and inviting criticism.

It is wiser to compliment too little than too much.

And with people whom we know very slightly it is best to go slowly, to wait until we find out just what sort of compliments they like. Above all we must be certain to take no liberties. All of us, as an extreme case, would be annoyed if a complete stranger were to express approval of our hair or of our finger nails.

One kind of compliment which is always safe is the one that is given *indirectly*.

Are we not all pleased to be told that so-and-so has made an agreeable remark about us *behind our backs?* Had we heard it at first hand, it might perhaps have embarrassed us or we might have doubted whether it was sincere. But coming indirectly it is highly acceptable — and it rings true.

When Bismarck, "Iron Chancellor" of Germany, wished to win over a hostile subordinate, he systematically praised him to others who would, as he knew, repeat to him what had been said.

This strategy, Lord Chesterfield observes, is "an innocent piece of art; that of flattering people behind their backs, in the presence of those who, to make their own court, much more than for your sake, will not fail to repeat, and even amplify the praise to the party concerned. This is of all flattery the most pleasing, and consequently the most effectual." [6]

There is another way of offering a compliment indirectly. Newton D. Baker, the Cleveland attorney, former secretary of war, used it recently in a Chicago courtroom. Presenting his case before a foreign-born judge, he took care to make a casual but very flattering remark about foreign-born citizens of America. A keen attorney who was present noticed this move as well as several others by which Baker very successfully gained the personal good will of the judge.

It is a simple enough plan. If John Smith is proud of his skill in telling good stories, we please him by praising this same ability in some other man. The knack of it, says Lord Chesterfield, lies in "commending those virtues in some other person" in which our man "either thinks he does, or at least would be thought by others to excel." [7]

We get a similar result when we praise a man directly in such a way that he is not called upon to acknowledge it.

Woodrow Wilson used this device during his campaign for the Democratic presidential nomination, when there was danger of a disastrous rupture between himself and Bryan. Someone had dug up and published a letter written years earlier by Wilson in which he expressed the desire to "knock Bryan once for all into a cocked hat." Wilson made no direct effort to heal the Great Commoner's feelings. But shortly after, at a banquet in Washington, at which Bryan was present, he included in his speech a high tribute to Bryan's character and the widespread admiration which he commanded. A little later, Bryan put his arm through Wilson's and told him not to worry about the letter.

Compliments and praise are among the stoutest tools which the leader employs in managing men and in binding them to him.

Most sure of all to be effective, perhaps, is the praise we give to those people whose success or failure depends largely upon our verdict and who are uncertain of themselves until we speak. Few women, for instance, ever grow weary of hearing their husbands praise their skill as housekeepers. Few men but what prize the approval of their superiors in business. Everyone longs for appreciation. We find most great leaders liberal in giving praise to subordinates.

Why John D. Rockefeller Praised a Man Who Failed

Edward T. Bedford, partner of John D. Rockefeller, has scored a failure. He is one of the "Old Guard" who has helped Rockefeller build the Standard Oil Company. But this time he has over-reached himself.

Then something happens that surprises him.

"I was leaving 26 Broadway one afternoon," says Bedford, "when I noticed Mr. Rockefeller and Mr. Pratt some distance behind me. I just continued on, as I was in no mood to discuss my profitless enterprise. But they called to me. Mr. Rockefeller gave me a hearty slap on the back and said:

"'Fine, Bedford! We have just heard about your South American affair.'

"I thought they might be twitting me or that they might be misinformed.

"'But that was a great loss. We just managed to save 60 per cent of the investment.'

"'Yes, and that was splendid. It was the way you handled it which saved that much for us. We do not always do so well upstairs.'" [8]

So with a chance to criticize, John D. went out of his way to find something to praise.

Praise of a subordinate is a powerful means of gaining and holding his good will. But it is far more. One of the greatest stimulants to renewed effort is a sense of achievement. And this feeling can be most easily developed in subordinates by giving them praise and credit.

Of Andrew Carnegie, Charles Schwab has said, "Mr. Carnegie was always one to take you by the hand and encourage and approve. . . . In my wide association in life, meeting with many and great men in various parts of the world, I have yet to find the man, however great or exalted his station, who did not do better work and put forth greater effort under a spirit of approval than he would ever do under a spirit of criticism." "I wonder if you reflect how you yourselves — how every other man responds with his best efforts under such conditions? . . . Now Mr. Carnegie understood this great thing early in life, and it was this fine philosophy, which he practised always, that made him a great commercial success." [9]

In the hands of Charles Schwab, Carnegie's pupil, praise of subordinates became a source of extraordinary power.

In explaining the enthusiasm among the workers when Schwab became head of the Emergency Fleet Corporation, Stockbridge says: "From managers to riveters . . . they knew that he would deal out praise and approbation, express appreciation publicly for good work in such a way as to be worth more to the man receiving it than any money reward."

When all records were smashed at the Camden yards and the *Tuckahoe* was built in twenty-seven days, Schwab gathered around him all the men who had worked on the ship. He made a speech of congratulation, presented each man with a silver medal and a letter from President Wilson. Then turning to the superintendent in charge, "Tommy" Mason, Schwab pulled his own gold watch from his pocket and handed it to him as a "little token."

"It's just this sort of personal contact, personal praise, appreciation, reward, stimulation and inspiration," said Stockbridge at the time, "that Mr. Schwab is relying on for success in his new job, just as they have brought him success in his previous jobs." [10]

To the subordinate, praise from a chief is like food to a hungry man. It is among these things in life upon which he sets the highest value of all.

Walter Strong, publisher of the *Chicago Daily News*, has told the authors that he keeps in his safety deposit vault three notes which he received from his predecessor, Victor Lawson, during twenty years of association. "All of them," he said, "were commendations for something I had done — recognition which was perhaps unnecessary."

Some executives make their praise hard to earn — and there may be sound strategy in this, particularly for a man of the reserved type.

Edward Bok said of Cyrus Curtis, famous publisher of the *Saturday Evening Post*, that he is "slow to criticize" and "likewise slow to praise."

But all great executives have discarded the old, stupid idea that results can be secured by constant criticism and by inspiring fear.

Neither are they worried by that ancient bogey man of the executive: that liberal praise of a subordinate may result chiefly in a demand for more money. "Expressed appreciation does not increase the expense account," says James H. Rand, Jr., head of Remington Rand, "but it is very apt to result in increase in profits." [11]

There are, of course, men whom it is dangerous to praise: Such men as we have already discussed (p. 136) who puff up and go to pieces. At times the executive must bring men of this sort down to earth by rough handling. Criticism plays its part in dealing with these men as well as with all men.

Another important point is this: The leader who is *disliked* usually defeats his own purpose by praising his subordinates. When someone whom we hate voices approval of what we are doing, our natural impulse is to stop doing it. But the true leader is not troubled by this hazard: His first objective, as we have seen, is to win the personal liking of his followers.

Among the six rules laid down by H. Hobart Porter, the noted public utility man, to guide his treatment of workers, we find these: "Give them full and public credit for all they do" — "Praise them in public." [12]

In America's two greatest railroad builders, in those stern men, James J. Hill and Edward H. Harriman, we find this same attitude. Hill, we are told by Pyle, was "expectant and appreciative" toward his men and one of Harriman's outstanding traits, as we have already noted, was "his unfailing recognition and appreciation of ability in any form."

By complimenting people from time to time in a way which pleases them, you gain their good will. Remember that they enjoy, most of all, praise on points about which they themselves are uncertain.

It is wiser to compliment too little than too much. Do not be an "incense swinger." Remember that only the very vain man wants constant praise.

With subordinates, praise is a powerful method of stimulating interest and loyalty. Give them credit for what they do. The one important precaution is this: Remember that some men, a minority, puff up under praise and go to pieces. Be on the lookout for them.

CHAPTER XXI

HOW TO GET CREDIT FOR
WHAT YOU DO

Coolidge Packs "His Little Black Handbag"

Why Benjamin Franklin Pushed a Wheelbarrow

Myron T. Herrick Claims Credit for Honesty

IN TWO WELL KNOWN INCIDENTS from the life of Calvin Coolidge, we find the clue to an interesting type of strategy. The first of these incidents is often used to illustrate the modesty for which Coolidge has been justly celebrated. The other illustrates a point which seems, on the surface, in sharp contrast to his modesty. Here is the first story:

In his last year at Amherst, Coolidge won a gold medal — an honor of national importance awarded by the American Historical Society. But he mentioned it to no one, not even to his own father. His employer after graduation, Judge Henry P. Field of Northampton, learned about it only when he happened to read an account of it in the *Springfield Republican* six weeks after Coolidge had received the medal.

Throughout Coolidge's career from a Vermont village to the White House, he has been noted for this same sort of sincere modesty, this unwillingness to claim the credit.

And yet there is another side of Calvin Coolidge. Here is the second story:

When he was up for re-election as Massachusetts state senator, Coolidge suddenly packed his "little black handbag" on the night before the election and was seen "striding toward the station" in Northampton. He had suddenly heard that the office of president of the Senate was vacant. Two days later he returned from Boston "and in his little black handbag he had the signed pledges of a majority of the senate to vote for him as president." [1] So Coolidge took his first big step ahead in politics, became president of the Massachusetts Senate: At the right time, with the right people, this modest man pushed himself most actively and speedily, claimed credit for all he was worth.

In these two stories, we see what appears to many as a conflict: on the one hand, genuine modesty; on the other, a talent for self-promotion. Let us observe another man who was famous for modesty: "Stonewall" Jackson, the Confederate general of the Civil War, who is now ranked with Robert E. Lee among the world's great soldiers.

The "innate modesty" of Thomas Jackson was an outstanding trait. At West Point he was "noted for his humility." On his deathbed he asserted vigorously that the term "Stonewall" belonged to his brigade and not to himself. And when, during the Mexican War, the commander-in-chief, General Scott, paid him a public and overwhelming compliment on his gallantry, Jackson never afterward mentioned it — not even to his family nor to his most intimate friends.

Yet, from the very beginning of this war, Jackson's letters to his sister were full of his plans for creating a reputation and for securing newspaper publicity — also full of his difficulty in accomplishing this purpose as a mere brevet second lieutenant. And in his pursuit of fame this brave and sincerely modest man made a clever move. He took a step which led directly to the compliment from General Scott and also to several rapid promotions: He had himself transferred from his regiment of regulars to an independent battery, believing that "the officers thereof would receive personal credit for whatever the company accomplished." [2] A few years later we find him exerting all his efforts to secure a professorship at the Virginia Military Institute largely because he considered the position "conspicuous."

In Jackson, as in Coolidge, we once more observe what seems to be a "conflict": sincere modesty *vs.* shrewd self-promotion. And this same seeming "conflict," of course, is found in the careers of all great leaders. But actually there is no conflict at all — only sound common sense.

It is about the many things that are sure to be *noticed* that these men are silent. But they go into action when they believe that their merit is almost certain to be *overlooked*.

We have no space to consider the moral aspects of building a good reputation. But it may be worth while to review a few familiar points. The foundation, of course, is what counts in the long run — soundness of character and real ability. But virtue is not its own reward in the world of practical affairs. The "violet by the mossy stone" is apt to remain unnoticed. And if we possess sound qualities and abilities and fail to make them known, we are in a way cheating not only ourselves but also others.

First and foremost, however, the genuine desire of able men is to be modest, to let their achievements speak for themselves whenever possible.

John D. Rockefeller for example, on being asked the "secret of his success," replied: "The time and chances were favorable. . . . One did not need to know much." [3]

So unassuming was the manner of Edward H. Harriman, the railway builder, even after some of his most brilliant triumphs, that an old acquaintance supposed that he was still only one of hundreds of more or less successful brokers until he happened by accident to learn the real facts from others.

All truly great men are noted for modesty of this sort.

It is only the weak man, the short-sighted man, who preens himself publicly upon such things, who is forever calling attention to what he has done or to how much he knows. He is moved only by the desire to gain a brief sense of self-importance.

The big man is above such silly vanity. Moreover, it always defeats itself. People long to strip the vain man of his glory. It is the modest man whom they delight to honor. All other considerations aside, the best way to get credit for most things is to be modest about them.

Few men, for instance, have ever effaced themselves more thoroughly than General Goethals, builder of the Panama

Canal. Public ceremonies he dodged altogether. When the first ship passed through the canal, he was observed in his shirt sleeves at the Pedro Miguel locks and he ran off when a cheer was raised for him. Yet few men have ever received more complete credit for a job well done than Goethals. We find the key to it all in this remark which he himself often made when the work was criticized: "We will answer them all later — with the canal." [4]

Goethals, like Lindbergh, our hero of today, let his achieve- ment and his merit speak for themselves. It is through their modesty that successful men build a large part of their repu- tation.

People, moreover, do not trust the man who is vain and boastful. His judgment is open to question. Because he appears to *over*rate himself and his ability, they feel that he is likely to form incorrect estimates in other matters. The same is true of the man who *under*rates himself too much, who is excessively modest and shy. False modesty is often only false pride — a form of vanity.

The able man is modest — but he understands the art of self-promotion.

Why Benjamin Franklin Pushed a Wheelbarrow

At the age of twenty-four, Benjamin Franklin struck out for himself. With borrowed money he bought out his partner and became sole owner of a printing business and of that small sheet, the *Pennsylvania Gazette.*

This genial, pleasure-loving lad, who was to become our first "self-made" man and one of the greatest Americans of all time, was now out on his own, sink or swim. Heavily burdened by debt, he had to establish his personal standing among business men.

And Franklin determined at once not only to lay firm hand on his faults — but also to make certain that others noticed what he was doing.

"In order to secure my credit and character as a tradesman," he says, "I took care not only to be in *reality* industrious and frugal, but to avoid all appearances to the contrary; I drest plainly; I was seen at no places of idle diversion. . . . and to show that I was not above my business, I sometimes brought home the paper I purchased at the stores through the streets in a wheelbarrow. . . .

"Thus being esteemed an industrious, thriving young man and paying only for what I bought, the merchants who imported stationery solicited custom; others proposed supplying me with books and I went on swimmingly." [5]

So by showmanship, Franklin deliberately called attention to his good points.

Able men know that good reputations do not grow on trees. They are built. Of Marshall Field, Elbert Gary says: "He built up a reputation of being unqualifiedly honest and exact; and it was because of this reputation that people bought from him." [6]

A device known to many was used by Herschel V. Jones, late owner and publisher of the *Minneapolis Journal*, to build the reputation that enabled him to launch himself as a newspaper proprietor. When he was still a reporter on the *Journal*, Jones opened his program by borrowing from a bank fifty dollars which he *did not need*.

"That," says Jones, "was the first of a series of borrowings which continued over a period of years, for no other purpose than to establish my credit. I never used these borrowed sums. When the notes came due I paid them off with the very same money that had been loaned to me. Gradually I increased the amounts I asked for, finally getting as much as 2000 dollars at one time.

"I didn't want the *money;* but I did want the *credit!* I wanted the people to understand that when Jones borrowed, he would pay!

"The test of my theory came when I decided to start publishing a commercial paper of my own. To put such a paper on a paying basis, I needed fifteen thousand dollars — and five thousand was all I had. I went to the cashier of a bank where I was well known through my frequent borrowings, and explained the project to him."

The cashier was disposed to lend the ten thousand dollars, but said that Jones would have to consult the directors. In the end, it was a comment made by the president of the bank that settled the question:

"'I also am in favor of letting Mr. Jones have the money,' he said. 'I don't know him very well personally, but I have noticed that for a good many years he has been a borrower from this bank and *he has always paid.*'

"For fifteen years or more," observes Jones, "I had been following my plan, hoping that some man of consequence would notice my record and, at the critical moment for me, would say just what these officials did say." [7]

Jones took care to *demonstrate* that he could be trusted.

Myron T. Herrick Claims Credit for His Honesty

A small precaution of this sort helped one young lawyer on his way to high place and fame.

We all remember Myron T. Herrick as our brilliant and beloved ambassador to France who recently died. But it was as an attorney in Cleveland that he began his career.

Now during those early days of struggle which all youthful lawyers must face, a misfortune fell upon Herrick.

He was called upon to meet a note for several thousand dollars which he had endorsed for one of his clients.

When a collector from the bank presented this note in a somewhat curt manner, Herrick showed him the door. For, as it happened, he was no longer legally liable. The time limit set by law had expired a few days before.

That Herrick, in spite of this loophole, drew on his slender resources and made good the amount is evidence of his high integrity.

But Herrick did more than this. He took no chances about getting full credit for his action. He did not rely upon the bank clerks, guilty of the error, to spread the news. In person he impressed upon the officers of the bank just what he had done and why.

The outcome was that Herrick soon secured through this

same bank a volume of business which more than offset his losses.

Herrick was a modest man. But he took care to *build* his reputation by claiming credit for qualities that might well be overlooked.

In this spirit, Al Smith, as governor of New York, kept in his office a series of illustrated reports which he was forever showing to people. In pictures and in words they presented vividly the splendid work he had done in giving his state wonderful new asylums, hospitals, and other public institutions.

In many different ways, able men make known those traits in themselves which people value. Nearly all leaders, for instance, have had the priceless reputation of always keeping their promises. Yet many a man fails in this, not because he is less honest — but largely because he is more careless. Able men adopt this simple safeguard: They are slow to bind themselves and they make as few promises as possible.

To dodge "ill-considered" promises Abraham Lincoln used to parry by asking people questions and telling them stories. Woodrow Wilson was "very reluctant to make a promise." Calvin Coolidge is reported to have a positive "dislike" for them.

It pays to be careful in such matters. The honesty of one man known to the authors has sometimes been questioned merely because he is painfully shy. In making an important statement, he often lets his eyes wander, fails to look the other man in the face. Now as we have already noted (p. 146), this habit, as a rule, actually reveals weakness of some kind. This man, and others like him, can profit by the strategy which Lord Chesterfield recommends:

"Always look people in the face when you speak to them; the not doing it is thought to imply conscious guilt." [8]

Many precautions of this sort aid the successful man in building his reputation.

To establish a good reputation and gain the respect of others, bear in mind that modesty and sound self-promotion go hand in hand.

Take especial care to be modest about those things you have done, or those qualities you possess which are already recognized, or which are bound to be noticed. Remember that the credit which others give you of their own accord is always greater than any credit which you may gain by making a claim yourself. Try to be modest and to establish a reputation for modesty.

If, however, certain of your worth-while achievements or traits are fairly certain to be overlooked altogether or not recognized in any way, follow a different plan. See to it that they come to the attention of the right people at the right time.

CHAPTER XXII

CREATING YOUR REPUTATION

*Andrew Carnegie Faces "Disgrace" and
"Criminal Punishment"*

*An "Upstart" Lieutenant Defies the
Secretary of the Navy*

Why "Joe" Cannon Claimed to Have Hayseeds in His Hair

*How "Hell and Maria" Aided Dawes to
Become Vice President*

A SMALLISH, TOW-HEADED LAD is facing a difficult decision. More depends on it than even he himself can realize. Andrew Carnegie has risen from a messenger boy to be telegraph operator and clerk to Thomas A. Scott, division superintendent of the Pennsylvania Railroad at Pittsburgh.

This morning on reaching the office he has discovered that traffic is in a serious tangle, that a wreck has tied up the line. And Scott is not on hand.

What shall Carnegie do? The safe thing is to do nothing. Only the division superintendent is allowed to issue train orders. "I knew," said Carnegie himself in later years, "that it was dismissal, disgrace, perhaps criminal punishment for me if I erred." [1]

But meantime freight trains are at a standstill. Passenger expresses are seriously delayed.

Carnegie takes the plunge. He breaks one of the strictest rules of the road. Train orders go flashing out signed with Scott's own initials.

189

When Scott himself arrives, the blockade is cleared. Everything is running smoothly. He is amazed, says nothing.

But soon Carnegie hears indirectly that Scott is delighted with his "little white-haired Scotch devil."

This event is a turning point for Carnegie. Even John Edgar Thomson, president of the Pennsylvania, hears of his "train-running exploit." Carnegie becomes Scott's private secretary. At twenty-four he himself is superintendent of the division.

"The battle of life is already half won," says Carnegie, in commenting on this incident, "by the young man who is brought personally in contact with high officials; and the aim of every boy should be to do something beyond the sphere of his duties — something which attracts the attention of those over him." [2]

A young railway mail clerk, like many hundreds of others, is distributing mail by primitive methods. Letters are sorted and routed largely by guesswork. Many are needlessly delayed for days, even weeks. But this clerk starts thinking. He works out a map of connecting routes, tacks it up in the car. He develops a new system of assembling mail for various points. The clerk is Theodore Vail. And this simple act is one of the big events of his career. His "charts" and "schemes" attract notice. Soon he is promoted. Five years later he is assistant superintendent of railroad mail service, — soon to be general superintendent, and already on his way to become head of the American Telephone and Telegraph Company.

To do more than is expected, to take extra care, to assume extra responsibility, to look beyond the day's work — this is the way that such men gain the attention of their superiors.

It was largely by out-thinking his job, Charles Schwab tells us, that Eugene Grace rose in eight years from switching engines to millionairedom and became president of Bethlehem Steel.

Charles Markham, chairman of the Illinois Central Railroad, began his climb one day when he was sweeping a station platform in blue shirt and overalls. Some officials observed the way he went about it. One of them said later that he handled this job "like a brisk piece of engineering."

"The man who attracts attention," says Schwab, "is the man who is thinking all the time and expressing himself in little ways. . . . not the man who tries to dazzle his employer by doing the theatrical, the spectacular." He mentions one employee in the "works" who was promoted merely because, when his shift went off duty, he always stayed "until he had talked over the day's problems with his successor." [3]

Very simple precautions, obvious ways of meeting the employer's needs more fully, often set a man apart from others. Marcus Bell, for example, who rose rapidly and became vice president of the Rock Island railroad as a very young man, finds one reason for his success in this fact: When he received an order he did not try to lean on his boss in carrying it out. No matter how complicated the order might be, he always took care *not* to ask "how" to execute it.

The president of a bank with four thousand employees, Eugene M. Stevens of the Continental Illinois of Chicago, recently described to the authors his problem in finding men "to bear greater responsibility."

He spread his hands apart on the top of his desk: "Suppose," he said, "I had a thousand men here standing in line with a commander in front of them. To the commander they all look alike. He cannot judge them as individuals. Only if certain of them step forward can they become marked men.

"I am always on the lookout for someone to step forward from among the employees in this bank. If these men could only know it, their greatest problem is to get the attention of the boss. The initiative and the courage are required to do something different — something that has not been ordered."

Sometimes, as in the case of Carnegie, it is worth running risks in order to "step forward" and gain prestige.

An "Upstart" Lieutenant Defies the Secretary of the Navy

The navy can't shoot for beans! — this is the gist of a remarkable letter which a youthful lieutenant once sent to President Roosevelt.

In writing it he ripped through miles of red tape, went directly over the heads of his commanding officers and of the Secretary of the Navy. These gentlemen had declined to listen to his ideas. Now William Sowden Sims, at the risk of punishment, was placing his plans before the President himself.

This was the first important step in the brilliant career of Admiral Sims, commander of our war-time fleet in European waters, called "the ablest figure of our generation in the sea establishment."

The immediate result was that five battleships of the Atlantic squadron were placed at the disposal of this "upstart" lieutenant. Next, he himself was promoted to the rank of commander and made inspector of target practice.

Sims had sound ideas — and he demonstrated them.

But equally important, he had the courage to smash red tape.

By this one act, he won the attention he deserved, "stepped forward" from the crowd, and laid the groundwork of his reputation.

This is a dangerous form of strategy. In using it we must be sure that we can meet a real need. But when we are certain, the risk we run is often richly repaid.

"A man who does not break a rule to save the maker is a poor one," [4] Andrew Carnegie once said. Often he promoted men merely because they used common sense in breaking some iron-clad rule. "If a man can't see the need for breaking rules, . . . I recognize that he has reached the limit of his ability." [5]

There are necessary exceptions to every rule in a business. And in most businesses also, certain rules and customs exist which have ceased to serve any useful purpose. All too many men observe them closely merely because it is safe and easy to do so. Yet to challenge such a "sacred cow" is often a simple way to serve the employer's best interests and to gain prestige. Obedience and discipline are essential, of course, in every organization. The subordinate must obey orders — and often blindly. But when something is going wrong, the able subordinate who hopes to get ahead starts out-thinking his job.

Of Cyrus Curtis, the publisher, Edward Bok says this:

"There are two kinds of men in Mr. Curtis's estimation who never amount to anything, the one kind that cannot do as they are told, and the other who can do nothing else." [6]

A decisive move, made without the least support from higher authority, played an important part in the career of James W. Young, well known Chicago advertising man, former president of the American Association of Advertising Agencies.

Starting as office boy in a publishing house at thirteen, Mr. Young had become chief copy-writer in the Cincinnati branch of the J. Walter Thompson Company.

And now the head of the branch, Stanley Resor, had been called to the main office in New York to become general manager.

Three men in Cincinnati were candidates for the position which Mr. Resor had left vacant. But for several weeks no decision was made. The branch remained without a head.

About this time Mr. Young had an idea. And he acted on it. He moved into Stanley Resor's abandoned office.

Quietly he stepped forward into the leader's empty shoes.

Later all three of the men were asked to cast votes to see who should have the position — each naming his first choice next to himself. The result of this ballot was never disclosed in detail. But James Young got the job.

He had taken a risky step — and it worked.

It is fatal to assume authority which will not be respected, or to issue orders which will not be obeyed. But the man who can put it across is amply repaid.

There are many ways of "stepping forward," of gaining prestige within an organization. This whole strategy centers in a simple point: to *plan* for promotion. Daniel Woodhull, president of the American Bank Note Company, believes that promotion comes to a man "fifty per cent . . . because he deserves it, and *fifty per cent because he asserts that he deserves it*. Knowing your own value," he says, "and knowing when and how to assert it are two difficult matters. Tact comes in their proper joining." [7]

A whole program for winning promotion has been laid out by Lawrence A. Downs, the rodman who has made himself president of the Illinois Central Railroad. "'It's . . . a man's business,'" he says, "'to bring himself to the employer's attention, quietly but successfully, as one worthy of promotion.'" Among the points which he emphasizes are these: "Do your stuff on the job you've got," and "Size up the job ahead, and prepare yourself to fill it." [8]

Above all, we find the truly ambitious man taking care to place himself where higher positions are likely to open up. Not only does he avoid "dead-ends," the jobs that lead to nowhere; but also he tries to get into businesses that are growing.

No man, perhaps, offers us a more striking example of this strategy than David Sarnoff. At the age of nine he reached this country in the steerage unable to speak a word of English. At thirty-two, he became general manager of the Radio Corporation of America and is today its president. Years ago, he decided that radio was destined to be the "great development of the near future" and as a boy he started work in this field — and stuck to it. Chiefly because he entered a rapidly growing industry, Sarnoff has been able to *make known* his real ability early in life.

Why Joe Cannon Claimed to Have Hayseeds in His Hair

Joseph G. Cannon is making his first speech before the House of Representatives.

This young man is to become the "Uncle Joe" beloved by cartoonists, speaker of the House for eight consecutive years. But now he is just one more new member, an obscure person from Illinois.

And he comes in for some ragging.

"The gentleman from Illinois must have oats in his pocket," suggests one humorous member.

There is a laugh. But Cannon retorts quickly:

"I not only have oats in my pocket but hayseeds in my hair." [9]

And with this one quip, Cannon steps into the limelight. The "Hayseed Member!" His fame spreads from coast to coast. By doing something different, something unusual, Cannon captures widespread attention and gains lasting prestige. Perhaps it is all an accident. But it is a type of strategy, risky and fascinating, which is often used: personal showmanship.

One of the chief dangers of it is this: Many a man who tries to employ personal showmanship is in actual fact only showing off. He is carrying out no careful plan of self-promotion, but merely behaving in some extraordinary or peculiar manner because it tickles his vanity to attract notice.

Cannon's true showmanship was very different: He created for himself a trade-mark which pleased millions, a trade-mark which stuck.

Theodore Roosevelt used this same method. He has been called "the most successful political showman since Napoleon." [10] It is no accident that he was so often depicted as a Rough Rider. "He knew when to wear . . . his rough rider suit," says Merriam. "Perhaps without the special train, the brass cannon and the khaki uniform, he might not have become governor of New York." [11]

And that other trade-mark of Roosevelt's, the "strenuous life," was no accident either. Boyden Sparkes, for instance, was once with Roosevelt at Oyster Bay, when a moving-picture machine was set up near by: "He spoke a few sentences with his hands in his pockets," says Sparkes. "Then the camera began to whir as the operator ground away at the crank. Instantly Mr. Roosevelt's hands were out of his pockets and he began to gesture with them as busily as a prize-fighter defending a championship. That was not only spontaneous; it was presence of mind; it was, if you please, acting." [12]

A well known photographer has pointed out that Roosevelt always declined to *pose* for him. He insisted on being snapped *in action* no matter "whether his face was contorted or his attitude awkward." So Roosevelt established and kept alive one of his trade-marks.

We can all think of many examples of this strategy.

Who can forget the many photographs of our former vice president, our present ambassador to England, Charles Gates Dawes, with that famous *underslung* pipe gripped between his teeth?

A Chicago banker, John Farson, "one of the best beloved men in the city" once explained to the sports writer, Hugh Fullerton, "that he always wore a red neck-tie so that people would remember him," and advised Fullerton himself to develop some such trade-mark.

It is interesting to observe that there is no sham, no pretense about the trade-marks established by these men. Cannon, the "Hayseed Member," had a somewhat rustic appearance and he represented many farmers. Roosevelt was genuinely wedded to the "strenuous life," had actually been a cowboy and a rough rider. Likewise Dawes' underslung pipe and Farson's red necktie certainly *grew out* of these men's natural habits and preferences. Many men who find that such personal traits and tricks of behavior arouse pleasant comment, later emphasize them without perhaps being fully aware of it. The great mistake in establishing a trade-mark is to be insincere. In using this strategy, just as in using all other strategy, successful men observe one rule: "Be yourself."

Can a young man in business use methods of this sort to attract the notice of his superiors? The danger of silly stunts has been pointed out, and very justly, by many executives. But sometimes, at least, a device to gain attention is effective.

John R. Morron, president of the Atlas Portland Cement Company, is said to have got his start by such a device when he was a clerk in the P. D. Armour's packing plant.

Knowing that Armour had a habit of coming down to the plant very early in the morning, he himself did this also and instead of the usual business clothes of the other clerks, he wore a *red sweater*. One day Mr. Armour inquired, "Who is that?" and was told. So Morron caught the boss's attention — was singled out from among all the other clerks in that big establishment. Now he had a chance to make known his abilities.

Queer behavior of this sort is risky business. But occasionally it pays.

Sometimes even unfavorable notice gets results.

The much loved author, Mark Twain, once astounded the nation by walking the streets of Washington during a snowstorm dressed in a white flannel suit. At the time he was doing a bit of lobbying to induce Congress to pass a certain bill on copyrights. And this queer costume was part of his plan of action. His white flannels, white as the snow, became, "not only the talk of the town," Champ Clark tells us, "but of the whole country." Everywhere they were a "resounding theme," "written up and cartooned" by many newspapers. As a result Mark Twain's bill was widely discussed, and, in the end, somewhat amended, it became a law.

To win notice for his project, Mark Twain thought it worth while to make himself mildly ridiculous.

Henry Ford took a similar view of those many jokes about Ford cars at which millions of people used to laugh. "They are all good advertising," [13] he said to B. C. Forbes.

We find another instance of this strategy in a little newspaper which George Cohan published to advertise his plays. In this paper, Cohan devoted much space to attacking unfriendly critics with the sole purpose of inducing them to denounce him at greater length. "Week after week, I'd go after them," says Cohan. "Week after week, they'd come back at me. This sort of thing went on for a couple of years till they got on to the fact that they had slipped me at least a million dollars' worth of advertising free of charge." [14]

"A million dollars' worth of advertising," is an amiable exaggeration. But Cohan made a fortune as a playwright and a producer. And this principle of his was sound. Those who publicly and loudly damn anything or anybody are apt to fail — merely because they focus widespread attention on the target of their shafts. How people rush for the play or the book that has been censored!

In one of the few big mistakes of his career, Edward Bok discovered this fact to his own cost. At the time when aigrettes on women's hats were fashionable, he launched a crusade in the *Ladies' Home Journal* to persuade women to cease wearing them on the grounds of humanity. He ran photographs of the killing of the mother bird and the starving young ones. But after four months of the campaign the only result was this: Sales of aigrettes had more than quadrupled! Bok had merely advertised them to thousands of women "who looked upon the aigrette as the badge of fashion." For him the crusade was a boomerang, but for the dealers in aigrettes it worked just as the Ford jokes worked for Ford, or the newspaper attacks for Cohan.

Getting unfavorable notice is not strategy which we can use frequently. But it is worth understanding. It helped Ford, Cohan, Mark Twain and the aigrette dealers for several reasons:

First, they all had something to offer that met a need. Ford, his low-priced cars; Mark Twain, his bill; and Cohan, his highly entertaining plays. Even the aigrette dealers were giving women something they really wanted.

Second, they all attracted attention by one of the most certain of methods — by stirring up an emotion. We do not easily forget the things that rouse us to scorn or anger.

Third, our feelings change quickly. Many a woman who in the morning boiled with genuine rage at the brutal aigrette hunters, was, in the afternoon, cheerfully planning an aigrette for her new hat.

Charles E. Carpenter, a brilliant speaker, once said that when he failed to arouse an audience in any other way he deliberately made his hearers angry. The speaker who cannot get attention is lost. But the man who stirs up the wrath of his hearers has their attention for sure and also a reasonable chance of switching their anger into friendly interest and liking.

To gain people's attention in this way by rousing an *unfavorable* feeling is clearly a risky matter. And this is true of all other methods of building prestige which rest primarily on attracting notice. It is vital to get attention. But it is also vital to be sure that this attention will *result* in a *favorable* feeling for ourselves.

How "Hell and Maria" Aided Dawes to Become Vice President

Charles Dawes' big chance came when he returned to the United States after the War. As purchaser of supplies at the front, he was called before a Senate committee which was trying to show that the War had been wastefully conducted.

What he said and did there made him a national figure over-night.

"David Belasco never staged a performance with more care or a nicer sense of the dramatic values," says Anderson. "At just the right moment he leaped to his feet.

"'Hell and Maria!' he shouted explosively. 'We were winning a war, not keeping books! Suppose we did lose a few carloads — what of it? We won the war, didn't we? Can't you understand that men were dying under shell fire? When we got a call for a carload of ether for the field hospitals do you think we stopped to put it down in the right column of the proper ledger? Hell and Maria, no — we shot it along!' and so on for about an hour.

"He stalked up and down the committee room, waving his fists. . . . he literally blew the investigation out of the water. His honest indignation struck a tremendously popular chord. . . .

"Close observers reported a twinkle in the eyes of the victoriously retiring General, and something like a chuckle issued from the region of his underslung pipe. The country had a new hero." [15]

Dawes had started a fight.

"His art of catching the public eye is studied," says another keen observer. "The 'Hell and Maria' testimony which ultimately made him Vice President was a calculated bit of self-advertising." [16]

After he became vice president, Dawes once more used the same device. Everybody recalls his sensational speech attacking the Senate's rule of procedure. Just what Dawes himself said about his strategy has been told to the authors by Melvin Traylor, president of the First National Bank of Chicago.

"Many people thought Dawes was simply crazy," said Mr. Traylor, "when he made his famous speech before the Senate. However, he told me personally why he did this. He wanted to focus public attention on the abuse which he wished to correct and this he certainly succeeded in doing. He did not care what the Senate thought about it."

That speech made many senators indignant. But it re-echoed throughout the country.

Once more Dawes gained prestige by starting a fight. There

is perhaps no more certain way of securing widespread notice. Whether in the Senate or in a club meeting, in an office or on a street corner, the man who is fighting somebody or something is given the center of the stage.

"There is something elemental in all of us," says Kent Cooper, general manager of the Associated Press, "which responds to the spectacle of a man in conflict with a foe." "One reason why the sporting pages have such a grip is because human beings love a contest or a fight." [17]

Such men as Roosevelt, Lloyd George, and Woodrow Wilson, from the beginning of their careers won and held the public eye by a series of fights. Many newspaper and magazine publishers have sent circulation leaping up merely by launching a crusade.

When this strategy is used, we sacrifice the object of our assault. And it is risky business. To employ it successfully, we must be able to answer "Yes" to these questions: Is our cause worthy? Are we sincere in supporting it? Will the response we secure be *favorable* to us among the people who really count?

Quite different from this strategy, yet also risky, is another method of building prestige that has helped countless men to succeed. Many have used it without being aware of it. Many have used it deliberately. It is simply this: being dignified.

Let us examine dignity for a moment — this trait which we nearly always find in the successful man.

Of Thomas Edison, when he was a mere candy butcher on the Grand Trunk railway, we are told that his "boyish dignity always won respect."

George Washington from his earliest years was much helped by his "impressive" appearance. Also he was "jealous of his rights and privileges." That he was generous in spirit, and ready to overlook slights, we all know. But also he was quick to protect his dignity if the occasion arose. During the French and Indian War, for instance, Washington resigned his provincial commission as colonel and retired from the army when he found that he was to be outranked by any and all British officers with the King's commission.

Similarly Theodore Roosevelt, keen for public service as he was, remained aloof on his ranch after leaving the New York Legislature, and declined an offer to head the New York City Board of Health, because he considered it beneath his dignity.

"A sense of dignity" is placed among the essentials of success by Eugene Stevens, president of the Continental Illinois Bank of Chicago. And Walter Frew, president of the Corn Exchange Bank of New York, has said that dignity is one of the three points that he looks for first of all in hiring a man: "presence. . . . a bearing that will induce people to put their trust in him."

All of us value our dignity. It is our way of showing that we understand and respect our own true worth; also that we know our rights and are prepared to defend them if necessary. It is a means of winning people's confidence and of building prestige.

If a man seems lacking in respect for himself, people are slow to trust him. They suspect perhaps that he will allow himself to be imposed upon. And if he will not protect his own interests, he surely cannot be counted on to protect the interests of others.

Yet what pitfalls surround this matter of dignity! We only have to look about us to see men who are stiff or pompous, haughty or conceited, firmly believing themselves to be dignified. Without realizing it, they are strutting and showing off, trying to cover up their own sense of inferiority or their own timidity. Instead of inspiring trust, they merely get themselves disliked.

A Chicago business man, who was extremely short and apparently sensitive about it, was forever trying to bolster his dignity by a silly method of this kind. Frequently when a visitor came into his office by appointment the executive would be found pacing up and down by the window. For a time he would pay no attention to the other man, not even greet him nor ask him to sit down. Some people he may have succeeded in impressing with his importance by this discourtesy. But many, known to the authors, left with disgust and dislike.

The really big man does not make such mistakes. Above all, he wants the good will of others. And he refuses to permit any notion about dignity to interfere. He wins that genuine respect which is made up both of liking and of trust.

Of Nicholas Longworth, speaker of the House of Representatives, Duff Gilfond has said: "He can switch from Mr. Speaker to Nick with the angle of his hat." [18]

Two things combined, dignity with personal charm, are what we find in highly successful men.

Those jokes that Abraham Lincoln cracked in the White House, those humorous yarns with which he was forever delighting people, were said to lower his dignity. Friends told him this and he himself mentioned it to Chauncey Depew — but he also mentioned that he intended to continue telling the stories.

True dignity is not achieved by the man who forces himself to seem solemn or awe-inspiring. Just as charm arises naturally from a sincere interest in others, so dignity grows naturally out of sincere self-respect.

Leaders, as we have seen, take great care in building prestige, in creating their reputation. But whatever the method they use, whatever their position in life, this is their first step: to consider the other fellow and his viewpoint, and to make sure that they will get a favorable response.

If you are working in an organization, try to plan for your own promotion. To gain the attention of those above you, do things that are not required of you, take extra care or assume extra responsibility. Do not hesitate even to break rules if you are sure that you are safeguarding the interests of your superiors, carrying out their real plans.

Study the job ahead of you and prepare to fill it. Try to get into a growing business where higher positions are likely to open up.

Be dignified and protect your dignity, but remember that it is even more important to be well liked.

CHAPTER XXIII

PUTTING YOUR IDEAS ACROSS

*How the Window of a Skyscraper Helped
Charles E. Mitchell Sell Bonds*

Why Edison Said Electricity Was Like a Dachshund

A Nursing Bottle Makes History

E VERY ONE HAS HEARD of Charles E. Mitchell, the ten-
dollar-a-week clerk, who has made himself chairman of
the board of one of America's largest banks.

A type of strategy that helped him get there, he himself
once described to Bruce Barton.

The two men had been lunching together at the Bankers
Club in New York. At the time, Mitchell was not yet head of
the National City Bank. He was head of the subsidiary bond
house, the National City Company.

"We stood for a minute," says Barton, "at a window looking
out over the tops of New York's skyscrapers. I made some com-
monplace remark about the eternal fascination of that view,
. . . I am not sure that he heard me. The panorama was
suggesting another thought to him.

"'Every once in a while one of our bond men comes into my
office and tells me he can't find any bond buyers,' he said.
'When that happens I don't argue with him, I say, "Get your
hat and come out to lunch." Then I bring him up here and
stand him in front of one of these windows, "Look down there,"
I say. "There are six million people with incomes that aggre-
gate thousands of millions of dollars. They are just waiting
for someone to come to them and tell them what to do with
their savings. Take a good look." ' " [1]

203

"Take a good look!"   In these words of Mitchell's is the key to strategy that we all understand but often neglect.

With his discouraged salesmen Mitchell did not rely upon words alone.

He *showed* them something.   He reached them *not only through their ears, but also through their eyes.*

It was largely because a particular man happened to *see* something that James J. Hill was able to swing that historic deal which made him the "Empire Builder," creator of the Great Northern Railway.   In Hill's daring purchase of the bankrupt St. Paul and Pacific, everything hinged on this one man, George Stephen, the Canadian banker who not only became a partner but also supplied the essential banking credit and facilities.

While Stephen was still lukewarm about the project, he was induced to ride westward from St. Paul with Mr. Hill over the "two streaks of rust."   Soon they passed beyond villages and settlements out into open and uninhabited prairie.   Now Stephen, says Pyle, "shook his head ominously.   Whence was business to come to the railroad?"

The decisive moment arrived when the train reached the station of De Graff.   Around "a rude but good-sized structure there were crowds of people; the trails leading toward it were covered with conveyances." [2]

This was Bishop Ireland's famous colony.   But that did not matter particularly.   The bare fact of it was well known.

What mattered was this: By accident it was Sunday and the colonists were going to church.

Stephen *saw* the colonists and for this reason his imagination was fired.   Now he could *picture* for himself the rush of immigrants into this "barren waste."

From that moment he was won over.

To get people's attention and convince them, we must, as already noted, first of all make contact with their experience. The surest way to do this with most people is to reach them through their eyes, to *show* them things.   Time and again we find able men going out of their way to use this strategy.

The noted trial lawyer, Joseph Choate, tells gleefully how he once saved an American diplomat from his creditors by taking care to display to the judge of a marine court this gentleman's commission adorned with a seal "which looked as big as a large platter." The point of law which Choate made was later "laughed . . . out of court" when the case was appealed. But meantime the diplomat had reached South America.

John Hertz, the cab driver who made himself a multimillionaire with his Yellow Cab system, clearly owes much to his skill in appealing to our eyes. He called upon scientists to help him find the most conspicuous color for his taxicabs.

In his cash register plant at Dayton, Ohio, John Patterson kept a pile of registers locked up behind glass "as an object lesson for all time." They were machines that had been sent back as faulty after a disastrous shipment to England. "Throughout his immense plant . . ." Isaac Marcosson reported, "you observe the words, 'We teach with the eye.'" [3]

To put across points to a listener, Theodore Vail, late head of the American Telephone and Telegraph Company, was forever "diagramming his talk" with a pad and pencil as he sat at his desk. Al Smith, Democratic leader, has this same habit of illustrating his thoughts as he talks. How Smith used his picture books to make people aware of the institutions he had given his state as governor, we have already noted. "'Figures and talk aren't enough these days,'" he said to Ida Tarbell. "'People have to have pictures to understand.'" [4]

This same strategy is employed by successful salesmen. They know that the one best way to sell is to *show* things whether they are dealing with corner grocers or directors of a bank. Letters, portfolios, photographs, charts, samples, printed statements, anything that can be *looked at*, they seize upon eagerly.

"A picture, with a few words of explanation, will make it possible to get over an idea in one minute that would require two minutes without the picture." So Overstreet explains this method in *Influencing Human Behaviour.* [5]

It is when we *see* as well as hear, that a fact or a set of facts moves us most deeply.

Finding at one time that a certain executive would not even pay attention while he described a plan Leffingwell, the management engineer, changed his tactics. He very easily sold this same plan to the executive by taking him to the office of another firm where it could be *seen* in operation.

After holding several rather unsuccessful meetings of employees, Theodore F. Merseles, as president of Montgomery Ward, finally found a way to crack their "veneer of indifference." At the next meeting he had them "sitting up straight" to quote his own words. One after another, Merseles asked the executives who were with him on the platform to stand up and tell how they had started with the firm at three dollars or ten dollars a week and had risen to high-salaried positions.

"Use of the power of example," says Merseles, "is one of the big things I have learned during the many years I have been directing other men." [6]

To teach better methods of work, Henry Heinz, the pickle king, was forever setting an example, wandering around the plant and joining in the tasks of his employees. He even showed them quicker ways of handling bricks and lumber by laying aside his coat and helping on the job as a volunteer.

Mussolini, dictator of Italy, says Marcosson, "expounded the doctrine of restraint on food and drink and in consequence leads the simple life." "He launched a drive for more babies and set the example by becoming a father himself." [7]

Even in reprimanding, John Wanamaker used this plan. "One day in the course of his rounds," says Gibbons, "Wanamaker noticed that a woman was standing in front of a counter vainly endeavoring to attract the attention of two saleswomen who were chatting with the wrapping clerk. The man whom Philadelphia considered its most eminent citizen stepped behind the counter and asked what was wanted. He had begun to bring out boxes when the girls suddenly realized what was happening. When they rushed up he yielded his place to them with a smile. He said nothing. He did not have to." [8]

It is by showing people things that we can, as a rule, most easily get their attention and cause them to remember. It is through the other fellow's eyes that we can usually reach him most effectively whether we are teaching or selling, persuading or rebuking.

Why Thomas Edison Said That Electricity Was
Like a Dachshund

Thomas Edison was once trying to explain an invention to a royal visitor.

It was necessary to make his distinguished guest understand the nature of electricity.

"Your Royal Highness," he said, "I think the best explanation of the nature of electricity was one which I heard an old Scotch line repairer once give to his assistant.

"'If you had a dog something like a Dachshund,' he said, 'only long enough to reach from Edinburgh to London, and you pulled his tail in Edinburgh, he would bark in London.'

"That," the inventor went on to say, "is as far as I can get. I can't tell you exactly what goes through the dog or over the wire." [9]

Edison painted a picture with words. He made a vague idea clear by comparing it to something simple and familiar — something that the other man had *seen*.

Of John J. Raskob, the one-time stenographer who has made himself a millionaire executive in the du Pont interests, a keen observer has said: "He thinks in pictures. . . . I am not so sure that this ability to picturize simply is not responsible for much of Mr. Raskob's business success. Even when he is discussing economics, he never deals in academic abstractions, but always reduces everything to people and situations — to pictures." "Mr. Raskob not only thinks in pictures but in simple pictures that are understandable to crowds and children." [10]

We cannot always give people something to look at. But we can always build a picture with words if we will take the trouble.

The trick of it is to talk in terms of objects — things that people can see. It is sometimes called being concrete or specific. It is strategy used by all great writers and speakers as well as able men in business and in the professions.

Joseph Choate, for instance, was once defending a man who had been accused of fraud — of restoring and doctoring certain genuine antiques to such an extent that they had little real value. "Who ever heard of anyone raising checks downward?" [11] asked Choate. And with this word picture, he made clear how absurd the charges really were. One of Choate's greatest powers as a trial lawyer, says Martin, was his "rich gift of illustration." [12]

A salesman, chiefly by discovering how to use this method in his daily work, soon made himself salesmanager of a company doing an annual volume of over two million dollars.

For two days Archibald McLachlan had been trying to sell Square D. safety switches to the chief electrician of a large manufacturing company. Suddenly, as he sat at this man's desk racking his brains for something to say, the news came that an employee in the works had been injured on an open knife switch.

The two men hurried to the hospital. Here they found the doctor, the safety engineer and the general manager.

Accusations and denials flew back and forth. The man died. And that same day McLachlan got "an order so large that it startled him."

"Finally," says B. C. Forbes, "it dawned on the young man that if a workman were to be *killed* whenever the salesman was trying to convince an obdurate electrician, safety switches would become standard factory equipment within short order! But actually to kill a workman every time a sale hung fire was neither possible nor desirable. So he decided that henceforth he would kill them verbally.

"He did. And the sales made by Mr. McLachlan during the few months that followed stand as the record for the Square D. company, pioneers in the production of safety switches. When, a short time later, he was made salesmanager, the entire sales force was trained in his methods." [13]

McLachlan won by killing men "verbally." He made pictures with words.

It is when we build a picture with what we say, that our message is most likely to be understood, remembered and acted on. This is one of the reasons that stories offer such a powerful method of putting ideas across.

A Nursing Bottle Makes History

Had it not been for the story of a nursing bottle, the Panama Canal might never have been built.

"The mismanagement, red tape, and stupidity" of the first few years of work are today widely known. But at the time few people understood the facts. A commission in Washington was still in charge, "issuing 'requisitions' and interfering by cable." Even Dr. Gorgas' vital work of exterminating yellow fever was in danger of never being accomplished.

At this time Dr. Charles A. L. Reed, a former president of the American Medical Association, was sent to Panama by that organization to conduct a quiet investigation. Soon Dr. Reed returned with a report. And in it, he related an incident which was to make history.

It started, says Hendrick, with a woman in one of the hospitals who needed a nursing bottle for her newborn child. "The nurse applied to Major La Garde for a rubber nipple and a nursing bottle; he had none — the requisition of last September had not yet been filled; he made out a requisition, took it to Colonel Gorgas for endorsement, then to Mr. Tobey, chief of the bureau of materials and supplies, for another endorsement, then to a clerk to have it copied and engrossed; then a messenger was permitted to go to a drug store and buy a nursing bottle and nipple, which finally reached the infant two days after the necessity for their use had arisen."

And the nursing bottle, which was worth not more than thirty cents, Dr. Reed pointed out, actually cost the government in the neighborhood of $6.75, figuring in the time of all the people concerned — "due to the penny-wise-and-pound-foolish policy of the Commission."

"Trifles have overthrown ministries and sometimes destroyed nations," continues Hendrick. "The story of the nursing bottle had tremendous results on the building of the Panama Canal. It was published in every newspaper in the United States, and commented upon, usually in hilarious and indignant fashion. . . . In particular it made a deep impression upon the energetic gentleman then occupying the White House. The

Reed report carried its inevitable lesson. . . . With one blow President Roosevelt applied the official axe, and all seven heads of the first Commission rolled into the basket. They no longer encumber the story of Panama." [14]

As nothing else could have done, this story about the nursing bottle brought home to the people of the United States the unbelievable conditions at Panama.

Considering people as a whole, one of the most certain ways to bring an idea home to them is with a story.

First of all, a story paints a picture: a moving drama of people and objects. And, secondly, it makes an idea *easy* to understand. Most people, as we have seen, have the *habit of laziness*. It requires effort to grasp a new idea, to relate it to their own experience. The story relieves them of this effort. If it is interesting in itself, they listen to it gladly, and the idea is painlessly absorbed.

Abraham Lincoln, as we have noted, was careful not to use his stories with people of unusually keen and active intellect. But, with this exception, he made his point clear day after day with those homely yarns of his: "Plain people," he himself once said, "take them as you find them, are more easily influenced by a broad and humorous illustration than in any other way." [15]

One amusing story which is much quoted was told by Lincoln to illustrate the military situation at a certain time during the Civil War: "A bull was chasing a farmer around a tree. The farmer finally got hold of the bull's tail and both started off across the field. The farmer could not let go for fear he would fall and break his neck, but he called out to the bull, 'Who started this mess, anyway?'" [16] Lincoln said that he had got hold of the bull by the tail and that while the Confederates were running away, he dared not let go. This summed everything up in a way that the whole country could understand.

Nearly all leaders use this method. And they realize, as Lincoln did, that the number of people who are too clever for it, is very small indeed.

At one time Hoover, as head of the Belgian relief, found that one of his food ships had been sunk by a German submarine and another menaced by an airplane. He "went straight to Berlin," says Welliver, "to demand that this sort of thing stop . . . and requested that the submarine and air commanders be notified to respect the Relief Commission's flag. He was assured with all appropriate unction that it had been a regrettable mistake, which couldn't occur again.

"'I know,' quietly replied Hoover. 'I am reminded of the man who was attacked by a neighbor's dog, and complained.

"'Oh,' replied the neighbor, 'don't worry about that dog, he'll not bite you. He isn't that sort of dog.'

"'I know all about that,' replied the man, 'and I know that you understand all about it; but does the dog understand it?'

"Even with a German official that story was worth more than a long argument. The functionary excused himself briefly, and on returning said:

"'I have just been communicating with the dog, and he knows now.'" [17]

Woodrow Wilson was noted for his use of this same sort of anecdotes to drive home his points. When, for example, a delegation of prominent men came to him in May, 1916, to oppose his plan of widespread military training, on the ground that it endangered American standards of personal liberty, Wilson settled the question in this way:

"You remind me of the story," he declared, "of the Irishman who had a million dollars left him. He took a room in a hotel and asked the boy to call him at seven o'clock in the morning and tell him that the boss wanted him. When he was called he said, 'Tell the boss to go to the devil; I don't have to come.' That was his idea of liberty." [18]

We know that anecdotes do not need to be humorous to drive home a point. Who can forget the stories told by that greatest Teacher and Leader of them all to send His message echoing down the centuries: the parables of the prodigal son, of Lazarus and the rich man, of the good Samaritan . . .

Stories not only make ideas easy to understand and remember, easy to pass on to others; but also, as we have seen, they save people the trouble of thinking out abstract points and carrying them in their minds.

It is for these same reasons that such expressions as "safe for democracy," "back to normalcy," "safety first," have had great influence. By presenting an idea in a new way, moreover, striking phrases and epithets of this sort attract widespread attention to it; and by making the issue very clear, they tempt people to think about it. Nearly every one, unfortunately, likes labels better than bare ideas.

No one perhaps understood the power of epithets and phrases more clearly than Roosevelt. Few men have used them more successfully: "nature fakers," "square deal," "the strenuous life," "weasel words," — these and many others are still alive and kicking.

When we explain a plan, it is often only the striking phrases which have any real effect. We must be careful to make them do justice to our idea. One construction engineer, says Leffingwell, who was presenting a sound project to an executive committee by means of charts, failed completely because he constantly referred to the shaded areas which he wished to emphasize as "this pink stuff." Another engineer who was designing a director's room ruined his chances by speaking of his arrangement as "the House of Lords' plan" — a phrase which stuck and which the directors feared because it suggested a "high and haughty way" of acting.

Just as such epithets and phrases strike home chiefly because most people have the habit of laziness, so this same human trait gives power to another more important form of strategy: the concrete proposal.

The value of offering a definite plan in order to get action is generally recognized. Let us suppose that we want our club to provide itself with better quarters. If we merely agitate the subject, we are likely to be ignored: We are asking our fellow members to do some difficult thinking — an act which most people postpone as long as possible.

But if we present a complete plan showing the others just how our idea can be carried out, what it will cost and what the results will be, our chances are ten times better. We easily get their attention, because we have saved them the trouble of thinking, and have made it easy for them to reach a decision.

They may change and amend our plan. But essentially all they need to do is to say "Yes" or "No."

Also our definite proposal, like all others, is a sort of ultimatum. It presents a clear-cut issue and carries a trace of unspoken threat: "If you don't do this you may be sorry."

Salesmen and doctors, lawyers and bank presidents, all successful men employ the concrete proposal in getting others to decide and act.

At one time when the followers of Pizarro, conqueror of Peru, were exhausted and faint-hearted from hunger, it was by this strategy that he held the ones who really counted loyal to his cause. With Peru still undiscovered, they were waiting on an island in the Pacific for a ship with supplies and new recruits. Instead there came a ship sent by the Governor of Panama. The commander of it told them that every one in Panama considered the expedition a failure and that the Governor had ordered them all to come home.

But Pizarro walked out before his men on the beach and with his sword drew a line in the sand. Those who wanted to come with him, he said, were to step across the line — the rest of them could go home! And Pizarro won.

Another advantage of using a concrete proposal is this: You safeguard yourself against that risk which is so common — the risk of being misunderstood.

Ivy Lee, America's foremost publicity man, recently told the authors that, for this reason alone, he invariably makes a specific proposal whenever possible. He pointed out as an example that in working out plans for announcing medical discoveries with Dr. Simon Flexner, director of the Rockefeller Institute, he and the doctor sometimes disagree when they have occasion to talk over a project in the theoretical stage, but that there is rarely any difference of opinion after the material has been put in concrete form.

Let us review the various types of strategy which successful men employ in putting across their ideas:

To focus the other fellow's attention on your ideas, to make him understand them and act on them, give him something to look at whenever possible. Plan to reach him through his eyes as well as through his ears. Show him things — objects, pictures, people, letters, charts — things of any kind which convey your idea or illustrate it.

When you can do so, use your own actions or the actions of others as examples.

In talking or writing try to paint pictures with your words. Be concrete and specific.

Frequently the best way to drive home an idea and make it stick, is to tell an interesting story to illustrate it.

In reaching groups of people, it is very helpful to employ striking phrases or epithets which make your thought sharp and clear and thus save others the trouble of thinking deeply about it.

When you desire to get prompt action on a project, take care to present it in a definite form, as a concrete proposal. Offer a complete program or a clear-cut issue.

CHAPTER XXIV

HAVE YOU A POKER FACE?

How Henry Ford Kept His Own Hand Hidden

Abraham Lincoln Extracts Information

*James Rand, Jr., Points Out Why Many Men
Fail to Rise*

NOT LONG AGO a young man named Davis called on Henry Ford at his River Rouge plant to sell him a piece of industrial real estate.

Ford, wearing rubber boots, cocked up his feet and listened. The property was a logical one for him to buy, being surrounded by land which he already owned. And Davis made a good presentation.

Then something happened which surprised Davis, something which he did not understand in the least until later on.

Ford made no direct reply but picked up a small piece of fiber-like material lying on his desk and tossed it over to him.

"Do you know what this is?" [1] he asked.

When Davis said, "No," Ford began telling him all about it. It was a new type of material which he was considering for use in the bodies of Ford cars.

For fifteen minutes Ford proceeded to talk about this material and also most frankly about his plans for next year's model. Davis was puzzled — but pleased.

Then Ford remarked that he did not care to buy the property, and ushered him out of the office.

So without revealing his reasons, and without argument of any kind, Ford turned down this offer most decisively. Yet he sent the other man away happy.

Ford's strategy, of course, is clear. That confidential chat about his plans was intended to charm the other man — as it did. But most important of all, it was a sort of smoke screen: a screen behind which Ford came to his decision, and which saved him from betraying his own thoughts and feelings.

The man who cannot learn to keep his thoughts and feelings to himself when necessary can, of course, never become a highly successful leader. To control others, as we have noted, he must first of all control the feelings which he himself displays. It is strategy which is vital in managing people.

We find such men as Ford and Schwab and Lincoln using many simple devices to keep their cards hidden until they are ready to show them. And always, when possible, they try at the same time to gain the other man's good will.

Of Charles Schwab, for example, Strawn says: "The reporters rarely have difficulty in obtaining an interview with him, though more than one reporter on his way back to his office, has suddenly awakened to the fact that instead of getting the information he was sent after, he has been listening to an endless collection of funny stories." [2]

And when Abraham Lincoln "wished to parry questions which no foresight could then safely solve, he became the questioner himself or sent his caller away with an apt story." [3]

One young reporter who used often to interview Commodore Vanderbilt, the founder of the Vanderbilt fortune, tells how he would leave him time after time without a scrap of information yet would forget all disappointment under "the charm of his geniality." Vanderbilt's method was to compliment the lad on his shrewdness and by tactful questions to lead him on to "confidences and revelations" about his own affairs.

By getting the other man to talk, by telling stories, by questions, by offering him confidences along a safe and different line, by the very methods that charm him, these leaders often baffle his efforts to get behind their guard. It will be interesting to see what other strategy they use for this same purpose.

James Simpson, the one-time clerk who has made himself chairman of the board of Marshall Field and Company, was sent in his earlier days to represent Field at a meeting of business men.   There he smoked so many cigars that Field himself was told about it.

"I hear," he said, "that you smoked more cigars than anyone else there."

"Yes, I did," replied Simpson, "but I smoked them, Mr. Field, so as to be sure I'd keep my mouth shut." [4]

Many of us need to take some such precaution, not only to avoid saying too much, but also to prevent the expression of our faces from betraying us.   It is vital, at times, to be able to listen non-committally.

"Finding some outside object on which to fix the attention while listening, such as sketching idly on a note pad, will make one's air appear casual," [5] says Royal Munger, a close observer of business methods.

A successful New York attorney told the authors that he uses Simpson's method: "During negotiations, I always smoke a cigar to conceal my feelings."

On rare occasions it is necessary to freeze the other fellow out by giving no response whatever.   Giannini, famous founder of the Bank of Italy, remarked once that he does this simply by continuing to think on whatever subject is in his mind, letting the "conversation go in one ear and out at the other" [6] without interfering with his own mental machinery.

Nearly all such men try to master the knack of the poker face.   Pringle said of John J. Raskob, when he was chairman of the Democratic National Committee: "He learned long ago, fortunately for the peace of mind of his associates, that there were times when it was wise to look knowing and say nothing; it is a trick acquired by industrial giants as well as by campaign strategists." [7]

Often when we are cornered, yet when it is unwise to commit ourselves in any way, a bit of irony offers an escape.

In 1917, for instance, when Colonel House had retired to his summer home and when this separation from Wilson "gave rise to the usual rumors of a break between the two," he told the reporters who demanded an explanation, that the rumor was "somewhat belated" as it generally came "about midsummer along with the sea serpent stories."

And the Duke of Wellington, conqueror of Napoleon, when he was later shown the French plans of the battle around Toulouse — plans which reflected little credit upon himself — and was asked to approve them as a matter of historical interest, merely remarked with great gravity: "What a beautiful plan! . . . and so perfectly drawn! Really it is wonderfully done. Pray return it to Marshal Suchet with my compliments and thanks." [8]

At times, also, in order not to be misjudged, it is necessary to do entirely innocent things in such a way that they cannot later be laid at our door by those who may wish to injure us.

Albert A. Sprague, head of a large Chicago wholesale house, has told the authors how Marshall Field once handled this problem. As a young man, Sprague went to Field, an old friend of his family, for advice about investments. Now Field, who was a director in many companies and had extensive inside information, could not well afford to place himself on record as recommending any particular stock. So, from time to time, he would merely tell Sprague what he himself was buying or selling with some such remarks as these: "I don't suppose this would be of any interest to you, . . ." or "I don't want you to pay any attention to what I tell you, but . . ."

On other occasions when it is vital to disguise not so much the thing we do but rather our reason for doing it, we may find it necessary to set up a dummy motive. During those stormy years after the Civil War when President Johnson was defying Congress and frustrating the law with his reconstruction policies in the South, Ulysses Grant, as head of the army, was placed in a difficult position. Strongly opposed to Johnson's actions, he nevertheless did not want to discredit the administration by an open break. Accordingly he used strategy. When Johnson dragged him off on a speaking tour, refusing to accept excuses, and forced him to sit on the platform in silent support of his policies, Grant's "disgust was so great that he became half unwell, and pleading illness, left the party." [9]

Even the old dodge of a pretended sickness sometimes serves both a useful and worthy purpose.

Grant "could dissimulate as well as any man that ever

lived," says General Badeau, his military secretary; "that is, he could prevent all but those who were absolutely closest to him, and sometimes these, from penetrating further than he wished into his thoughts or purposes or desires." [10]

Abraham Lincoln Extracts Information

Grenville M. Dodge tells of a long interview which he once had with Abraham Lincoln, without even guessing until years later what it was that Lincoln really wanted.

Dodge, a general in the Union army of the West, had just spent two weeks with General Grant in the East at City Point. Then, merely to pay his respects, he called on President Lincoln at the White House.

This was after the campaigns of the Wilderness and the Potomac, "in the darkest days of Grant's career in the East."

After a short talk with Lincoln, Dodge rose to go. But Lincoln detained him, disposed of a crowd of visitors, and led him into another room.

Seeing that Dodge was ill at ease, Lincoln took a book from his desk. "He opened the book," said Dodge long afterward, "crossed his legs and began to read a portion of a chapter, which was so humorous that I began to laugh and it brought me to myself. When he saw that he had gotten me in his power, he laid the book down and began to talk to me about my visit to the Army of the Potomac and what I saw."

Then, keeping Dodge with him for lunch, Lincoln extracted from him every shred of fact and opinion he possessed about General Grant and his army.

"The purport of all this," says Dodge, "came to me in after years." "I did not know then that Lincoln's table was piled with letters demanding the change of Grant, . . . wanting to have a different commander sent, etc." [11]

So, without making known his purpose or his own feelings, Lincoln secured the information he needed.

Alfred H. Smith, former president of the New York Central Lines, once made this comment: "One of the best ways to learn things is by acquiring the knack of making everybody feel so at ease that they will just naturally open up and talk to you frankly and freely." [12]

Very often it is vital to obtain information without revealing why we want it. And the strategy of it is simple. "Direct questions may frequently fail to get results," Frank O. Wetmore, late chairman of the First National Bank of Chicago, recently remarked to the authors. "But by merely showing an interest in the other man's business you may frequently get what you want."

General Dodge tells of another encounter with Abraham Lincoln, this time at Council Bluffs, Iowa, before the Civil War when Dodge, as an engineer, had been "making reconnaissances west of the Missouri for the Union Pacific Railroad. . . ." "Mr. Lincoln . . ." says Dodge, "sought me out, and on the porch of the Pacific Hotel, for two hours, he engaged me in conversation about what I knew of the country west of the Missouri River, and greatly impressed me by the great interest he displayed in the work in which I was engaged. He stated that there was nothing more important before the nation at that time than the building of the railroad to the Pacific Coast. He ingeniously extracted a great deal of information from me, and I found the secrets I had been holding for my employers in the East had been given to him." [13]

All leaders have understood and used this kind of strategy. Frequently they conceal the fact that they even desire information.

A business man who has had many contacts with outstanding executives was asked by the authors which of the methods used by these men had most impressed him. He said it was their way of securing information about another man without letting people realize that they were especially interested in him. They would bring up the man's name casually, or with some remark calculated to draw others out and then simply sit back and listen.

This method is often highly important. At times we may defeat the very purpose for which information is needed if we betray a too active interest in our subject.

James Rand, Jr., Points out Why Many Men Fail to Rise

Not long ago a group of prominent men at the Union League Club of New York were discussing the problems of the young man in business. What they had to say has been described by James Rand, Jr., head of Remington Rand. "One of them," he says, "put the question, 'Why is there such a scarcity of young men for the big positions in business?'" Argument ensued that lasted for the balance of the afternoon.

"These leaders of business, men well known in the world of commerce and finance, finally agreed on the answer. They were unanimous on the fact that 'The young man cannot keep his mouth shut!'"

In the course of the discussion, one of the men in the group told of a youth who seriously damaged his prospects and ruined a deal with which he had been entrusted, merely because he had not been able to resist the temptation to talk about it in the club car of a train.

"Absolute frankness," continues Rand, "is advisable between the individuals directly connected with a business deal but talking about it to others is a high 'crime and misdemeanor' that often has fatal consequence. . . . In fact, I do not believe it is possible for a man to succeed in a large way who talks 'confidential company affairs' even to his wife." [14]

As Lord Chesterfield remarks, to tell any other person a "secret with which they have nothing to do, is discovering to them such an unretentive weakness as must convince them that you will tell it to twenty others, and consequently that they may reveal it without the risk of being discovered." He also observes that *"nine in ten of every company you are with will avail themselves of every indiscreet and unguarded expression of yours, if they can turn it to their own advantage."* [15]

We cannot control people if we are not willing and able to keep certain information to ourselves. Nearly all leaders have been noted for their care in guarding secrets.

Ford and his son, Edsel, for example, work together in running the huge Ford interests and "no one," says Crowther, "knows what part each has in arriving at any decision. . . . It is certain that they do have differences of opinion." "But never in specific instance has it been revealed whether Henry Ford or Edsel Ford has taken the initiative." [16]

And Ulysses Grant, says his secretary, Badeau, had secrets from every one he knew and without doubt died with emotions and beliefs which he never revealed to any one whatever.

Why is this strategy so difficult for some people? Why is it that secrets so often leak out?

Actually people betray a secret or a confidence largely because it is pleasant to do so: First, to offer an unexpected revelation is, as we have seen, often a means of winning other people's good will; second, the man who does this gains from his act a brief sense of self-importance. His vanity is tickled for the moment.

People who cannot keep secrets nor respect confidences are largely the victims of their own *ego*.

Able men, of course, are not interested in this silly form of vanity. Moreover, they know that a man who, without good reason, reveals confidential facts, is usually distrusted by others. Those to whom he betrays such secrets, even about himself, will not, if they have good sense, thereafter trust him with their own. One of the important points to establish in building a reputation is the ability to keep a close mouth.

Some people fall into another grave error in this matter of secrecy: They make a great show of having information which they cannot reveal.

"Take care," says Chesterfield, "never to seem dark and mysterious — which is not only a very unamiable character but a very suspicious one too. If you seem mysterious with others, they will be really so with you, and you will know nothing." [17]

The man who tries to seem mysterious is, as a rule, merely showing off.

We do not find the leader trying to seem mysterious. On the contrary, his object is to keep secrets without appearing to do so. To be frank is an admirable and amiable trait, — also a way of getting confidences in return. We can all be frank without telling things which are nobody else's business.

Of Donald A. Smith, one of the builders of the Canadian Pacific railroad, later Lord Strathcona, Preston says: "In accepting confidences and giving none, while appearing to be most unreserved in his manner, he had no peer in British North America." [18]

On occasions, a parade of secrecy or a display of mystery is useful to create suspense and arouse curiosity about something which is to be revealed later on. But the man who does this as a matter of habit or simply to please his vanity, is making a serious mistake.

"Have a real reserve with almost everybody and have a seeming reserve with almost nobody," observes Chesterfield, "for it is very disagreeable to seem reserved and very dangerous not to be so. Few people find the true medium; many are ridiculously mysterious and reserved upon trifles, and many imprudently communicative of all they know." [19]

To guard a secret successfully calls for a number of precautions. Sometimes, we must do a bit of acting.

During the War, for example, Woodrow Wilson made a point of "composing his face" and "trying to look surprised" when the Spanish Ambassador presented a secret peace offer from Austria. It was essential for him to conceal the fact that the offer had been intercepted by the British Intelligence Service and that he himself already knew all about it.

In your dealings with others, particularly in trading or in contact with those who are in search of information, learn to conceal your thoughts and feelings when it is advisable to do so.

Sometimes it is helpful to throw out a smoke screen: to get the other fellow to do most of the talking, by asking him questions and drawing him out; or to engage his attention along another line by telling him stories or harmless confidences.

At other times, you may be aided in controlling your expression by some outside activity such as sketching on a pad or smoking.

Often it is important to secure information without revealing your reason for wanting it. To do this, it is usually best to put the other fellow at ease by displaying an interest in his affairs and encouraging him to talk. As a rule this method is more successful than direct questions.

Sometimes, however, it is necessary to obtain information about another man or a particular subject without even showing that you yourself are especially interested. You can do this by bringing up the man's name or the topic very casually, perhaps offering some remark which will stimulate conversation.

Make it a point to learn how to keep secrets. Remember that other people are on the alert to profit by your unguarded remarks and also that few will respect your confidences.

Be careful to avoid seeming mysterious. It is easy to keep to yourself what is nobody else's business, and at the same time to be genuinely frank and open. To parade a secret is a form of showmanship that is sometimes useful in order to arouse curiosity. But ordinarily this method merely creates ill will and cuts you off from the confidences of others.

CHAPTER XXV

PLAYING YOUR CARDS TO WIN

Why John D. Rockefeller Bluffed with His Check Book
Westinghouse Rescues His Company from a Receivership
Joseph Choate Makes Himself a Partner in the Firm

JOHN D. ROCKEFELLER has told how a simple bit of bluffing
helped him become an overlord of oil.

His chance came when he was only thirty-five, when
his Standard Oil Company in Cleveland was still just one
among many refineries.

That this ex-clerk with his slender resources managed to buy
out his competitors and found the Standard Oil industry which
we know today is one of the great exploits of business history.

The critical moment always came when a price had been
agreed upon and it was time to pass title. And Rockefeller's
plan of action was simple. Both Forbes and Winkler tell how
he himself explained it in later years:

"'We had to do a lot of bluffing with our check book in those
days.'" [1]

"'Yes, it does seem amusing now, although it was a matter
of grave concern to us then. I would whip out our check book
with rather a lordly air and remark, as if it were a matter of
entire indifference to us: "Shall I write a check or would you
prefer payment in Standard Oil Shares?" Most of them took
the shares — very wisely as it turned out. . . .'

"'What did you do when cash was demanded instead of
stock — you were always short of capital?'" Forbes asked
Rockefeller.

"'We managed to scramble through somehow. By this time we had learned fairly well how to get banks to lend us money.'" [2]

So Rockefeller won — by offering to write checks for money that he did not possess. And because he made the offer with a "lordly air" of indifference, it was seldom necessary to write them.

Yet it is important to observe that this was no empty bluff. When he was called, Rockefeller could "scramble through."

We have all done bluffing of this kind. And it is, of course, a recognized tool of leadership. It works like all other methods of managing people. The purpose of it is to control their emotions. By making a bold show of strength, the leader arouses in other men either confidence or fear as the occasion demands.

Rockefeller, by concealing his own doubts and displaying confidence, inspired his competitors with faith in his future.

Of this particular art he was a master.

In his early days, as a produce merchant, he once induced a rich man to loan him five thousand dollars to meet current expenses, by first convincing him that he himself could be counted upon to invest twice that sum in the rich man's business!

It was by a similar stroke that Herbert Hoover got his first job after leaving college.

When he applied to the noted engineer, Janin, in San Francisco, Janin told him that he needed no assistants and had a long waiting list. He added, however, that another typist was needed in his office.

Hoover, interrupting, said he would take the job as typist — but stated that he couldn't start until Tuesday, four days later.

Yet at that moment Hoover did not even know how to run a typewriter! It was by a bold display of confidence that he got his start with Janin. He banked on learning how to type in his four days of grace — and did so.

Walter Chrysler had a similar experience in his early days when he was a youthful shop-hand at 30 cents an hour in a railroad roundhouse at Salt Lake City. In an emergency, on a morning when a large part of the force was off duty, Chrysler was asked whether he could put a certain locomotive into condition and have it ready to operate by three o'clock that afternoon. The work was far beyond his experience — but he gave no signs of his astonishment. Like Hoover, he concealed his doubts and put up a bold front. He asked for some men and set to work. The engine was ready by three.

This event, Mr. Chrysler told the authors, was a turning point in his career.

Three months later, as a direct result of it, he was offered a job as general foreman in the shops of another railroad. And at thirty-three he became the youngest superintendent of motive power on record in the Chicago Great Western system. He was on his way to become one of the outstanding industrial leaders of America. The first steps had been taken.

In the careers of able men we find many examples of this strategy.

When Thomas Preston, widely known Tennessee banker, had, at twenty-five, worked his way from messenger to manager of a small outlying bank in Chattanooga, it was by this method that he saved his bank from failure. In that panic year, 1893, ten of the seventeen banks in Chattanooga went under. And runs began on all of them. When the line of anxious depositors formed outside Preston's doors, he "didn't beg or plead," says Gwinn. Far from it. Knowing that his bank was sound, if only he could stop the run, he announced that he was ready to pay every one. More important still, he stated that he wanted no depositor "who lacked faith." When one heavy depositor tried to call his bluff, Preston took him to his vaults and counting out $16,000 in gold, insisted that he take it home with him. And Preston kept insisting until the other man begged him to keep it and then went out to tell the others what fools they all were.

Sometimes the leader shows his strength by emphasizing the difficulties which he faces. When George Westinghouse was first bringing natural gas to Pittsburgh, people were slow to invest in his enterprise because they doubted that he could supply enough gas. An estimate was published that thirty million feet a day would be required by the city: a figure which left the good citizens breathless. Westinghouse countered "not with denials and evasions" but with the startling announcement that *four hundred* million instead of thirty million feet would soon be needed every day! And the very boldness of his statement created the confidence he desired.

To inspire confidence and courage in others — this is the task of every leader. He does not shut his own eyes to risks and dangers ahead. Not at all. He appraises them carefully. But once having seen that he will succeed if only the others stand by, then he acts as though there could be no question of the outcome. We find able men observing this precaution even in very minor matters.

The noted auctioneer, Fred Reppert, for example, once remarked that on meeting an owner before a sale he always told him that he felt fine, gave him his "heartiest handshake and a cheerful grin," no matter what the actual state of his health might be. "If I am not feeling up to the mark," said Reppert, "I never let on." [3]

It is, of course, by taking care not to "let on" that successful lawyers frequently offset damaging evidence in jury trials. "It is related of Rufus Choate," says Donovan, "that on one occasion when a witness gave evidence that was obviously greatly detrimental to his case he required the witness to repeat slowly the testimony while he carefully wrote out the words uttered." [4] By this bit of bluff Choate made the jury feel that he found "something of importance in it to his side of the case."

T. E. Lawrence, hero of the *Revolt in the Desert*, even when utterly exhausted or nearly overcome by heat on long marches, used to make a point of pretending to be unwearied and even of playing about as though he were enjoying himself. He bluffed in order to give new vigor to his equally tired and discouraged Arabs.

This sort of bravado the strong man engages in with his eyes open and as part of a definite program. It is only the weak man who does it blindly — merely to show off. Lawrence, for instance, refused absolutely at one time to take the place of a missing machine gunner when the pilot of an airplane seemed to expect him to do so. He would rise to no dare, spoken or unspoken. "No!" he says, "I was not going up to air fight no matter what caste I lost with the pilot. He was an Australian, . . . not an Arab to whose gallery I had to play."

The vain man four-flushes about many things just for the silly pleasure he gets out of it — about how much he knows, for example. But if the true leader ever bluffs a bit about this, it is only to accomplish a worth-while purpose. In commenting on the skill of John T. Delane, famous editor of the *London Times*, in securing inside information, Sir Edward Cook says: "Delane gave freely because, I imagine, he wanted to receive freely. The way to get information . . . as every diplomatist and editor are aware, is to know, or at least to seem to know, much already."

Just as it may be good strategy, on occasions, to bluff a little about how much we know, so, also, it is sound at times to bluff by being positive and aggressive in making statements. As we have already seen (p. 106), the man who habitually uses this cocksure manner in advancing his ideas usually defeats his own purpose. But in the hands of an able man, the brusque, dogmatic statement is very often an effective means of inspiring confidence.

A well known Chicago business man has told the authors about an advertising agent who recently saved an important account by this method.

The client, who happened to be an Englishman by birth, came to him to announce that he had taken the business away from him and had placed it in the hands of another agency.

"Why have you done this?" asked the advertising man.

"Because the advertising you have given us has not been good."

"Is that the only reason?"

"Yes."

"Well, I refuse to accept that reason. I say that our advertising *has* been good. You have been in the manufacturing business all your life while I have been in the advertising business all my life. I ought to know. Moreover you are an Englishman and I am an American. I know how to plan advertising for the American people."

And through this blunt, positive assertion of superior knowledge, the advertising man succeeded in restoring his client's confidence; caused him to undo what was already done and to give him back the account.

There have been a few men endowed with overwhelming force of intellect and will who have employed this method day in and day out. E. H. Harriman, the railroad builder, was one of these. Through his "crushing directness," his overbearing gruffness, he awakened in other men unlimited confidence in himself. But he made many needless enemies, aroused much needless opposition and died at sixty-two largely as a result of "overwork and undue nervous strain."

Brusqueness or dogmatism is a powerful device when correctly used — especially in emergencies. But it is a fighting weapon.

Now all great leaders are fighters, ready to strike when necessary. But it is on tact, on kindliness and shrewd understanding of human nature that they rely primarily to establish their influence over men.

Westinghouse Rescues His Company from a Receivership

George Westinghouse faces failure — the same Westinghouse whom we have just observed earlier in his career introducing natural gas into Pittsburgh.

The panic of 1907 has put the Westinghouse Electric Company into the hands of receivers.

But visitors, says Leupp, see "the men busy the next day at their usual tasks, and the chief wearing an unclouded brow."

Westinghouse interviews one of his lieutenants. At the end of the meeting he exclaims: "By the way, McFarland, I've got an idea now for our turbine that will make a sensation when we bring it out." [5]

No sign of worry in George Westinghouse! His confidence spreads to subordinates, spreads to stockholders. Soon comes the critical move, a new issue of stock, *and five thousand of his own employees subscribe over six hundred thousand dollars!*

So by concealing his fears and doubts, by putting up a bold front, Westinghouse rescues his firm.

At all times, of course, it is the confidence of the leader that sweeps forward his followers. On him rests the burden.

No leader but has his fears and worries. But the true leader does not reveal them. Especially in the dark hours, he goes out of his way to display serene confidence before his associates and subordinates. And this outward show, this *doing things* to exhibit his confidence, not only inspires the rest. Even more it is the surest way to dispel his own doubts, to make his confidence real.

When Harriman in the midst of a business depression took the daring step which changed the "dilapidated and run down" Union Pacific into one of the most splendid railroad properties of the country, it was only through a striking display of confidence that he secured the support of his timid executive committee. Before the members of it had even passed the great appropriation for improvements which he demanded, he committed himself, at his own personal risk, to spend large parts of it. Also he purchased for himself five thousand shares of the preferred stock of this railroad which was barely out of the hands of the receivers and took care to tell the others about it.

At the battle of Gettysburg, wounded General Sickles steadied his wavering corps and saved the day, by having himself carried up and down the lines on a stretcher, while he smoked a cigar, made cheerful remarks.

The night before the battle of Waterloo, with even the position of the enemy in doubt, Wellington danced until the last moment at the Duchess of Richmond's ball in Brussels.

Admiral Rodman, in tense, breathless moments during the World War, used to give his orders sharply, then would start telling some "absurdly irrelevant story to another officer on the bridge."

Feelings are contagious. A tiny sign of fear or worry in the leader strikes home to his followers. And so do signs of confidence.

It is when the odds are desperate that we see the able man most carefully masking his doubts, playing his part like an actor; laughing away the fears of others — and his own. In the careers of all successful men from Alexander the Great and

Napoleon to Andrew Carnegie and James J. Hill, we discover such dramatic moments.   And we find this method used by all true leaders from the humblest young department head to the most illustrious bankers and industrial captains.

In a fight or contest, of course, this same strategy is used for an entirely different purpose: Then the leader uses a bold display of strength in order to arouse fear in his opponents.

When strikes were threatened during the building of the Panama Canal, Goethals merely remarked that any man not back at work in the morning would be permanently dismissed. And he won out.   There were no strikes.

Like Rockefeller with his check book, Goethals bluffed.   But it was no empty bluff.   He too was prepared to make good if necessary.

E. H. Harriman, in his dealings with other business leaders, won many a bout by boldness of this kind.   "Mr. Harriman," says Otto Kahn, "was not averse to something like bluffing, in fact he rather enjoyed the sport; but he never indulged in that pastime without having previously been careful to put himself in such a position that, if a test of strength was called for, he could, if not win, at least give such an account of himself, that his opponent would become imbued with a wholesome respect for his fighting capacity, and would be extremely disinclined to tackle so formidable and resourceful an antagonist in the future." [6]

An incident from the career of Mussolini, dictator of Italy, illustrates this strategy very clearly: "In December, 1924," says Motherwell, "after the Matteotti murder had cost Mussolini the support of all parties save his own, he was the most thoroughly licked man in Europe.   The army, public opinion, and the greater part of the organized force of the country, were against him.   His own supporters were weak and nervous.   He had no weapon left but bluff.   In cabinet meetings his opponents demanded his resignation.   'Very well,' he replied, 'here is my resignation.   But if it is accepted, in half an hour I shall be in the streets of Rome at the head of my militia.'   He spoke like a man with victory in his hand.   The request for his resignation was withdrawn." [7]

It was through a different kind of bluff that Calvin S. Brice, ex-senator from Ohio, sold Vanderbilt the Nickel Plate railway. This line paralleled Vanderbilt's own road, but it was on the verge of bankruptcy, and Brice only got a laugh when he made his first offer. Vanderbilt said he would wait for foreclosure and buy it from the sheriff.

Then Brice induced Jay Gould to help him spring a joke on Vanderbilt: Gould was merely to say nothing when the newspapers announced that he intended to buy the Nickel Plate. Furthermore, he was to ride slowly over the line, with a wise look, smoking cigars on the rear end of an observation car. It worked. "Before Gould had reached Chicago," says Brown, "Vanderbilt, in a fit of hysterics, wired Brice he would take the Nickel Plate . . . and Brice was saved." [8]

A bluff that has made history was staged by Napoleon after his victory at Friedland. Because he was now hard pressed by the uprising in Spain, his representative, Daru, agreed to let off defeated Prussia with a much lighter indemnity than had been mentioned at the start. But Napoleon, weakened as he was, surrounded by enemies and unsteady allies, won out by a daring stroke: He refused to ratify Daru's treaty. He *raised* instead of lowering the Prussian indemnity.

Joseph Choate Makes Himself a Member of the Firm

It was no accident that Joseph Choate, at the age of twenty-seven, became a partner in New York's leading law firm.

Not only was he able, but also, and equally important, this future leader of the bar played his cards shrewdly.

Only a few years earlier, he had started as a clerk with this same firm — Butler, Evarts and Southmayd. Then he had left them and struck out for himself, "seeing no prospect of any further advance in that office." And this was a sound move.

But it is in Choate's way of returning to this firm that we find the most interesting point.

Very soon, his old employer, Evarts, indicated that he would like to have him return.

And Choate pretended not to understand.

The more actively Evarts threw out hints, the less Choate responded.

Choate himself has described the whole transaction: "In the meantime," he says, "Mr. Evarts began to approach me with new overtures, asking at first if I did not know of any young man whom they could get to come in with them to help in the business of the firm. Of course, I said I did not. But he from time to time continued his approaches, and finally said: 'You don't seem to understand what I am after. We want you back in the office, and to come in as a member of the firm.'" [9]

At last the definite offer for which Choate had been waiting! He got what he wanted from Evarts by a familiar device: by making the other man show his hand first.

To conceal our own interest and wear a mask of indifference, is often the surest way to control the other fellow's feelings. We find able men frequently using this method, especially in trading.

Thomas Edison hit on this strategy by accident — and thereafter used it regularly in marketing his inventions.

In his early twenties, as electrician of the Gold Stock and Telegraph Company, Edison invented and patented many improvements on the tickers then in use.

"One day," says Rolt-Wheeler, "two of the directors of the company stopped Edison in the brokerage room and asked him to come to the office of the president, stating that they wanted to take up with him the question of purchasing the title to his inventions and improvements of the gold ticker. 'I had made up my mind,' Edison has since said, 'that five thousand dollars would strike me about right, but I would take almost anything, rather than not sell, as I needed the money sorely for further experiments. "Well, Mr. Edison," General Lefferts said, "how much do you want for your devices?" "I do not know how much they may be worth to you," I answered. "Make me an offer." "How would forty thousand dollars strike you?" I believe you could have knocked me down with a feather, so astonished I was at the sum!'" [10]

It was with this $40,000 that Edison was first able to set himself up as an independent manufacturer and inventor. And he never forgot that lucky bit of strategy which enabled him to get it.

"Make me an offer!" this became Edison's unchanging answer to all overtures. By this plan he sold Orton of the Western Union Telegraph Company two different devices, each for $100,000.

Like Choate, Edison won out by making the other man show his hand first. We have all used this method to secure the strong position in a trade. Always we find successful men shifting the burden to the other fellow when it is possible to do so.

That is how Louis Sudler, well known Chicago real estate man, recently closed a big deal. Most of us know those last-minute objections and reasons for delay, which people often raise when final papers are to be signed. All these troubles Sudler nipped in the bud.

By appointment he entered the office of the principal in the deal with the contract ready in his pocket. But he did not take it out at the start. Instead he led the talk around to baseball, golf, and other topics in which he knew his customer to be interested.

Finally, the other man, unable to contain himself any longer, said: "Well, what about the contract?" [11]

Sudler produced it. And it was immediately signed. He had shifted the burden to the other man, forced him to make the first move.

At times, the only possible way to persuade people to act as we desire is to conceal our own interest. If we seem indifferent, people may regard our plan as an opportunity for themselves; but if we urge it upon them, they may become wary.

For this reason Harvey Firestone, in his early days, posted himself on the plans of a man named Christy, pursued him to Chicago, registered at the same hotel, kept out of sight one whole evening and part of the next morning, all with one object in view: to meet this man "by accident" as he entered the dining room for breakfast.

"We had breakfast together," says Firestone. "He inquired about our business. One thing led naturally to another, and before breakfast was over he had bought $10,000 worth of stock. Later, Mr. Christy bought around $50,000 worth of our stock, became our president, and was of immense help to us at a time when we needed all the help we could get.

"And he sold himself! All I did was to fall in with him at the right time." [12]

So largely by concealing his own eagerness, Firestone laid a cornerstone of the great tire business which bears his name today.

Often indeed, to accomplish their purpose, able men remain completely in the background. John L. Motley, for example, in paving the way toward his appointment by President Grant as minister to England, sent letters containing his campaign speeches not to Ulysses Grant himself, but to Grant's friend and secretary, Badeau, who was sure to show them to him. Many are the times when statesmen and diplomats give information not directly to the people in whom they are interested but rather to someone who they believe will pass it on to them.

On occasions, indeed, we find the leader giving his facts to such a go-between in the strictest "confidence," knowing that the other man will not be able to resist the temptation to talk.

In this way, Leonard Wood, as governor of Cuba, induced the unwilling and suspicious Cubans of a certain town to participate in the American administration after the war with Spain, and to produce a Cuban to serve as mayor. He asked a merchant who happened to call on him if it were true that the Cuban gentlemen were "very indifferently educated" and "afraid to accept civil offices." Also he requested the merchant to keep this conversation "private." As a result, these remarks of his, which he would not have dared to make openly, spread through the whole town. A few days later one of the leading Cuban citizens accepted the challenge and was appointed mayor.

No methods used by leaders are more interesting than those which depend upon keeping hidden their own thoughts and feelings. And no other methods, perhaps, are more widely discussed. But all strategy of this type is less easy than it seems: It calls for real understanding of the other fellow and of how he will probably react, close observation of his re-

sponse and, finally, a nice judgment to draw the line between legitimate shrewdness and mere trickery.

In order to inspire confidence in other people, especially in subordinates, conceal your own doubts and worries. Also be ready at times, especially in moments of stress, to make a display of personal confidence and serenity.

Do not shut your eyes to the dangers and risks before you. Appraise them carefully. But having decided to go ahead, then act as though success were assured.

In emergencies, brusque, dogmatic statements are of value in restoring or creating confidence. But it is important to remember that positive assertions of this sort, if used regularly, arouse needless opposition and are usually a sign of weakness.

In a fight or contest, it is often effective to bluff about the strength of your own position — but only if you can give a good account of yourself, should the bluff be called.

In trading and in many types of negotiations, it is frequently helpful to conceal, wholly or in part, your own interest. When possible, try to shift the burden to the other man and make him show his hand first.

CHAPTER XXVI

MISTAKES TO AVOID IN USING HUMOR

Lincoln Comes to the Rescue with a Joke
Will Rogers Gives Dwight Morrow a Lift

A GENTLEMAN FROM OHIO, named Brand, once found himself unpleasantly embarrassed during an interview with President Lincoln.

While they talked, a regiment arrived outside the White House and Lincoln was called on for a speech.

He asked Brand to accompany him and continued to hold him closely in conversation. But when they reached the portico and the regiment raised a cheer, an aide stepped up to Brand and told him it would be necessary for him to drop back a few steps. Quick as a flash, Lincoln said: "You see, Mr. Brand, they might not know which was the President." [1]

In that awkward moment, Lincoln came to the rescue with his kindly humor. By this small joke on himself, he relieved an embarrassing situation.

Everybody knows the value of humor in putting people at ease and in winning their good will. And, like Lincoln, many leaders have been famous for their ability to make people laugh. Humor has been one of their recognized methods of controlling men.

To understand their strategy it is important to remember this fact: Humor is an edged tool; it can be used to fight with as well as to please. We find a striking example of this point in the career of Henry P. Fletcher, our recent ambassador to Italy. With one joke Fletcher did two things: He not only won over a group of men and scored a diplomatic triumph but also he punished an individual.

At a critical time, Fletcher arrived in Chile as minister. "The previous American Minister," says Collins, "had actually been withdrawn. Fletcher was finally dispatched as a forlorn hope in the effort to prevent war."

The Brazilian envoy, an old friend of his, took Fletcher to the leading club and introduced him to the business men. With no enthusiasm the prominent citizens of Chile came up to shake hands. One of them observed that he was glad to greet Fletcher as a private individual but not as a representative of the United States. Unaware that Fletcher spoke Spanish, he then remarked to his friends in this tongue: "As for his country I wouldn't buy a shoestring from her."

"Until now, Fletcher had not said a word." says Collins, "But this was his opportunity. Turning to the company and addressing them in perfect Spanish, he said: 'Gentlemen, I see that my mission is already a failure. One of the chief objects of diplomacy in these days is to create better trade relations between sister nations. But what can I do? Here, on the very first day of my arrival, I find that the shoestring market is all shot to pieces.'

"The surprise of being addressed in their own tongue, combined with the good nature and tolerance of this retort, so worked on the minds of these susceptible Latins that they burst into hearty laughter at the expense of their own countryman, and welcomed their American guest into the innermost circles of their club life.

"In the end, the man who had made the slurring remark became one of the American's best friends and supporters, and the Chilean government, controlled to a large extent by the members of that particular group of Santiago business men, settled at Fletcher's behest all of the matters over which the nations had been so long quarreling." [2]

Fletcher made these Chileans laugh *at the expense of their own countryman*. He gained the good will of the group by ridiculing one man. And if this man later became a friend, it was clearly not because he had enjoyed the joke but rather because he had received just the right amount of punishment.

To use humor successfully we must first ask ourselves this

question: Who is our victim and what, if any, will be the effect on him?

Calvin Coolidge learned this lesson early in life, when he was elected a sort of class jester at Amherst. "In accordance with custom," he says, "our class chose three of its members by popular vote to speak at the commencement. To me was assigned the grove oration which according to immemorial practice deals with the record of the class in a witty and humorous way. While my effort was not without some success I very soon learned that making fun of people in a public way was not a good method to secure friends, or likely to lead to much advancement, and I have scrupulously avoided it." [3]

The cutting edge of humor is, of course, well understood: When people laugh, they always laugh *at* something or somebody, and usually it is a somebody. A child giggles when we slip on the ice; we ourselves smile when cartoonists give the President a sly thrust. All laughter must have a butt. People enjoy it largely because it raises their *ego;* gives them an agreeable sense of superiority over someone else; and so fills their mind with pleasant thoughts about themselves.

That Henry Cabot Lodge never fully grasped this fact has been, says Lawrence, a "bit of tragedy" in his career. Like Coolidge, he found that a humorous address in college roused ill will. But in his case the animosity was so great that the ceremony of which his speech formed a part was thereafter discontinued altogether. And Lodge was never able to apply what he discovered. With his "thrusts of sarcasm, his occasional sharp wit" he continued throughout his career to stir up hostility without intending to do so.

One of the shrewdest blows we can strike at the other fellow's *ego* is to make him the butt of ridicule or laughter. Irony, sarcasm, satire are useful tools of combat. They are employed by the able man to snub and squelch those who impose upon him and to bring down opponents.

That popular pastime, "kidding," is, of course, a mock-combat in which two people each get a thrill from their own successful thrusts and in which they display their affection for each other like two small boys tussling and scuffling. The risk of all "kidding" lies in those accidental thrusts which occasionally strike too deep.

It is for these reasons that we find successful men taking great care to gauge the result of their shafts when they bring their sense of humor into play.

One type of humor that is always certain to please we have just watched Lincoln using: He charmed another man by a joke on himself. As we have already noted in an earlier chapter, this is a favorite device of the leader. Woodrow Wilson with his story of the squirrel whiskey (p. 118) delighted his listeners by making them feel superior to him. We cannot go wrong with a joke on ourselves. We accomplish much the same result by joining in the laugh when someone else springs one on us.

Another type of friendly humor we find in one of Calvin Coolidge's famous flashes of dry wit. During the summer which he spent in the Black Hills, he called together all the newspaper men and told them that since his birthday came on the Fourth of July, there was to be a party on that day to which they were all invited.

Every one was much pleased. Someone asked him if there were going to be fireworks.

"No," replied Coolidge with a twinkle, "we will leave the pyrotechnics for the gentlemen of the press," [4]

Coolidge turned the laugh on the newspaper men. But in his thrust there was a compliment.

Lastly we come to that class of humor which fills the comic strips of our newspapers and the pages of *Life* and *Judge*. Here is humor that is nearly always safe, for the target is some imaginary person or a person who is well out of range. Many leaders are famous for their skill in using jokes and stories of this type.

It is by giving a thought to the victim that able men make their humor effective in creating good will. They take care that their thrusts inflict no damage which they may regret. Kindly humor charms people and puts them at ease. It is perhaps unequalled as a means of relieving tension and drawing people together.

Will Rogers Gives Dwight Morrow a Lift

Some people were astonished when Dwight Morrow, as ambassador to Mexico, made Will Rogers his right-hand man.

Morrow's strategy and what Rogers did for him have been described by Bruce Barton: "Morrow put him up at the Embassy, and in twenty-four hours the government of Mexico discovered yet another side to the American character. In the palace, on the President's private car, and in the offices where nothing had been heard from Americans for a long time but dignified diplomatic complaints, a new noise resounded. All business was suspended while everybody laughed. . . .

"The President was to make a trip of several days in his private car, and . . . Morrow and Rogers, as well as members of the Cabinet and army officers were invited to go along. It was at a rather tense period following the elimination of three Presidential candidates via the rifle route. Rogers, brought forward to meet the President, drew back and called loudly for an interpreter.

"'I want to get straight with this bird,' Rogers exclaimed, pointing to Calles: 'I want to make him understand that I am down here just to see the sights and have a little pleasure. I am positively not a candidate for anything.'"

"Calles roared with laughter. . . .

"After Rogers left for home there was no tenseness in the conversation when the American Ambassador had business with a member of the government. You can't keep men from getting on well together when they have laughed at the same funny stories." [5]

"Frequently I have told jokes and stories for the purpose of bringing two people together," Frank Wetmore, late chairman of the First National Bank of Chicago, recently told the authors. "I don't know any other system that works so well when you want two people to like each other."

In opening his cabinet meetings, Grover Cleveland used almost always to start with a free and easy chat "running off into story telling." "Every member," says Herbert, "had his own sense of humor and now and then his good story to tell." [6]

As vice president, Charles Gates Dawes, now our ambassador to England, turned himself into "a sort of court jester for
social Washington." And in his days as a banker, many were
the stiff business gatherings which he loosened up with his stories
and jokes.

No matter what a man's job may be, humor of the right kind
will help him in dealing with people.

Said A. L. Merritt, as superintendent of the New York subway: "A good-natured, joking, quick-thinking man on a
crowded platform is worth ten policemen with clubs. And this
good humor, in an employee, . . . is contagious. We have one
man who, by the funny inflection of his voice — half-sarcastic,
half-joking — as he requests people to 'Step forward, plenty
of room in the center of the car,' can load that car to capacity
and even beyond in jig time. The less room there is in the car
the funnier it becomes, and the passengers grin as they obey." [7]

In passing, it is of interest to note that the real butt of this
man's humor was not the passengers, but rather the subway
company itself with its inadequate facilities.

As Merritt observes, good humor is as catching as measles.
The man who is pleasant and cheerful does not need to crack
jokes to raise our *ego*. He can do this simply by being near us.
By his very manner he makes us think of pleasant things about
ourselves. Just to see someone smile makes us *feel* like smiling;
just to hear someone laugh makes us *feel* like laughing.

*By making people laugh, by stirring their sense of humor, you can
raise their ego and thus please them and gain their good will. As a
means of putting others at ease, relieving tension and drawing people
together, humor of the right kind is most effective strategy.*

*When you use humor be sure to consider the butt of your joke. Remem-
ber that you are wielding an edged tool: to expose another man to
laughter is a method of fighting. Be careful not to arouse ill will which
you may regret later. The safest types of humor are these: the joke
on yourself, the joke that conveys a compliment, the joke about imaginary
people or people who are entirely out of range.*

*You can win people's esteem just by being good-humored and pleasant;
emotions are contagious.*

CHAPTER XXVII

WHEN AND HOW TO PUT UP A FIGHT

Lincoln Throws a Man Out of His Office
Horace Greeley Scores a Bull's-Eye
Rockefeller Makes an Angry Man Feel Foolish

AN INTERESTING and unusual incident in the career of Abraham Lincoln was once described to Joseph Bucklin Bishop, by Lincoln's former secretary, John Hay:

"I was sitting with him on one occasion," said Hay, "when a man who had been calling on him almost daily for weeks in pursuit of an office was shown in. He made his usual request, when Lincoln said: 'It is of no use, my friend. You had better go home. I am not going to give you that place.'

"At this the man became enraged, and in a very insolent tone exclaimed, 'Then, as I understand it, Mr. President, you refuse to do me justice.' At this, Lincoln's patience, which was as near the infinite as anything that I have ever known, gave way. He looked at the man steadily for a half-minute or more, then slowly began to lift his long figure from its slouching position in the chair.

"He rose without haste, went over to where the man was sitting, took him by the coat-collar, carried him bodily to the door, threw him in a heap outside, closed the door, and returned to his chair. The man picked himself up, opened the door, and cried, 'I want my papers!' Lincoln took a package of papers from the table, went to the door and threw them out, again closed it, and returned to his chair. He said not a word, then or afterward, about the incident." [1]

"As he was closing it, the pen of the editor slackened slowly, then stopped, and glancing over his shoulder, with his face wreathed in a childlike smile, Mr. Greeley said soothingly:

"'Don't go! Don't go! Come back and *free your mind!*'" [5]

Chauncey Depew tells how Lincoln, in this same quiet way, literally flayed a man who made an effort to increase his difficulties during the Civil War. He was a congressman named Ganson who, it happened, was totally bald and whose face also was hairless. In a gloomy period of the Civil War he came to Lincoln and made a lengthy demand that, in return for the support which he had given the administration, he should be told at once the exact conditions at the front, good or bad. "Mr. Lincoln looked at him earnestly for a minute and then said, 'Ganson, how clean you shave!' That ended the interview." [6]

A similar shaft of ridicule helped insure victory for that great trial lawyer, Joseph Choate, in what he himself considered his most important case. Choate succeeded in reversing a sentence of guilty pronounced by a court-martial sixteen years before against General Fitz-John Porter. In opposition there appeared as a witness no less a person than the Adjutant-General of the army "in full regimentals with cocked hat, epaulets and spurs." He brought forward lengthy and weighty arguments.

"Mr. Choate," says Strong, "in his inimitable manner of childlike simplicity, began his argument by saying: 'We have listened with patience to the remarks of the distinguished Adjutant-General of the United States army. His long argument reminds me of the advice once given to the graduating class in the Theological Seminary of Tennessee: "Now boys, remember one thing, do not make long prayers; always remember that the Lord knows something."'" [7]

On some occasions, when they have to deal with people who are imposing upon them, such leaders as Choate use a simple and direct rebuke. But only, as a rule, when the other man has left himself without a comeback.

By this plan Choate brought down to earth a judge who refused to listen to him in an important case. This judge had an exasperating habit of talking to his associates on the bench while the attorneys were delivering their arguments — especially if they were young attorneys. No one had ever dared to protest. But one day the judge happened to try his trick on Choate.

"Choate," says Brown, "ceased speaking immediately, folded his arms and gazed steadily at the judges, his handsome face a trifle paler than usual. A hush fell upon the court-room. Judge Van Brunt, noticing the stillness, turned around and looked inquiringly at the silent advocate.

"'Your honor,' said Choate, 'I have just forty minutes in which to make my final argument. I shall not only need every second of that time to do it justice, but I shall also need your undivided attention.'

"'And you shall have it,' promptly responded the judge, at the same time acknowledging the justice of the rebuke by a faint flush on his cheeks." [8]

We find an interesting example of this same method in the early days of Frank Davis, the insurance salesman who became "commander-in-chief of the eight thousand agents" of the Equitable Life and later western production manager of Penn Mutual.

"On one occasion," says Crowell, "he had made a definite appointment with an important business man. Arriving promptly on the minute, he was kept waiting in the corridor. Eventually the executive strolled out.

"'What can I do for you?' he asked. 'Make it brief.'

"'I can't talk standing up,' said Davis, 'and I don't intend to try. I have a definite appointment with you. If you see fit to keep your word and listen to the kind of service we can render you, I am at your command. Otherwise, I shall say good day.'

"The business man blinked. Then he held out his hand.

"'You're right, my friend; come inside,' he said.

"Inside of three minutes Davis left the office with a signed contract for fifty thousand dollars of life insurance in his pocket." [9]

Another familiar device by which able men sometimes subdue a man is simply to keep silent and ignore him.

Rockefeller Makes an Angry Man Feel Foolish

In John D. Rockefeller's early years, says Bruce Barton, an angry man once rushed into his office, "strode up to his desk, hit it a mighty thump and exploded:

"'Mr. Rockefeller, I hate you,' he cried. 'I have a thundering good reason for hating you, and, by heaven, you are going to hear the truth about yourself from me.'

"With that he launched into a ten-minute diatribe which made Cicero's remarks on Catiline sound like a prose poem. The clerks in the office could hear the whole thing, and waited expectantly to see John D. hurl an ink well at the intruder or have the porters throw him out. But John D. did neither. He laid down his pen and looked at his assailant with an air of benevolent interest, which the increasing bitterness of the outburst seemed to merely intensify. He leaned forward as if eager to catch every single word.

"The visitor was mystified.

"In spite of himself he began to miss on a couple of cylinders, for wrath, unfed by denial, cannot maintain itself indefinitely. At length he stopped with a final gurgle, and waited for a reply.

"Still John D. remained silent. His enemy gulped. He had prepared himself for a battle. In his own mind he had gone over every possible reply which John D. could make, and was ready with a hot retort. But how can you argue with a man who says nothing?

"He gave the desk a couple more good blows, which obviously lacked real conviction, and then, looking decidedly foolish, he rose, and slumped toward the door. As it slammed behind him, John D. hitched his chair a little nearer the desk, picked up the pen, and started in at the precise point where he had been interrupted. Neither upon that day nor later did he so much as refer to the incident." [10]

On many occasions it is possible, as we know, to quell people by this simple method. To ignore a man and make it stick, is to strike a decisive blow at his *ego*.

There are many examples of this strategy.

One of the richest men in America at one time offended Colonel House by using his name "too loosely." For a while thereafter, says Arthur D. Howden Smith, "House was always busy when he telephoned. . . . Afterward I watched him employ the same tactics on several occasions. They seemed to work." [11] With the very rich man this was what happened: He was heard to complain of the treatment he was getting and to wonder whether House were "sore." This, House explained to Smith, was his method of punishing people who needed discipline.

A bumptious editor, at a dinner in company with William E. Gladstone, once made an openly slighting remark to this great English statesman. Gladstone had observed pleasantly that he had received a note from the editor a few days earlier. But this person insisted that it could not have come from him — though possibly from his secretary. Gladstone said nothing, but from that time on was unable either to see him or to hear him. And as Gladstone led the conversation, the editor was completely sunk for the evening.

An effective plan which leaders sometimes employ with an adversary is to goad him into losing control of his temper, by appearing utterly indifferent themselves.

Disraeli, Gladstone's famous political opponent in Parliament, used this plan. When Gladstone rose to attack him, he would, says Murray, "sit immovable with folded arms, save from time to time he conveyed by some trivial gesture — a glance through his carefully adjusted glass at the clock, or a polite rearrangement of articles displaced on the table by his adversary's angry fist — a contempt more galling than the most furious retort." [12]

In the court room, Joseph Choate was highly skilled in this trick of seeming indifferent and thereby flustering an opponent.

One of the reasons that successful men so often win their fights is because, while the other man loses his grip, they themselves remain calm. They keep their own anger well in hand, using it like gunpowder behind a carefully aimed bullet. With them, an outburst of temper is usually a matter of strategy. They let fly only when this is the best way to win out.

How Charles Dawes employed this method during the World War, when Pershing sent him as his representative to an important conference in London, has been described by James O'Donnell Bennett:

"Dawes," says Bennett, "was only a lieutenant-colonel then. When he presented himself to the British military mightiness with whom he was to negotiate, that exalted man, pointedly gazing over and beyond the Lieutenant-Colonel's head, puffed:

"'Where is General Pershing? General Pershing should be here! General Pershing's presence here is of the first importance!'

"'I'm here!' said Dawes, 'to represent General Pershing — and here with all his power, *God damn you!*'

"Was Dawes killed on the spot? He was not. He and the mightiness promptly got into fruitful negotiation, and in '19 the mightiness not only recommended for Dawes the most distinguished British decoration he received, but crossed the Atlantic solely to attend a banquet in Dawes' honor." [13]

And this same strategy, of course, Dawes employed in that famous "Hell and Maria" speech before the Senate committee, which we have already observed (p. 198). Not only was his outburst coolly planned, but also, in paving the way for it, he used another shrewd bit of tactics that has helped many a man win a fight. He deliberately "led the committee on to nag him with trivial questions and carping criticisms" [14] until they had put themselves completely in the wrong and had laid themselves wide open to his counterblast.

The calculated outburst of rage is a weapon which Napoleon used most skilfully. He employed it at one time after his victories in Italy to compel the Austrian envoys to accept his terms when they had hesitated and argued for weeks. Finally he growled at them that he had been too lenient, and then, says Ludwig, "to give them a salutary fright, he bursts into rage, dashes a vase to the ground, and thus forces them to sign the peace in which everyone gets what Napoleon had promised six months before." [15]

Some men set loose their anger like a child touching off fireworks, merely to ease their feelings or to tickle their vanity. But the leader expends his temper like valuable ammunition.

During his ranching days, Theodore Roosevelt was once threatened by a saloon bully with two drawn guns who insisted that "four eyes" should treat the crowd to drinks. Eventually Roosevelt came out from his seat behind the stove and struck three rapid blows to the jaw which sent the bully down "like a tree," firing his guns wildly.

To those swift blows Roosevelt's anger gave terrific force. But it is certain that this was no outburst of blind rage.

The real fighter knows how to control and use his anger. For each person, for each situation he chooses the best method of attack. Before striking he plans his campaign. And more important still, he decides first of all whether fighting of any kind is the right strategy.

To manage people successfully, it is important to know not only *how* to fight, but even more *when* to fight.

The able man rises above many petty slights, many shafts of criticism from others. He is patient and kindly and he knows simple methods of giving useless anger and peevishness a safe outlet. First and foremost his purpose is not to fight but to conciliate; not to strike fear into men but to gain their good will; not to compel but to inspire.

On the other hand, he cannot and will not permit people to impose upon him beyond a certain point. And when engaged with an adversary, he stays to the finish.

Make it your first objective to control people by gaining their personal esteem and their willing co-operation.

But if and when they impose upon you beyond reasonable limits, be ready to strike.

Keep in mind the various methods that can be used to win a victory. Try to choose the easiest and most certain method in the light of the man whom you face and the situation as a whole. Remember that the knockout blow may range all the way from a bit of ridicule or a calm rebuke to a crack in the jaw.

Also make it a point not to indulge in outbursts of temper, except for a specific purpose when you feel sure that this is the best way to handle a situation.

APPENDIX

Because of the great number of books and magazines on which the authors have drawn, it has not been practical to list the sources of all the data which have been incorporated in this book. Below, however, are given page references for all quoted passages of a sentence or more in length. The number in brackets preceding each reference corresponds to the superior number in the text. Here and in the text itself, these numbers run serially by chapters.

In designating titles of magazines the standard abbreviations are employed as they appear in the *Readers' Guide*. The abbreviation "Int." is used to indicate the word "Interview" and means that the material was supplied to the authors by a responsible individual — usually by one of the principals in the happening described or by an eye witness.

FRONTISPIECE. [1] Charles Merriam, *Four American Party Leaders* (Macmillan), p. 35. [2] Merle Crowell, *Am. M.*, 82 (Oct. 1916), 12.
CHAPTER I. [1] Paul R. Leach, *Youth's Companion*, 103 (1929), 410. [2] Merle Crowell, *Am. M.*, 82 (Oct. 1916), 12. [3] Charles Merriam, *Four American Party Leaders* (Macmillan), p. 35. [4] Alfred Grunberg, *Am. M.*, 83 (June, 1917), 77.
CHAPTER II. [1] Benjamin Franklin, *Autobiography* (Houghton), pp. 126–127. [2] Andrew Carnegie, *Autobiography* (Houghton), p. 120. [3] Lillian Eichler, *Book of Conversation* (Doubleday, Doran), Vol. 1, p. 76.
CHAPTER III. [1] Dr. Victor Rosewater, *Theodore Roosevelt As We Knew Him*, ed. by Frederick S. Wood (Winston), p. 304. [2] Isaac F. Marcosson, *Am. M.*, 94 (July, 1922), 103. [3] Wm. A. McGarry, *Sat. Eve. Post*, 200 (Oct. 15, 1927), 66. [4] Thomas Beer, *Hanna* (Knopf), pp. 137–138. [5] Edward Bok, *A Man From Maine* (Scribner), p. 111. [6] Lord Frederick Hamilton, *The Vanished Pomps of Yesterday* (Hodder), p. 46. [7] Hugh S. Fullerton, *Am. M.*, 95 (Feb. 1923), 182. [8] Isaac F. Marcosson, *Am. M.*, 92 (Sept. 1921), 140. [9] Int. [10] Oscar King Davis, *William Howard Taft* (P. W. Ziegler), p. 134. [11] Phillips Russell, *Benjamin Franklin* (Brentano's), p. 74. [12] Andrew Carnegie, *Autobiography* (Houghton), pp. 23–24. [13] E. T. Raymond, *Life of Arthur James Balfour* (Little, Brown), p. 232.
CHAPTER IV. [1] Annie E. S. Beard, *Our Foreign-born Citizens* (Crowell), pp. 62–63. [2] Andrew Carnegie, *Autobiography* (Houghton), p. 124. [3] Keene Sumner, *Am. M.*, 102 (Sept. 1926), 151. [4] Bruce Barton, *Am. M.*, 102 (Aug. 1926), 72–73. [5] Hugh Leamy, *Collier's*, 80 (Dec. 24, 1927), 42. [6] Bruce Barton, *Am. M.*, 102 (Aug. 1926), 72. [7] Catharine MacKenzie, *Alexander Graham Bell* (Houghton), p. 76. [8] Int. [9] Arthur Edward Phillips, *Effective Speaking* (Newton), pp. 28–30.
CHAPTER V. [1] Bruce Barton, *Collier's*, 82 (Aug. 4, 1928), 9. [2] Merle Crowell, *Am. M.*, 82 (Oct. 1916), 64. [3] John K. Winkler, *W. R. Hearst* (Simon & Schuster), p. 15. [4] J. B. Bishop, *Notes and Anecdotes of Many Years* (Scribner), pp. 60–61. [5] Horace Green, *Life of Calvin Coolidge* (Duffield), p. 53. [6] Arthur D. Howden Smith, *Real Colonel House* (Doran), p. 139. [7] Isaac F. Marcosson, *Am. M.*, 94 (July, 1922), 49, 100. [8] Frederick L. Collins, *Am. M.*, 105 (June, 1928), 139. [9] Duff Gilfond, *American Mercury*, 11 (1927), 451. [10] Samuel Pennypacker, *Autobiography of a Pennsylvanian* (Winston), p. 106. [11] Lillian Eichler, *Book of Conversation* (Doubleday, Doran), Vol. 1, p. 86. [12] T. E. Lawrence, *Revolt in the Desert* (Doran), p. 250. [13] Isaac F. Marcosson, *Am. M.*, 93 (May, 1922), 162. [14] Charles Seymour, *Woodrow Wilson and the World War*, in *Chronicles*

Reeves, *Personality* (Feb. 1928), 33. [16] B. C. Forbes, *Am. M.*, 92 (Sept. 1921), 16. [17] J. C. Penney, *Am. M.*, 88 (Aug. 1919), 51, 95, 97. [18] Arthur D. Howden Smith, *Real Colonel House* (Doran), p. 168. [19] W. S. Dutton, *Am. M.*, 104 (Aug. 1927), 141. [20] Edwin Wildman, *Financial World*, 49 (1928), 864. [21] Frank Parker Stockbridge, *World's Work*, 36 (1918), 248, 250.

CHAPTER XVII. [1] Clinton W. Gilbert, *Collier's*, 80 (Dec. 17, 1927), 9. [2] Charles Schwab, *Succeeding With What You Have* (Century), p. 24. [3] B. C. Forbes, *Am. M.*, 93 (Apr. 1922), 301. [4] *Personality in Business* (A. W. Shaw), p. 137.

CHAPTER XVIII. [1] Hermann Hagedorn, *That Human Being Leonard Wood* (Harcourt, Brace & Howe), pp. 90–91. [2] *Ibid.*, p. 94. [3] Frank Barkley Copley, *Frederick W. Taylor* (Harper), p. 84. [4] Earl Chapin May, *Sat. Eve. Post*, 201 (Mar. 9, 1929), 145. [5] Albert Sidney Gregg, *Personality* (June, 1928), 43. [6] B. C. Forbes, *Men Who Are Making America* (Forbes), p. 180. [7] Jonathan N. Leonard, *World's Work*, 58 (1929), 64. [8] Samuel Crowther, *Am. M.*, 97 (Apr. 1924), 114. [9] W. S. Dutton, *Am. M.*, 106 (Aug. 1928), 82. [10] Russell H. Crowell, *Romantic Rise of a Great American* (Harper), pp. 98–99. [11] William Hard, *Who's Hoover* (Dodd), p. 18.

CHAPTER XIX. [1] B. C. Forbes, *Am. M.*, 95 (Jan. 1923), 62. [2] Int. [3] Samuel M. Vauclain, *Sat. Eve. Post*, 201 (Mar. 23, 1929), 132.

CHAPTER XX. [1] Charles Seymour, *Woodrow Wilson and the World War*, in *Chronicles of America* Series (Yale Press), Vol. 48, p. 16. [2] Carl Sandburg, *Abraham Lincoln* (Harcourt), Vol. 1, pp. 253, 272. [3] Fred C. Kelly, *Am. M.*, 84 (Dec. 1917), 15. [4] E. G. Johnson, *Best Letters of Lord Chesterfield* (McClurg), p. 61. [5] Fred C. Kelly, *Am. M.*, 84 (May, 1917), 16. [6] E. Haldeman-Julius (ed.), *Letters of Lord Chesterfield*, Little Blue Book, No. 194 (Haldeman-Julius Co.), p. 32. [7] E. G. Johnson, *Best Letters of Lord Chesterfield* (McClurg), p. 199. [8] John T. Flynn, *Collier's*, 80 (July 2, 1927), 44. [9] Samuel M. Crowther, *System*, 41 (1922), 679. [10] Frank Parker Stockbridge, *World's Work*, 36 (1918), 252. [11] James H. Rand, Jr., *Assuring Business Profits* (Forbes), p. 90. [12] James C. Derieux, *Am. M.*, 98 (Dec. 1924), 24.

CHAPTER XXI. [1] Horace Green, *Life of Calvin Coolidge* (Duffield), pp. 45–46. [2] Thomas Jackson Arnold, *Early Life and Letters of General Thomas J. Jackson* (Revell), p. 95. [3] M. K. Wisehart, *Am. M.*, 106 (Dec. 1928), 144. [4] Joseph Bucklin Bishop, *Notes and Anecdotes of Many Years* (Scribner), p. 223. [5] Phillips Russell, *Benjamin Franklin* (Brentano's), pp. 120–121. [6] Keene Sumner, *Am. M.*, 101 (June, 1926), 16. [7] James H. McCullough, *Am. M.*, 97 (Jan. 1924), 16. [8] E. G. Johnson, *Best Letters of Lord Chesterfield* (McClurg), p. 107.

CHAPTER XXII. [1] Andrew Carnegie, *Autobiography* (Houghton), p. 71. [2] *Ibid.*, p. 73. [3] Charles M. Schwab, *Succeeding With What You Have* (Century), p. 12. [4] David R. Craig and W. W. Charters, *Personal Leadership in Industry* (McGraw-Hill), p. 127. [5] Charles R. Flint, *System*, 44 (1923), 753. [6] Edward Bok, *A Man From Maine* (Scribner), p. 145. [7] Helen Christine Bennett, *Am. M.*, 95 (Apr. 1923), 20. [8] Neil M. Clark, *Am. M.*, 104 (July, 1927), 37. [9] L. White Busby, *Uncle Joe Cannon* (Holt), p. 133. [10] James Kerney, *Political Education of Woodrow Wilson* (Century), p. ix (Intro.). [11] Charles Edward Merriam, *Four American Party Leaders* (Macmillan), p. 38. [12] Boyden Sparkes, *Elks Mag.* (Oct. 1928), 42. [13] B. C. Forbes and O. D. Foster, *Automotive Giants of America* (Forbes), p. 101. [14] George M. Cohan, *Twenty Years on Broadway* (Harper), p. 200. [15] Paul Y. Anderson, *Outlook*, 149 (May 2, 1928), 4–5. [16] Gentleman at the Keyhole, *Collier's*, 79 (Mar. 26, 1927), 35. [17] Bruce Barton, *Am. M.*, 102 (Aug. 1926), 73. [18] Duff Gilfond, *American Mercury*, 11 (1927), 452.

CHAPTER XXIII. [1] Bruce Barton, *Am. M.*, 95 (Feb. 1923), 16. [2] Joseph Gilpin Pyle, *Life of James J. Hill* (Doubleday), Vol. 1, p. 206. [3] Isaac F. Marcosson, *Am. M.*, 93 (May, 1922), 160. [4] Ida M. Tarbell, *Collier's* 81 (May

APPENDIX

257

19, 1928), 8. [5] H. A. Overstreet, *Influencing Human Behavior* (Norton), p. 55.
[6] G. A. Nichols, *Ptr. Ink*, 143 (Apr. 5, 1928), 26. [7] Isaac F. Marcosson, *Sat. Eve. Post*, 201 (Jan. 26, 1929), 90. [8] Herbert Adams Gibbons, *John Wanamaker* (Harper), Vol. 2, p. 45. [9] Francis Rolt-Wheeler, *Thomas Alva Edison* (Macmillan), pp. 90–91. [10] Editorial, *Mag. of Business*, 54 (1928), 249. [11] Edward Sandford Martin, *Life of Joseph H. Choate* (Scribner), Vol. 1, p. 349. [12] *Ibid.*, Vol. 1, p. 85. [13] B. C. Forbes, *Am. M.*, 93 (Apr. 1922), 34. [14] Marie D. Gorgas and Burton J. Hendrick, *William Crawford Gorgas* (Doubleday), pp. 193–194. [15] Chauncey M. Depew, *My Memories of Eighty Years* (Scribner), p. 57. [16] Russell Conwell, *Why Lincoln Laughed* (Harper), pp. 121–122. [17] Judson C. Welliver, *R. of Rs.*, 61 (1920), 260–261. [18] James Kerney, *Political Education of Woodrow Wilson* (Century), p. 366.
CHAPTER XXIV. [1] Int. [2] Arthur Strawn, *American Mercury*, 12 (1927), 138. [3] Henry B. Rankin, *Personal Recollections of Abraham Lincoln* (Putnam), p. 220. [4] Neil M. Clark, *Am. M.*, 94 (Sept. 1922), 164. [5] Royal F. Munger, *Chicago Daily News*, 53 (Aug. 16, 1928), 34. [6] B. C. Forbes, *Men Who Are Making the West* (Forbes), p. 226. [7] Henry F. Pringle, *Outlook*, 149 (Aug. 22, 1928), 645. [8] John Fortescue, *Wellington* (Dodd), pp. 205–206. [9] Adam Badeau, *Grant in Peace* (Scranton), p. 39. [10] *Ibid.*, p. 16. [11] Grenville M. Dodge, *Personal Recollections of Lincoln, Grant and Sherman* (Monarch Printing Co.), pp. 18, 19–20, 82. [12] B. C. Forbes, *Am. M.*, 92 (Sept. 1921), 132. [13] Grenville M. Dodge, *Personal Recollections of Lincoln, Grant and Sherman* (Monarch Printing Co.), pp. 10–11. [14] James H. Rand, Jr., *Assuring Business Profits* (Forbes), pp. 80–82. [15] E. G. Johnson, *Best Letters of Lord Chesterfield* (McClurg), p. 95. [16] Samuel Crowther, *World's Work*, 56 (1928), 391–392. [17] E. G. Johnson, *Best Letters of Lord Chesterfield* (McClurg), p. 107. [18] W. T. R. Preston, *Strathcona and the Making of Canada* (McBride, Nast & Co.), p. 97. [19] E. G. Johnson, *Best Letters of Lord Chesterfield* (McClurg), p. 57.
CHAPTER XXV. [1] John K. Winkler, *John D.* (Vanguard Press), p. 95. [2] B. C. Forbes, *Men Who Are Making America* (Forbes), p. 299. [3] Neil M. Clark, *Am. M.*, 102 (Aug. 1926), 116. [4] Judge J. W. Donovan, *Modern Jury Trials and Advocates* (G. A. Jennings Co., Inc.), p. xvii. [5] Francis E. Leupp, *George Westinghouse* (Little, Brown), p. 210. [6] Otto H. Kahn, *Our Economic and Other Problems* (Doran), p. 18. [7] Hiram Motherwell, *Plain Talk*, 2 (1928), 568. [8] Marshall Brown, *Wit and Humor of Bench and Bar* (T. H. Flood & Co.), p. 57. [9] Edward S. Martin, *Life of Joseph Hodges Choate* (Scribner), p. 125. [10] Francis Rolt-Wheeler, *Thomas Alva Edison* (Macmillan), pp. 74–75. [11] Int. [12] Harvey S. Firestone and Samuel Crowther, *Men and Rubber* (Doubleday), p. 60.
CHAPTER XXVI. [1] Brand Whitlock, *Forty Years of It* (Appleton), p. 19. [2] Frederick L. Collins, *Am. M.*, 106 (Sept. 1928), 165. [3] Calvin Coolidge, *Autobiography* (Cosmopolitan), pp. 70–71. [4] Int. [5] Bruce Barton, *Collier's*, 82 (Aug. 4, 1928), 34. [6] Hilary A. Herbert, *Cent.*, 85 (1913), 741. [7] A. L. Merritt, *Am. M.*, 92 (Sept. 1921), 49.
CHAPTER XXVII. [1] Joseph Bucklin Bishop, *Notes and Anecdotes of Many Years* (Scribner), pp. 65–66. [2] Earl Chapin May, *Sat. Eve. Post*, 201 (Apr. 6, 1929), 28. [3] James O'Donnell Bennett, *Liberty*, 5 (Feb. 4, 1928), 28. [4] M. E. Hennessy, *Calvin Coolidge* (Putnam), p. 71. [5] Joseph Bucklin Bishop, *Notes and Anecdotes of Many Years* (Scribner), p. 18. [6] Chauncey M. Depew, *My Memories of Eighty Years* (Scribner), p. 59. [7] Theron G. Strong, *Joseph H. Choate* (Dodd), p. 155. [8] Marshall Brown, *Wit and Humor of Bench and Bar* (T. H. Flood & Co.), pp. 83–84. [9] Merle Crowell, *Am. M.*, 95 (June, 1923), 150–151. [10] Bruce Barton, *Am. M.*, 98 (Dec. 1924), 16. [11] Arthur D. Howden Smith, *Sat. Eve. Post*, 199 (Aug. 28, 1926), 73. [12] D. L. Murray, *Benjamin Disraeli* (Little, Brown), p. 164. [13] James O'Donnell Bennett, *Liberty*, 5 (Feb. 4, 1928), 28. [14] Paul Y. Anderson, *Outlook*, 149 (May 2, 1928), 4. [15] Emil Ludwig, *Napoleon* (Liveright), p. 104.

INDEX

Alcott, Louisa M., 16*ff.*
Allyn, Stanley, 60.
Archbold, John D., 145*ff.*
Armour, P. D., 171, 196.
Arthur, President, 163.
Astor, John Jacob, 56.
Astor, Lady, 102.
Atterbury, William Wallace, 147, 148.

Baker, Newton D., 129, 176.
Balfour, Arthur James, 21.
Bamberger, Louis, 164.
Barringer, J. H., 74, 100.
Barton, Bruce, 121, 203*ff.*
Beatty, Admiral David, 59.
Beck, Thomas, 121.
Bedford, Edward T., 177*ff.*
Beer, William, 15*ff.*
Bell, Alexander Graham, 28.
Bell, Marcus, 191.
Bickel, Karl A., 26.
Billings, Dr. Frank, 171.
Bismarck, Otto von, 123, 176.
Bloom, Edgar Selden, 97*ff.*, 161.
Bok, Edward, 16*ff.*, 23*ff.*, 107*ff.*, 179, 192*ff.*, 197*ff.*
Booth, Evangeline, 32.
Brice, Calvin S., 233.
Brown, Charles W., 32.
Brunker, Albert, 72, 145.
Brush, Matthew C., 5, 86.
Bryan, William Jennings, 110*ff.*, 177.
Butt, Archie, 175.

Calles, President, 35*ff.*, 242.
Cannon, Joseph G., 194*ff.*, 196.
Carnegie, Andrew, 8*ff.*, 20, 24*ff.*, 69, 76*ff.*, 122, 124, 127, 145, 147, 173*ff.*, 178, 189*ff.*, 192.
Carnegie, Thomas, 76*ff.*
Carpenter, Charles E., 114*ff.*, 198.
Carranza, Venustiano, 142.
Chalmers, Hugh, 20.
Chapin, Roy, 20.
Chase, Salmon P., 122.
Chesterfield, Lord, 64, 174, 175, 176, 187, 221, 222, 223.
Choate, Joseph, 11, 33, 204*ff.*, 207*ff.*, 233*ff.*, 247*ff.*, 250.
Choate, Rufus, 228.
Chrysler, Walter, 84*ff.*, 226*ff.*
Clemenceau, Georges, 77, 105, 108.
Cleveland, Grover, 108, 242.

Coffin, Charles A., 145.
Coffin, Howard, 20.
Cohan, George, 197.
Coolidge, Calvin, 19, 36, 63*ff.*, 64, 181*ff.*, 187, 240, 241, 246.
Cooper, Kent, 26*ff.*, 200.
Couzens, Senator James, 134.
Cox, Peter, 57.
Cummings, Amos, 30*ff.*,
Curtis, Cyrus, 16*ff.*, 179, 192*ff.*

Davis, Frank, 145, 248.
Dawes, Charles Gates, 57*ff.*, 119, 195, 198*ff.*, 243, 245*ff.*, 251.
Day, Joseph, 66*ff.*
Decker, Edward, 123.
Delane, John T., 229.
Depew, Chauncey M., 53.
Dimock, Anthony, 61*ff.*
Disraeli, Benjamin, 112*ff.*, 126, 250.
Dodge, Grenville M., 127, 219, 220.
Donham, Wallace B., 65, 78, 86*ff.*, 143*ff.*
Donnelley, Thomas E., 92*ff.*
Downs, Lawrence A., 136, 193*ff.*
Doyle, Conan, 105.
du Pont, T. Coleman, 139.
Durstine, Roy S., 79*ff.*

Edison, Thomas, 27, 75*ff.*, 200, 207, 234*ff.*
Edward VII, King, 11.
Eidlitz, Charles L., 99.
Evans, Edward S., 88*ff.*

Farquhar, A. B., 56.
Farson, John, 196.
Field, Judge Henry P., 181.
Field, Marshall, 83, 111, 141, 170, 185, 216*ff.*, 218.
Firestone, Harvey, 235*ff.*
Fiske, Bishop, 119*ff.*
Fletcher, Henry P., 103*ff.*, 238*ff.*
Flexner, Dr. Simon, 213.
Foch, Ferdinand, 85.
Fohr, Louis J., 153.
Foraker, Burch, 164*ff.*
Ford, Edsel, 221*ff.*
Ford, Henry, 5, 76, 111, 158, 197, 215, 221*ff.*
Forgan, James B., 144.
Foster, James H., 47.
Franklin, Benjamin, 7*ff.*, 19, 80, 106*ff.*, 116, 184*ff.*

Frew, Walter, 201.
Frick, Henry Clay, 132*ff.*
Frohman, Charles, 105.
Frueauff, Frank W., 139.
Fuller, Chief Justice, 174*ff.*
Fullerton, Hugh, 10, 18, 196.

Gage, Lyman J., 144.
Garfield, James A., 24.
Gary, Elbert H., 14*ff.*, 66*ff.*, 69, 83, 145, 185.
Gary, Theodore, 152*ff.*
Gates, John, 65, 145.
Giannini, Amadeo P., 217.
Gifford, Walter S., 54, 157.
Gillette, William, 105.
Gladstone, William E., 250.
Goethals, General, 19, 100, 183*ff.*, 232
Gompers, Samuel, 20, 163.
Gould, Jay, 233.
Grace, Eugene, 190.
Grant, Ulysses S., 126*ff.*, 145, 218*ff.*, 222, 236.
Greeley, Horace, 30*ff.*, 246*ff.*
Grozier, Edwin, 85*ff.*
Guggenheim, Daniel, 162.

Hamilton, Lord Frederick, 17.
Hamlin, Clay, 82.
Hammond, John Hays, 100*ff.*
Hanna, Mark, 15*ff.*, 47, 57.
Harding, Warren G., 63*ff.*
Harmon, William E., 95*ff.*, 106.
Harmsworth, Alfred, *See* Northcliffe, Lord.
Harriman, Edward H., 117, 124, 147*ff.*, 180, 183, 230, 231, 232.
Hay, John, 36, 48*ff.*, 54, 115, 244.
Hayes, Rutherford, 23.
Hearst, Senator, 100*ff.*
Hearst, William Randolph, 36, 43*ff.*
Heinz, Henry, 206.
Herrick, Myron T., 186*ff.*
Hertz, John, 205.
Hill, James J., 81, 180, 204.
Hoover, Herbert, 3*ff.*, 71, 94*ff.*, 137*ff.*, 166, 210*ff.*, 226.
Hopkins, George, 95, 112, 137.
House, Colonel, 36, 45*ff.*, 77, 105, 108, 110*ff.*, 136*ff.*, 150*ff.*, 217, 250.
Howard, Roy, 148*ff.*
Hutchins, Robert Maynard, 120.

Jackson, Thomas "Stonewall," 182*ff.*
Janin, Louis, 138*ff.*, 226.
Johns, William H., 79*ff.*
Johnson, President, 218.

Johnson, Tom, 129*ff.*
Jones, Hershel V., 185*ff.*

Kelly, Fred, 17, 174*ff.*
Kilbrick, Isaac, 90, 104.
Kingsbury, Prof. Forrest A., 143, 146.
Knapp, Joseph P., 121.
Kruttschnitt, Julius, 147*ff.*

LaSalle, Sieur de, 32.
Lasker, Albert D., 120.
Lawrence, T. E., 38, 228.
Lawson, Victor, 168, 179.
Leach, Paul R., 3*ff.*, 53*ff.*
Lee, Ivy, 102, 213.
Lee, Robert E., 126.
Leffingwell, W. H., 44, 46*ff.*, 106, 205*ff.*, 212.
Lincoln, Abraham, 44, 114, 122, 128, 146, 173, 187, 202, 210, 216, 219, 220, 238, 244, 247.
Littleton, Martin, 77.
Lloyd George, 81, 94*ff.*, 102*ff.*, 105.
Lodge, Henry Cabot, 58, 240.
Longstreet, General James, 126.
Longworth, Nicholas, 38, 202.

McBride, John, 169.
McCall, Peter, 38.
McCormick, Cyrus H., 29.
McCosh, Dr., 41.
McKinley, William, 47, 53, 111*ff.*
McLachlan, Archibald, 120, 208.
McLain, David, 41.
Marcosson, Isaac, 18, 37, 39*ff.*, 54.
Markham, Charles, 190*ff.*
Mason, Max, 75.
Maxim, Hudson, 123.
Merritt, A. L., 243.
Merseles, Theodore F., 206.
Mitchell, Charles E., 203*ff.*
Mitchell, Dr. David, 114.
Mitchell, John A., 125.
Morgan, Earl B., 87.
Morgan, J. Pierpont, 69, 156.
Morron, John R., 196.
Morrow, Dwight W., 35*ff.*, 156, 242.
Motley, John L., 236.
Munsey, Frank A., 63.
Murphy, Mike, 135*ff.*
Mussolini, Benito, 206, 232.

Napoleon, 70, 80, 163, 233, 251.
Nast, Thomas, 43*ff.*
Nelson, Horatio, 162.
Northcliffe, Lord, 100.

Obregon, President Alvaro, 142.

Paine, William Alfred, 37.
Parnell, Charles S., 108.
Paterno, Dr. Charles, 88.
Patterson, John H., 60, 81*ff*., 98*ff*., 205.
Peary, Rear Admiral Robert, 49.
Penney, J. C., 149*ff*.
Pennypacker, Governor, 38.
Pershing, General, 120, 245*ff*., 251.
Piper, Colonel, 8*ff*., 76*ff*.
Pizarro, Francisco, 213.
Platt, Thomas Collier, 131*ff*.
Porter, H. Hobart, 180.
Prentiss, Mark O., 141.
Preston, Thomas, 227.
Pulitzer, Joseph, 117.
Putnam, George Haven, 115*ff*., 172.

Rand, James H., Jr., 89*ff*., 179, 221.
Raskob, John J., 207, 217.
Récamier, Mme, 115.
Reed, Dr. Charles A. L., 209*ff*.
Reeves, James, 64.
Reid, Whitelaw, 48*ff*.
Reppert, Fred, 30, 228.
Resor, Stanley, 162, 193.
Rhodes, Cecil, 90.
Rockefeller, John D., 83, 124, 173, 177*ff*., 183, 225*ff*., 249.
Rockefeller, John D., Jr., 31.
Rodman, Admiral, 231.
Rogers, Henry H., 39*ff*.
Rogers, Will, 242.
Roosevelt, Theodore, 5, 11, 13*ff*., 18, 40, 54*ff*., 58, 103*ff*., 108, 131*ff*., 173, 175, 191*ff*., 195, 196, 201, 210, 212, 252.
Rosenwald, Julius, 90.

Sabin, Charles H., 100.
Sarnoff, David, 194.
Schwab, Charles, 5, 16, 29*ff*., 36, 69, 87, 124, 153*ff*., 157*ff*., 164, 178*ff*., 190, 191, 216.
Schweppe, Charles, 133*ff*.
Scott, Thomas A., 145, 189*ff*.
Scott, Walter Dill, 15, 17.
Scripps, E. W., 148*ff*.
Selfridge, Harry Gordon, 164, 170.
Sickles, General Daniel E., 231.
Simpson, James, 216*ff*.
Sims, William Sowden, 191*ff*.
Smith, Alfred E., 33, 81, 169, 187, 205.
Smith, Alfred H., 149, 219*ff*.
Smith, Donald, *See* Strathcona, Lord.
Sprague, Albert A., 218.
Stanton, Edwin M., 122, 145.
Stanton, Henry T., 10, 83, 145.
Steinmetz, Charles, 162*ff*.

Stephen, George, 204.
Stevens, Eugene, 73*ff*., 191, 201.
Storey, William, 5.
Storrs, Emory, 163.
Strathcona, Lord, 11, 223.
Strong, Walter, 59, 85, 179.
Suchet, Marshal, 218.
Sudler, Louis, 235.
Sumner, Charles, 44.
Swift, Gustavus, 117.
Swope, Gerard, 25, 167.

Taft, William Howard, 18*ff*.
Taylor, Frederick, 44, 114, 161.
Taylor, Moses, 62*ff*.
Thomson, John Edgar, 20, 190.
Thornton, Sir Henry, 32*ff*.
Todd, John R., 112.
Tomlins, W. L., 113*ff*.
Traylor, Melvin, 199.
Twain, Mark, 196*ff*.

Underwood, Frederick D., 145.

Vail, Theodore, 190, 205.
Vanderbilt, Cornelius, 216, 233.
Vanderlip, Frank A., 156.
van Dyke, Dr. Henry, 115*ff*.
Van Vlissingen, J. H., 92*ff*.
Vauclain, Samuel, 50*ff*., 58*ff*., 100, 161, 171, 245.
Von Moltke, Count, 122.

Walpole, Sir Robert, 174.
Wanamaker, John, 56, 87*ff*., 165, 206.
Washington, Booker T., 120.
Washington, George, 81, 200.
Wellington, Duke of, 218, 231.
Westinghouse, George, 145, 227*ff*., 230.
Wetmore, Frank O., 220, 242.
Whiting, Lawrence, 18.
Whitlock, Brand, 106.
Wilkinson, Melville, 124*ff*., 134*ff*.
William I, Emperor, 123.
William II, Emperor, 122, 151*ff*.
Wilson, Woodrow, 36, 45, 51*ff*., 77, 107*ff*., 108, 118*ff*., 136*ff*., 177, 187, 211, 217, 223.
Wood, Leonard, 21, 49, 160*ff*., 236.
Woodhull, Daniel, 193.
Woodward, Charles, 161*ff*.
Wrigley, William, Jr., 21, 61, 72.

Young, James W., 165*ff*., 193.
Young, Owen D., 5, 76, 90, 101, 145, 167.

Zukor, Adolph, 86.